ALEXANDER HAMILTON

ALSO BY NOEMIE EMERY

WASHINGTON: A BIOGRAPHY

ALEXANDER HAMILTON

An Intimate Portrait

Noemie Emery

G. P. Putnam's Sons
New York

Library of Congress Cataloging in Publication Data

Emery, Noemie, date.
  Alexander Hamilton:

  Bibliography: p.
  1. Hamilton, Alexander, 1757–1804.   2. Statesmen—
United States—Biography. I. Title.
E302.6.H2E47   973.4′092′4 [B]   81-22662
ISBN 0-399-12681-3   AACR2

PRINTED IN THE UNITED STATES OF AMERICA

Acknowledgments

For their assistance in the writing of this book I wish to thank the staffs of the Library of Congress, the New-York Historical Society, and the New York Public Library, the last for permission once again to use the facilities of the Frederick Lewis Allen Memorial Room. I also wish to thank Marilyn Marlow of Curtis Brown, Melissa Pierson of G. P. Putnam's, and my editor, Diane Reverand, whose suggestions, always in the direction of clarity and discipline, were an indispensable help. I also wish to thank Kathryn Brown for help in typing, and Mary McLaughlin, for permission to use her extensive library of works by and about Alexander Hamilton, and for the generous and extended loan of many old and valuable books.

I am indebted to the following, who supplied editorial judgment and moral support: Helen Emery, Joseph and Trude Lash, Nancy Milford, Madelon Bedell, Susan Brownmiller, Christa Armstrong, Grace Darling, Oliva Huntington, Laurie Morgan, and the late Allard Lowenstein, whom I will miss every day of my life.

IN MEMORY OF
Allard Lowenstein
(JANUARY 16, 1929–MARCH 14, 1980)

Author's Note

ALEXANDER HAMILTON is the great romantic of American history. Alone among our politician-statesmen, he would do well as the hero of a drama (*Coriolanus* would be a good example), a tragic opera or a ballet. From his bastard birth to his death by gunfire, with the intervening trail of scandals, confessions and self-induced crises, his life is rich in dramatic elements, and his death has the special quality of crystallizing his personality. He was never more in character than when, through a mixture of qualities heroic, great and simply silly, he accepted the challenge flung at him by Aaron Burr.

This book is written from the duel backward, in an effort to explore the qualities that led him, at the age of forty-nine and at the height of powers, to embrace his extraordinary death. As such, unusual attention is given to his later years, slighted in most biographies, which take here one quarter of the book. Emphasis is also given to the way the characteristics that drove him to the duel—his ambition, pride and love of order, stemming from his shattered and disordered childhood—changed the nature of the American government. History is never isolated from the characters of the men who make it, and the destinies of nations are determined by the compulsions of the great.

I

THE WEST INDIES lie off the American continent, arcing from Cuba to the coast of Venezuela in a chain of more than thirty islands, tropical in climate and brilliantly intense. Alexander Hamilton is linked to three of them: Nevis where he was born, St. Croix where he grew to young adulthood and St. Kitts (St. Christopher) where his forebears, fleeing their spouses or their creditors, were commonly accustomed to repair. All possess astounding beauty. Samuel Taylor Coleridge, visiting Nevis in 1825, found it "captivating," with its huge cone of mountains rising in a graceful curve from the ocean to pierce a crown of clouds, its churches and its planters' mansions dotting the descending hillsides and its lower country, brilliant with mango, guava and orange trees, and the translucent, light-green fields of sugar cane. Nearby lay St. Kitts, "the fertile isle," its interior dense and clotted with deep forests rising at the peak of Mount Misery to 3,792 feet above sea level, its slopes thick with wild orchids and so tangled with dense foliage that travelers to its summit had to crawl on hands and knees. St. Croix, to the north and somewhat larger, was at once more cosmopolitan and less exotic. The island had on its north coast not one but two port cities, including Christiansted, its capital, a small and bustling seaport of warehouses and shipping depots, small stores, churches and a fort. In all, the islands were a prospect to enchant the visitor—especially one like Coleridge, from the chill of Britain, who added to his journal this beguiling note: If a man would bring his "re-source" with him—"especially his wife"—he could live forever in serene retirement in the islands' "sweet recess."[1]

But there were other sides to paradise that Coleridge neglected to describe. Hurricanes could wrack the islands, fevers ravage them, summer heats breed indolence and disease. Worse still was an illness made by man. The white islanders—French, Dutch, Danes and British—a mixed race of European outcasts under an assortment of mixed crowns, straddled a suppressed black population, some native, some imported, who fueled the plantation economy of this green and lavish land. The problem was the pervasive canker of the American South, made by numbers infinitely worse. Nevis in Hamilton's time had a population of six hundred white settlers to ten thousand Negroes; St. Kitts, four thousand to twenty-six thousand, of whom only three hundred blacks were free. Treatment of these slaves was undeniably barbaric: At the docksides cargoes of blacks, washed and oiled, were paraded before prospective buyers to the incessant beat of drums. Charlestown in Nevis, where Hamilton was born, and Christiansted, where he lived later, were local centers of the slave trade. This appalling spectacle may have been one of his earliest and most enduring sights. As an American, he was to show a profound abhorrence of the slave system.

The story of Hamilton's island family is deep in mystery and myth. His maternal grandfather, one John Faucette, physician, "a man of letters and of polished manners,"[2] emigrated from France to the West Indies sometime before 1700. His dates of transit are somewhat fixed by history: he was a Huguenot, and the Edict of Nantes was revoked in 1685. After a century of mild tolerance, the Sun King had decreed a reign of storm and cloud. John moved to Nevis, became a planter and took a wife, Mary, producing among other children a daughter Ann, who married James Lytton, a wealthy planter of St. Kitts. Confusion reigns as to whether there were one or two Mary Faucettes, or two Faucette couples. One biographer has unearthed a deed of gift to "John and Mary Faucette" of Nevis in 1714; another a record of marriage between John Faucette and Mary Uppington of Nevis on August 21, 1718. This second Mary, who bore Hamilton's mother, was a strong-minded woman, probably of English ancestry, who injected a stream of Saxon element into Alexander's mix of Scots and French (and perhaps Jewish) blood. Dates point to the probability of two sets of wives and children: Ann Faucette Lytton was herself the mother of four children when she moved to St. Croix with her husband in 1738. The Faucettes now moved inland to a plantation near Gingerland, a fertile area rich in spice and cane. Here was born their daughter Rachel, perhaps in 1729.

Little today is known of Hamilton's mother, except by the traces of her extraordinarily stormy passage through her life. Tradition and likelihood have her a woman of refinement and temper, inheriting her father's graces and her mother's iron will. John Church Hamilton, Alexander's fourth son and first biographer, leaves this record of Rachel's impact on her son: "He spoke of her as vividly impressed upon his memory"[3] as a woman of intelligence, culture and elegance of form—qualities likely to impress Hamilton, as a child as well as an adult. Rachel was eleven when her world collapsed. Mary Faucette, depressed by financial losses or domestic squabbling, filed for separation from her husband on February 5, 1740, and fled with her daughter to the "fertile isle" of St. Kitts. The breakup was a disaster for the child. John Faucette had fought the separation, and the parting of father and daughter had been bleak. Doubtless it had left a void for both of them: John would make Rachel his sole heir and executrix of his will. What Rachel knew of domestic stability had its ending here: her life hereafter is a story of erratic stress. It had also set a pattern for the future: all three of Rachel's children were to grow up missing at least one parent; Alexander was to lose his father at the same age she had lost hers.

Mary's experience had not dimmed her enthusiasm for wedlock, at least where other people were concerned. Five years later she pushed her daughter into marriage with one Johan Michael Levein, a wealthy Danish planter many years her senior, who according to Rachel's biased but perhaps truthful grandson, "attracted by her beauty . . . received her hand against her will."[4]

The unhappy couple moved to St. Croix, and in 1746 their son Peter was born. Parenthood could not rescue the marriage, which had gone from bad to worse, deteriorating into a sequence of increasingly ill-mannered fights. What caused these dissensions is questionable. Events later suggest that Rachel's stubborn nature ran against Levein's desire to dominate and utterly control his wife. By 1749 the quarrels had become so violent that Levein in a show of brutal power had jailed her in the fort at Christiansted; perhaps his idea of discipline, surely his idea of right. Whatever his intentions, the results were disastrous. Released, Rachel fled her husband, son and marriage, and perhaps returned to her mother on St. Kitts. The provocation must have been extreme to make her leave her child, or perhaps she could no longer bear connection to anything that bore the imprint of Levein. Levein hung on—perhaps through malice,

15

perhaps through the idea of forcing a return to him—divorcing her nine years later when she was already the mother of two children by another man. The terms of the decree, that she had been "shameless, rude and ungodly . . . forgotten her duty . . . let her husband and child alone . . . [and] given herself up to whoring with everyone"[5] have a ring of great brutality, whether through common legal terminology or the special malice of Levein. On her death, with her young children penniless, he intervened in her estate and claimed the legacies that she had willed her other children for his son.

Whether Rachel had indeed "whored with everyone" is now unknown. It is more likely it was an invention of her husband's venom, based on events that occurred long after the marriage had collapsed. What is known is that sometime between 1750 and 1752 she had encountered James Hamilton, fourth son of Alexander Hamilton, laird of the Grange of Stevenson parish, Ayrshire, in Scotland, and set up a relationship with him.

James Hamilton at this time was in his mid to later twenties, in looks much like his son in adulthood, of engaging visage and facile charm. Family tradition has him gentle and helpless, a man of "generous and easy temper" whose indolence and incompetence at business led to indigence at an early stage in life. This mild term conceals a fatal weakness: the stability that had ruled generations of the secure and landed Hamiltons appeared to have eluded James. It had already cost him the regard of his family, the utter silence that prevailed between him and the lairds of Ayrshire suggesting an embittered and perhaps painful break. (The silence continued until one of the Scots Hamiltons wrote to his then world-famous cousin in 1797.) These failings in James may have at the time escaped Rachel, to whom his lack of fiber may have come as a relief. James and Rachel, both somewhat unstable and with more charm than may have been good for them, entered a common-law marriage by necessity (she was not yet divorced, and remarriage was forbidden her) sometime around 1751. The relationship appears to have been monogamous; people who knew them treated them as man and wife. The union produced two children who took their father's name: James, born in 1753; and Alexander, born January 11, 1755.

No records appear to have been kept of these children marked twice by indigence and shame. It is typical of the lack of care afforded records that for many years Alexander was believed to have been born in 1757, making him two years younger than he was. On the evidence of later appearance, he was physically fragile and emotionally intense, with much of his mother's magnetism and his father's careless charm. Doubtless he had already his dominant physical characteristics: blue eyes, delicate features, pink cheeks and chestnut hair, perhaps at that age red-gold. Precocious and charming, he rapidly outdistanced his lackluster older brother, and such funds and efforts as could be spared by his family were employed on his behalf. He was an early and voracious reader. Though his studies of necessity were miscellaneous, he became a passionate devotee of books. Such education as he had was scattershot, family finance and his illegitimate status preventing regular attendance at state schools. At least one happy memory appears to have survived. He later liked to tell his children of his attendance at a Jewish school, where he rattled off the Decalogue in Hebrew, standing on a table because he was so small.

At home, tensions, always latent, continued to increase. A move to St. Croix sometime in Alexander's early childhood did nothing to repair his father's inability to hold on to cash. Poverty, strain and uncertain finances inflamed problems caused by social ostracism, and James's hapless nature may have begun to grate on Rachel, who appears the more high-strung and forceful of the two. Suggestions that these tensions were absorbed by their young children were revealed in later years. There is a reference to "the tragedy of the unhappy couple"[6] in Alexander's letter to his fiancée years later, and a dry comment in a letter to his sister-in-law Peggy Schuyler in 1781: " 'Tis a very good thing when the stars unite two people who are fit for each other. . . . But it is a dog of a life when two dissonate tempers meet, and 'tis ten to one this is the case."[7]

Driven by debt or domestic harassment, James Hamilton left his family in 1765, fleeing to St. Kitts to drift about the islands in increasing indigence for the remainder of his life. He never saw his children or his "wife" again. It is not known if he discussed his move with them beforehand, or presented them with a surprise.

Alexander's sole written comment on his abandonment appears in a letter written to his Scots relatives in 1792: "My father's affairs at a very early day went to wreck . . . which occasioned a separation between him and me."[8] "Separation" is a word of deliberate neutrality, discounting blame on any side. Intermittent efforts at communication occurred in the years following, consisting mainly of transfers of money to the parent from the son. "I will cheerfully pay your draft on me for fifty pounds," Alexander wrote in one letter. "I wish it was in my power to advance the sum."[9] In 1785 he wrote to his brother, "I had written to our father, but had not heard of him since. . . . I had pressed him to come to America

17

after the peace."[10] Excuses were made by the elder Hamilton, on the grounds of poverty or illness, but more likely of disquiet at the proposed resumption of a connection so abruptly cut. He never came.

Alexander never allowed himself to condemn James Hamilton; he remained his "dear father" (at least in letters) to his death. That he blamed his father, and blamed him greatly, was revealed later: all his life he was to be extraordinarily sensitive to the plight of abused or abandoned women, or any woman brought into a harsh situation by a man. There is a wealth of condemnation in his warning to his sister-in-law not to marry a man "in whom you have not good reason for implicit confidence,"[11] and in his reaction to the (fraudulent) plight of Peggy Shippen Arnold in a letter written to his fiancée:

> She is apprehensive the resentment of her country may fall on her (who is only unfortunate) for the guilt of her husband. I have tried to persuade her her apprehensions are unfounded, but she has too many proofs of the illiberality of the state to be convinced. . . . At present, she forgets his crime in his misfortune, and her horror at the guilt of the traitor is lost in her love of the man. But a virtuous mind cannot long esteem a base one, and time will make her despise, if it cannot make her hate.[12]

Maria Reynolds, who later seduced him, gained entrée to his office in the first place with a story that her husband had left her deserted and penniless in a strange city, far from home.

Rachel may have appealed to her half-sister, who had married money, but the Lytton family had entered the first stage of its decline. The next generation of Lytton heirs would lose their share of their fortune, and one of Alexander's cousins would kill himself in 1769. She next rented a house in Christiansted and opened a shop, selling goods bought from her landlord and others to support herself and her two children, then aged twelve and ten. What resentments filled her or her children are conjectural, but they may have resulted in Alexander's later scorn for purely commercial pursuits, in his sense of merchants as tools to be used in the interests of the state. Years later in an outburst to his friend John Laurens he wrote, "You know I hate the money-making men."[13] Resentment, however, was soon the least of his troubles. He was barely one month past his thirteenth birthday when Rachel died of typhoid fever on February 19, 1768, at the age of thirty-nine.

Alexander himself had been desperately ill at the time of his mother's death. One can imagine his sensations upon recovering to discover this final loss. This was attended by a blow of a more subtle nature: no gesture appears to have been made by James. Rachel's small estate was meager. The brittle language of the court papers describes a scene of scarcity and want:

> The probate court met here in a house in town belonging to Thomas Dipnal, where an hour earlier a woman named Rachel Lewine died, in order to seal up her effects . . . a chamber containing her effects, together with a trunk . . . sealed in an attic storage room and two storage rooms in the yard . . . after which there was nothing more except some pots and other small things which remained unsealed for use in preparing the body . . . among them 6 chairs, 2 tables and 2 washbowls. The transaction was then closed.[14]

Three days later the court met to distribute her effects among her heirs. The records ring with barbs which contrasted "Peter Lewine, born in marriage with John Lewine, who is said for valid reasons to have obtained a divorce from her," with the "illegitimate children, born after the separation. . . . Peter Lewine has resided and still resides in South Carolina, and according to reports is about 22 years old."

Rachel had left her sons a small legacy, including three slaves willed her by her mother. Levein interceded and obtained them for his child, her "only lawfully begotten heir." Peter Lewein died in Georgia, in the country in which his half-brother had become a power, in 1782. "He dies rich, but has disposed of the bulk of his fortune to strangers," Hamilton wrote to his wife. "I am told he has left me a legacy, I did not inquire how much."[15]

What did this background mean to Alexander Hamilton, thirteen, financially embarrassed and bereft? Behind him lay a vast expanse of human wreckage, from which rose a complex of emotions, troubling and deep. Not all of this was readily apparent: there is some indication at this point (as in the instance of his father) that he had driven some of his emotions underground. On the surface was the innate pessimism that was to separate him from the believers in the benevolence of human nature, with whom he would be politically embattled later on. There was a complex attitude toward women, stemming from conflict involving his mother

19

and her life. There was an intense if guarded hunger for a father's hand. George Washington, strong, virile, responsible and perennially forgiving, would supply much of the parenting he missed. Yet Hamilton remained suspicious, vengeful, on the guard for slights. When the moody general declined to play the ever attentive paragon, Hamilton considered him "indelicate" and "cold."

There was another aspect of his character: he had begun to dream. Fueled by his own imagination or the thwarted longings of his disappointed parents he had begun to nurse the idea that the islands and his cramped condition were not to be the limits of his life. His reading would strengthen this vision, feeding his mental powers and providing necessary escape. Plutarch, an early and an enduring favorite, would point the way toward a public future: an ideal of honor in the ego's merging with the glory and traditions of the state. As yet the substance of these dreams was nebulous: he would call them his "Castles in the Air." The airy tone was suited to the child of thirteen. Nothing more tangible had as yet come his way.

Meanwhile, there was the immediate future to be faced. There was no money to send the orphaned boys to school. James was sent off to a carpenter—and thence into oblivion—Alexander to Nicholas Cruger, an importer and merchant, as an apprentice and a clerk. To his children Hamilton described him as an "opulent" merchant, perhaps to impress them, perhaps because he did seem opulent to him. Doubtless there was a sympathetic or proprietary interest: Cruger had supplied Rachel with dry goods in the days when she kept store. Hamilton was later to remember him as a kind employer—in America he would charge nothing for handling legal matters for Cruger's sons.

At the warehouse, Alexander gave the first full demonstration of the talents that were to create his dazzling career. The boy, who wrote poetry in his spare moments, could also calculate complex accounts of sales and imports, balancing the larger picture with a keen eye for detail. When Cruger took a trip in 1771 and left him alone to manage, Alexander showed an amazing grasp of business, sending off complete if breathless letters mingling accounts of shipments of staves, mules and caskets of vinegar with grim warnings of the *Guardas Costas* (privateers). He ventured with some audacity a tart comment on the captain, hired to keep pirates clear of Cruger's ships. "Give me leave to hint to you, that you cannot be too particular in your instructions,"[16] warned the sixteen year old. He added that the captain "seemed to want experience" in matters of the sort.

20

Still, what were staves and vinegar to Rachel's disappointed son? John Church's accounts of his father at this period show the unmistakable signs of thwarted will:

> He mastered its details [wrote John Church of the warehouse] but the inward promptings of his mind looked far beyond it. . . . He thought of immortality, and fondly contemplated from his island home those fields of glory and summits of honor which displayed themselves to his imagination from beyond the deep.[17]

The precise extent and passion of these imaginings had been confided earlier to Edward Stevens, a friend who had escaped to school in America when Hamilton was two months shy of fifteen years old:

> To confess my weakness, Ned, my Ambition is [so] prevalent that I contemn the grovelling condition of a Clerk or the like to which my Fortune, &c., condemns me, and would willingly risk my Life, though not my Character, to exalt my Station. . . . My youth excludes me from any hopes of immediate preferrment, nor do I desire it, but I mean to prepare the way for Futurity. Im no Philosopher . . . and may be jus[t]ly said to build Castles in the Air. My Folly makes me ashamd, and I beg youll Conceal it, yet, Neddy, we have seen such Schemes successful when the Projector is Constant. I shall Conclude saying I wish there was a War.[18]

The letter was prophetic of the entire nature of his life. He was ashamed of his musings: how could they not seem wildly unreal? Too unreal, and too embarrassing, to be admitted without backtracking and apologies, even to his closest friend. Yet they had acquired substance as the sustaining factor in his life. As important as this was a concurrent development: the merger of ambition and morality, which was to remain constant all his life. He must rise, but only under strict conditions—that he serve a chivalrous ideal. "My Life, but not my Character . . ." The line contained his fate.

Nothing might have happened if he had not met Hugh Knox. Knox was the Presbyterian pastor of Christiansted, a Scots-Irish émigré who had studied theology at Princeton under the tutelage of the son-in-law of

Jonathan Edwards. Ironically, the man who sent Alexander Hamilton to America was sent on his way to Alexander's island by the father of Aaron Burr. Knox was an expansive creature, a "Universal lover of mankind" whose concept of his duty went beyond the delivering of weekly sermons in his church. He once defined his own creed as "Teaching from House to House . . . [becoming] acquainted with every Person under his Care . . . [to] study their tempers and Dispositions . . . and take care that Children, who are the Hope of the next Generation, be brought up in the Nurture and Admonition of the Lord."[19] It was in this last role that he most saw himself: the mentor and protector of the young. Especially the young and gifted: he had once preached a sermon of praise to Maecenas, patron of Horace, Livy and Virgil, for "drawing these incomparable geniuses out of obscurity, and cherishing and developing their parts." Who on the island was at once more obscure and more promising than Alexander Hamilton, with his taste for poetry and his skill at figures, and his seemingly pathetic fate?

Knox made himself Hamilton's intellectual patron, giving him the access to his library. He encouraged him in the production of essays and verse. Alexander spent evenings in Knox's study, absorbing classics; Sundays at church, absorbing the Calvinistic creed that fit so well with his own experience of eternal sin, conditional redemption and the caprices of a willful God. This training complemented his intensity and pessimism, and its impact lasted for some years. Friends at college recalled him praying night and morning, quoting Scripture and arguing the virtues of "revealed religion" with persuasive force. Knox and his God would capture the part of his nature that craved absorption in a higher purpose and hold it until superseded by another—the "religion" of the cause of the United States.

On August 31, 1772, a hurricane struck the island with devastating force. As the short southern twilight was about to fall, winds and rain roared in from a northerly direction, raging with great violence till ten. There was a respite of an hour as the air grew deathly still. Then the winds, which had circled round the island, blew back in redoubled force, the aroma of gunpowder adding to the terrors and the wind-driven rains lashing the brackish yellow water on the shore. The experience terrified everyone, including Hamilton, who, as was his habit, translated emotion into words. "Good God! What horror and destruction!" he had written. "It seemed as if a dissolution of nature was taking place."

He continued with a vivid picture of meteors and of incessant lightning, played against the crashing sounds of falling houses and the piercing screams of the distressed. His images of God's fury were as vivid as his descriptions of nature's rage.

> Death comes rushing in in triumph, veiled in a mantle of ten-fold darkness. . . . on his right hand sits destruction, hurling the wind belching forth flames—calamity on his left, threatening famine, disease. . . . Where now, vile worm, is thy boasted fortitude? . . . See thy wretched state, and learn to know thyself. Despise thyself and adore thy God.[20]

This last was Calvinism, ingested from Hugh Knox. The color, the empathy, the tragic vision, were his own.

Ostensibly, the piece was written as a letter to his father, the by now long absent James. In reality, it was composed with some thought of publication, as other of his pieces had been. When it was printed in a local newspaper on September 28, it became an island-wide sensation. Though anonymous, it was quoted widely. The Governor wished to know his name. This wave of recognition was steered and monitored by Knox. Into the praise he insinuated questions—was this imagination to waste itself on ledgers and accounts? Other brilliant young people had been sent to college—people like Neddy Stevens, who had fathers with money. The horror of the hurricane was still alive in memory, and Knox played on the islanders with calculated skill. Exactly who contributed to the fund that was set up remains unknown, but the list included relatives, among them his cousin Ann Lytton Venton (later Ann Mitchell) to whom Hamilton showed kindness later on. The Crugers had put in an added sum: a percentage of the profits from their exports was to be set aside for his income with their trading partners, the firm of Kortwright and Co. in New York. Knox himself had high connections in the Presbyterian community in America and had written letters to his friends. Hamilton would be sent to college on the mainland in New Jersey or New York.

There was no anxiety about the choice of place. Reports had reached the islands in 1764 and 1768 of riots over taxes, but the dangers appeared to have been past. The city of Boston was still an armed garrison with a military governor and British troops, but with the repeal of all but one of the notorious Townshend Duties, the differences of the colonies with His Majesty's government appeared to be resolved. No obstacles remained to the voyage to America. He could sail by the new year.

What of Alexander Hamilton, seventeen, about to slip the prison of the islands for the world? On both sides was a solid background, broken by aberrant strains—his mother's fierce and violent, his father's indolent and weak. (Weakness was to be his special terror; "passion" his synonym for feared disorders in the state.) There was an ardent nature, warm and generous, inherited from his parents, matched uneasily with a love of order born of his observation of his parents' lives. There was a craving for legitimacy in all its forms. Out of his disordered childhood comes this passage on the marriage vows, written years later to his intensely loving fiancée:

> Those sacred ties which society has established and heaven approved has something delightful in it that I find myself incapable of expressing. . . . A sincere passion takes pleasure in multiplying the ties by which it is held to its subject, and every new sanction is a new gratification. It seems to think it can never be closely enough linked to what it loves.[21]

All his life he was to cherish the "sacred ties" of law.

There was a deep distrust of human nature running against his native ardor and underlying his veneer of lively charm. "I am restrained by the experience I have had of human nature," he once wrote to his fiancée. "Do not suppose I entertain an ill opinion of your sex. I have a much worse one of my own."[22]

Despite the vivacity, there was a desire to hold others at arms' length. This was the basis of his confession to John Laurens, like himself an aide to Washington, the closest friend of his war years and perhaps of his entire life:

> You know the opinion I entertain of mankind, and how much it is my desire to preserve myself from particular attachments, and to keep my happiness independent of the caprice of others. . . . You should not have taken advantage of my sensibility to steal into my affections without my consent.[23]

Thus the voice of the child victimized by those who had held power over him: the vengeful Levein, the father who deserted him, the mother who died and who, though she protected him, made the family vulnerable to scandal and disgrace. The "caprice" of others was something to avoid.

24

There was one thing more. His sense of his own private honor would fill the empty spaces in his past. In the wreckage of his family was a string of broken vows. Divorce and desertion, errant husbands and runaway wives, splits between parents and children ran back on both sides of his family in a pattern of appalling disarray. No one was completely innocent—even his mother, who had fled a vicious husband, left a child of her own behind. His condemnation of his shattered background would form the moral terrain of his own life. He would be a man of honor. He would honor contracts. He would discharge his debts, unlike his father, who had slipped off in the night.

Late in autumn he was ready to depart. Nothing survives of what must have been his tumultuous sensations as his escape emerged from vision into fact—the first sign of a solid foundation underneath his castles in the air. Ambition aside, there was another cause for pleasure. In a strange country he would not be known as the illegitimate child of a father who deserted him and a mother who had been called a whore.

As he left the tropic glory of the islands, he would be casting off his shame. In paradise the fortunes of his family had followed a descending scale. America, with its harsh seasons and its muted palette, could bring him nothing but release—from his harsh past and from his tethered future, from the "grovelling condition" of a clerk. One by one the conditions of his prophetic letter were taking shape before his eyes. He was born constant. He would reach preferment. All he needed was his war.

I I

HAMILTON'S PASSION for the American nation was the dominant emotion of his life. It was not only his country, but his religion, his home and his family as well. Significantly, it was with the start of the American Revolution that he lost all interest in the Presbyterian creed. He would not regain his interest in religion until he and public life had parted company, some years before his death. The reasons for this extreme attachment are complicated and diverse. He was a young man of deep emotions, who had as yet found little outlet for them save in frustration, ambiguity and rage. The islands, diverse and multinational, supplied no focus for patriotic feelings or ideals.

Three other events made this attachment preternaturally deep. Within weeks of his landing, he found himself in an atmosphere of wealth, power and social prominence that offered him his first experience of security and his first glimpse at an impressive future that he could hope to make his own. Second, the revolution brought the promise of a society founded on a firm moral basis, enshrining the order and balance that he longed for, and had so far in his life been denied. Third, it brought an outlet for the demands of his romantic nature, for the dreams that had been his solace in his lonely childhood and in the long drab hours at his desk. Together their appeal had a great power that produced a lifelong spell.

Hamilton's homes in the islands had been with people on the edge of fiscal, social and emotional disintegration. His first home on the American mainland was with people at the apex of society, blessed with talent, buttressed by money and reinforced by community prestige. William Livingston, Knox's old friend, was master of Liberty Hall, a prestigious mansion dominating the village of Elizabethtown, New Jersey, as Livingston himself, eccentric and literate, dominated its political and social life. He was a younger son of one of the great colonial families, which controlled large portions of the lower Hudson Valley, held high political offices in New York and New Jersey and counted half the great landowning families as kin. Livingston himself was known as a politician, lawyer, wit and scholar, as a relentless foe of imperial and governmental power and as a satirist with an acid, biting pen. In the Revolution he was to rise further, to a truly remarkable career. He served twice as delegate to the Continental Congress, as delegate in 1787 to the Constitutional Convention and as nine-term governor of his state. He died in office in his eighteenth year of power, in 1790.

Hamilton's first setting in America was not only aristocratic, but intensely political, leavened by intellectual esprit. Through Livingston's door passed the elite of the colonies: Elias Boudinot, his friend and neighbor, whose home at Boxwood Hall abutted his; Gouverneur Morris, from Morrisania, north of New York City; and John Jay, pale and solemn, courting Livingston's exquisite daughter Sally, whom he was to wed in 1774. It was Alexander Graydon, portraitist of Hamilton, who left the clearest picture of John Jay: the tall, lean body; the scholar's stoop; the aquiline nose and deep black eyes; above all, the serenity of the genuinely devout:

> His manner was very gentle and unassuming. His deportment was tranquil, and one who had not known him . . . would not have been led to suppose that he was in the presence of one eminently gifted by nature with intellectual power. . . . He thought and acted under the conviction that there is an accountability far more serious than any which men can have to their fellow-men.[1]

The impression left by Morris was of a different nature. The Marquis de Chastellux found him vivacious but "unfortunately maimed," alive with a robust and cynical humor; "an admirable companion at table . . . refined in the dark history of political intrigue."[2] The maiming was a leg, lost below the knee. When the husband of a woman friend

27

returned home unexpectedly early, Morris had fled through a window and jumped into his carriage, which had overturned. It was not the first time that this might have happened. "Gouverneur's leg has been a Tax on my Heart," John Jay had written of the incident. "I am almost tempted to wish he had lost something else."[3] Undeterred, Morris would go on to a full life as a lover and diplomat, becoming the lover of Talleyrand's mistress, and wedding at the age of fifty-seven Anne Cary Randolph, the blighted belle of a Virginia family (a cousin of Thomas Jefferson's son-in-law), a woman of brilliance and character, who had gone to trial for the murder of her child by her sister's husband in 1793. The marriage was fruitful and exceptionally happy. Nature, Chastellux had noted, had not formed Morris for "an inactive man."

Here was a portion of the government in embryo. Boudinot would serve as president of the Continental Congress and hold other high wartime offices; Morris became senator from New York and ambassador to France; Jay served as governor of New York and as first Chief Justice of the United States. The company was impressive, and to a young man from the provinces, perhaps intimidatingly rich. If Hamilton was dazzled, lost or even homesick, he has left no record. His letters to Hugh Knox, which run through the first years of the Revolution and might have served as testimony to his wonder, have been lost.

Hamilton studied at Francis Barber's, a Presbyterian academy near Elizabethtown, and then at King's College (now Columbia) in New York City, entering as a special student in 1773. He was a serious and an attentive scholar, studying to midnight in Livingston's library, rising at dawn in warmer weather to continue reading in the quiet of a nearby graveyard with his thin back resting on the stones. The reading habit was to be compulsive. Through the war he carried with him a battered paybook, filled not with accounts but with notes scribbled from his books— principles of economics, climates and produce of various countries, whole passages from Plutarch's *Lives*.

At King's he studied Latin and anatomy; he engaged a tutor to help him study math. There was relentless effort to improve himself. Robert Troup, whom he met in his first year at college, recalled him practicing oratory at a debating society he formed with four other students and continuing to read and compose verse. He began here his lifelong habit of walking back and forth as he absorbed his lessons or tangled with a mental problem, muttering to himself in a low voice as he paced. His new friends at King's were from the landed, professional and mercantile aristocracy of New York. All were connections to the society he was moving into, ambassadors from a world of tranquillity and balance, models upon whom to base his life.

Livingston had a family of six children, ranging from their teens into their twenties; Boudinot had three small daughters, aged nine, six and two. Hamilton for the first time had the experience of a normal household, untouched by bitterness, unbroken by separation or divorce. It was appealing, but it was the source of added tensions. He was *in* these families, but he was not *of* them, a difference that no amount of good intentions could conceal. It made his past and present circumstances stand out in relief more sharply: a foothold on the edge of power is not a comfortable state. Perhaps for this reason he was willing at age nineteen to leave for a less personal environment when King's agreed to take him as a special student, a concession nearby Princeton did not make. Yet they had laid claims upon him that he could not readily dismiss. When Boudinot's infant daughter died, he wrote a poem for the grieving parents. The night before the burial, he stayed up all night to watch the tiny corpse.

Hamilton was still at Liberty Hall on the night of December 16, 1773, when several hundred Bostonians, enraged at yet another effort of Parliament to impose external taxes on them, boarded three ships as they lay at anchor in Boston harbor and pitched hundreds of pounds of tea into the bay. With the shattering news days later that Boston was to be placed under military occupation, the colonies were plunged into a profound political agitation that was not to end until ten years later when all ties to Britain had been cut. On all sides, the moves brought frantic questionings involving claims of overlapping loyalties that were not easily resolved. Hamilton, émigré as he was, did not escape them, and his torment was intense. He had formed few of the ties that bound Americans to England, and likewise few of the resentments against the slights, insults and curtailments of colonial power. But he did have instincts that exercised another form of power and introduced complications of their own. He was not a rebel by nature, and an uncertain background had confirmed him in this trait. He loathed disorder, hated breakage, and the thought of rupture from what was openly referred to as the "mother country" held profound implications for him that he did not care to face. In his case, however, there were countervailing forces: his friends and patrons were impassioned rebels; a break with them was emotionally dangerous and would have orphaned and exiled him again. Becoming a rebel was not a natural development. A distaste for disruption, for uprisings against order, was to mark him all his life.

Hamilton was a compulsive writer, given to purging his emotions in

29

the press. Twice in his life it was to lead him into trouble; here it was to bring him early fame. As a rebel, he produced two remarkable defenses of the American cause—"A Full Vindication of the Measures of Congress," written in November 1774; and "The Farmer Refuted," an answer to a broadside by a Tory clergyman, in February 1775. They brought him to the attention of men like John Jay as an equal, winning their respect as well as their affection, and contributed largely to Washington's decision two years later to offer him a position as his writing aide. They also shed strange light on the making of a rebel who did not want to be one, and who remained conservative at heart.

In his broadsides Hamilton elaborated on the basic rebel posture, imbibed in Livingston's household and strained through the theories of John Locke: Government is a contract between the ruled and rulers; men exchange obedience for safety, guarantees and rights. But the agreement is not altogether binding: a breach by either party cancels the obligation to obey. The British constitution had declared that men could be taxed only by members of a legislature for which they had directly voted—the House of Commons in England and the colonial assemblies overseas.

This was a momentous issue: the English civil war had started with the attempt to raise "ship money," levied not by Parliament, but by the Crown, the imperceptive Charles I. To the Americans, there was an implication still more dangerous. They saw their right to deny money as their one check on imperial policy and feared their right of self-determination would be lost. Breach of contract was abhorrent to Hamilton, as was another fear inherited from childhood—the fear of being powerless, in the hands of those whose interests were not his.

All this was powerfully expressed in his pamphlets, which took on of necessity an autobiographical cast. Other qualities emerged which were peculiar in both a young man and a rebel: his cynicism, his passion for order and his gentle treatment of the king. Almost nowhere in these pages was there the resentment of authority, the restlessness, that is thought to typify the young. What was present was an icy, brutal cynicism that was brought to bear not only on the British, but on mankind as a whole.

This was the first appearance of the creed of "interest," which became the mainspring of his thought. Parliament, he said, was moved by selfishness—what its members feared was loss of office; what they hoped to gain were votes. Americans, who could neither punish nor reward them, were powerless to influence their dealings, and so should not be at the mercy of their laws.

We are without those checks upon the Representatives of Great Britain which alone can make them answer the end of their appointment with regard to us, which is the preservation of the rights, and the advancement of the happiness of the governed. The direct and inevitable consequence is, *they have no right to govern us.*[4]

To expect men with such powers to govern gently was to ignore history as well as the nature of the human race:

The people of Britain must . . . be an order of superior beings, not cast in the same mold with the common degenerate race of mortals, if the sacrifice of our interest to theirs be not entirely welcome . . . the philanthropy of their representatives will be of a transcendant and matchless nature, should they not gratify the natural propensity of their constituents, in order to ingratiate themselves.

Unchecked, this tendency would lead to cruel developments:

Parliament . . . would oppress and grind the Americans as much as possible. . . . Jealousy would concur with selfishness, and for fear of the future greatness of America . . . every method would be taken to drain it of its wealth.[5]

These are extraordinary comments for a young person. "Degenerate" is not the way the average young man of twenty views the human race. The pamphlets at first had been anonymous. Many guessed they were the work of William Livingston, a cynic nearly sixty years of age.

Surprisingly also, he was neither moved nor frightened by the king. In fact, he felt affection for him, laying the incursions on American liberties at the feet of Parliament instead. Parliament, he said, had greater "interest" in the subjection of America, and therefore was the more deadly foe:

The authority of Parliament over America would in all probability be a more intolerable and excessive species of despotism than an absolute monarchy. The power of an

31

absolute prince is not temporary, but perpetual. He is under no temptation to purchase the favor of one part . . . at the expense of another . . . but to treat them all the same.[6]

Carefully, he separated the monarch from the concept of tyranny, keeping them distant and apart:

You are mistaken when you confine arbitrary government to a monarchy. It is not the supreme power being placed in one instead of many that discriminates an arbitrary from a free government. When any people are ruled by laws in framing which they have no part . . . without in the same manner binding the legislators . . . they are in the strictest sense slaves.[7]

Lack of control of the agents of power was his sole criterion of tyranny, to which its forms were incidental. Britain, with its king ever more a figurehead, was never a despotic government, while France, though its form changed radically, remained so, alike under the Terror as in her reign of Bourbon kings. Hamilton was careful in his tracts to emphasize that while Parliament was a tyrannical power for the Americans, who did not elect it, it was a legitimate body for Englishmen, who did. And he retained a fondness, if not for George III, for the idea of the monarch as the paternal, all-embracing father, the symbol of unity and strength. The figure to him was benign, not menacing. So pervasive was his dream of order that he tried to re-create it in his own country in the form of a president, greatly powerful and placed in office for life. He was honestly astonished when his enemies denounced this as the seed of despotism and as a potential threat.

In the end Hamilton was able to accept his role as rebel only by a complex accommodation of his own. In his mind Britain became the revolutionary, by overturning long-standing laws of nature and of its own constitution to satisfy its passing interest and its greed. He could rebel only in the name of tradition and stability, against a power without reason or restraint. The specter of disorder haunted him even on his own side of the quarrel. He did not regard intensity of belief as an excuse. There was a rumor that he saved the Tory president of his college from being tarred and feathered. When patriots wrecked the presses of a Tory printer, he sent a troubled letter to John Jay:

I am always more or less alarmed at every thing which is done of mere will and pleasure, without proper authority. Irregularities I know are to be expected, but they are nevertheless dangerous, and ought to be checked by every prudent and moderate mean.[8]

He insisted later that the Revolution had been an act of order, taken to restore a balance that had been wantonly destroyed. Britain had broken faith with the laws of God, justice and her own constitution; the Americans had gone to war only for "rights and privileges *antecendently* enjoyed."[9] The distinction was an important one; he insisted they had broken no new ground. In time he came to deny the name of revolution in itself. When the Chevalier de Pontgibaud, a French officer who had served with the Continental army, visited America in 1797, he recorded this conversation in the course of a visit with his friend.

Our separation cannot be called a revolution [Hamilton had told him]. There have been no changes in the laws, no one's interests have been interfered with. . . . All that is altered is that the seat of government is changed.[10]

Hamilton's delight in military action became the driving passion of his life. In time this was to frighten many of his adversaries: John Adams, in a slighting reference to his size, his appearance and his unabashed hunger for battlefield glory, referred to him as "the Bloody Buoy." Some historians have agreed with Thomas Jefferson, who saw in him a Caesar manqué, too eager for combat, with a hidden urge to govern by the sword. It is certain he was sometimes thrown off balance. He was wrong, for instance, in his urgings in the late 1790s that the United States go to war with France.

Not only were his manners martial—he always moved and stood just like a soldier—so were the patterns of his mind. Military standards were in part his standards, by which he judged other people and himself. George Washington was a great man because he was cool in battle. It was easy for him to hate Horatio Gates, the enemy of Washington and of his future father-in-law Philip Schuyler, because Gates had a reputation for cowardice and had once in battle run away. The dream of conquest, of himself as hero, was never very distant from his mind. Though repelled by the politics of Caesar and Bonaparte, he saw them as heroes. Later he would be drawn almost fatally into the schemes of Francisco de Miranda, a South American adventurer, to free Latin America from Spain. Following his example, his surviving sons would enlist in most of the wars in their lifetimes; one, James Alexander, making a valiant effort to join the Union army at the age of seventy-five. There is a persistent feeling in his correspondence as well as in his children's writings that people like Thomas Jefferson, who shied from battle, were not completely men.

But there were softer parts to this enthusiasm that cut its iron edge. He disliked brutality, or the idea of causing pain. He was invariably generous to prisoners. At Yorktown he stepped between his soldiers, who had lost a favorite officer, and their British captives to keep them from taking their revenge. In 1782 he sent Henry Knox an anguished letter protesting rumored plans to kill British prisoners in reprisal for enemy atrocities. He insisted that the murder of the helpless was not moral, that Americans did not do things like this. As did Washington, he showed more anger toward American speculators than toward British soldiers. He disliked men less for politics than for qualities of heart. In politics he showed signs of hatred toward the French Directory, but this had its basis in that regime's excessive cruelties, in the blood-soaked horrors of the guillotine.

He saw war as a chivalric exercise, a stage for him to act on and to display the qualities of selfless courage that would win him honor, love and the accolade of a place in history with the people he had read about in books. It was not the men he killed, but the chances he took in daring other men to kill him that mattered, and that gave his passion those extreme romantic underpinnings, as lethal and compelling as a drug. Alexander Hamilton at twenty-one, captain of artillery in the Continental army after months of training in a volunteer company, was ready to embrace his fate.

There were few shots at glory in the calamitous first year of war. The army, plagued by indiscipline, inexperience and the political weakness inherent in the structure of thirteen colonial governments trying to make themselves a nation, suffered the inevitable problems when confronted with British regulars augmented by Scots regiments and hired soldiers from the German province of Hesse-Cassel. In March 1776 George Washington, named commander-in-chief by Congress in June 1775, drove the British from Boston with a massive cannonade from the heights of Dorchester, ending a siege of eleven months. But on coming to New York in spring, he was confronted with a British army twice as large as his, infinitely more experienced and backed by the massive power of the British fleet.

On August 26 the British demolished an American outpost stationed on Long Island; by September 30 they had driven the entire rebel army from New York. In October the Americans were harried through Westchester and across the Hudson River. In November there was a desperate retreat through New Jersey that took on the nature of a rout. Supplies dwindled and desertions were rampant; on December 22 Washington crossed the Delaware into Pennsylvania with barely twenty-five hundred men. On Christmas night, in a march that began at eight P.M. in a driving snow storm, he recrossed the river, marched all night to Trenton, reached the town just as dawn was breaking and in a lightning bombardment of artillery, captured a Hessian cantonment of twelve hundred men. On January 6 he struck again at Princeton in a repeat performance, this time seizing British regulars. He had rolled back the British lines from the outskirts of Philadelphia to just below their stronghold at New York.

Hamilton's artillery was conspicuous in both engagements, and he himself was becoming widely known. "I saw a mere boy," wrote one soldier, "with small, delicate and slender frame, cocked hat pulled down upon his eyes . . . [who] marched behind his cannon, patting it now and then as if it were a pet horse or plaything."[11] His very fragility set off his martial fervor. He looked like a child playing war.

One officer saw his company marching into Princeton. "It was a model of discipline, at their head was a boy, and I wondered at his youth, but what was my surprise when he was pointed out to me as that Hamilton of whom we had heard so much."[12] He was living his fantasies, as were others of Washington's young troops. If there was an extreme note in his behavior, it was written off as the war fever common to others and did not yet seem strange.

Only the oldest among his acquaintances sensed the presence of something desperate and strained. Edward Stevens, who had sailed for medical school in Edinburgh before the onset of the Revolution, was appalled when he learned from Hugh Knox that Hamilton had become a soldier in the field.

> How are you [he wrote to Hamilton] and how have you been since I saw you last? If you are in good health, then all is well with you. . . . I have been greatly tormented by thoughts of your health, which has been very dear to me since the start of our friendship. I don't know how you will be able to survive the fatigues and hardships of a winter campaign in America. Surely your constitution will never

35

sustain these severities, without the aid of some extraordinarily strong force.[13]

Stevens was then a qualified doctor, who had known Hamilton since he was very young. If his health had been a worry since childhood, and in the warm climate of the islands, it points to a systemic weakness that made involvement in military ventures a constant danger to his life.

The winter campaigns were especially hazardous: the attacks on Trenton and Princeton had each involved a frigid predawn march. Afterwards in winter quarters he had a two-month illness of unknown nature that he described to Hugh Knox only as "severe." One year later, after another campaign involving forced marches, two battles and a winter trip to Albany, he had another illness that is better documented. He collapsed at Peekskill with "violent rheumatick pains" throughout his body; he was thought to be dying; twice he was "cold high as the knees."

Not until the war had shifted to the southern sector did his wracking illnesses abate. Even then, in 1779, his friend James McHenry, who had also studied medicine, was prescribing a diet for a protracted stomach illness, "designed also to correct your wit."[14] After Yorktown, a campaign of no special hardship, he was ill for months, describing himself in December as "still in and out of bed." He was ill constantly, almost on a yearly basis, for the remainder of his life. Stevens in his letter had referred to a "délicatesse de constitution," suggesting many possible weaknesses; it is likely he had rheumatic fever when quite young. Thus, aside from the possibility of death by bullet, which he went out of his way to court on all occasions, he must have known that he faced risks beyond those run by others. His very presence on the battlefield was an enormous hazard to his life. There is here almost a wish to die. His early claim, that he would give his life to make his reputation, takes on an ominous new tone.

He was in a contest with his own mortality in which normal rules were void. His standards were fierce and he drove himself relentlessly, using his weakness as a goad to hazard more. He was living now the code of Caesar, which he had read in Plutarch when still young.

> There was no danger to which he did not willingly expose himself, no labour from which he pleaded an exception. His contempt of danger was not much wondered at by his soldiers, for they knew how much he coveted honour. But his enduring so much hardship, which he did to all appearances

36

beyond his natural strength, very much astonished them. For he was a spare man, had a soft and white skin, and was distempered in the head, and subject to an epilepsy. . . . But he did not make the weakness of his constitution a pretext for his ease, but rather used war as the best physic . . . whilst, by indefatigable journeys, coarse diet, frequent lodgings in the field, continual labourious exercise . . . he struggled with his diseases, and fortified his body against all attacks.[15]

While in hospital, he received an offer that altered the direction of his life—an invitation from George Washington to join the staff at headquarters, with the rank of lieutenant colonel and the position of aide-de-camp. His first reaction was to hesitate. He prized his independence, and he was reluctant to place his destiny in the hands of others, an act his experience had taught him was unwise. He loved his command and its chance for danger—there was little hope for glory at a desk. Washington was a lure, as was the idea of headquarters. He would have a bird's-eye view of operations at the very center of command. But appealing as this was, he felt a tremor. This was not his idea of war.

At twenty-two, he had evolved a code of honor that would control him all his life. He took the great for models, tried to emulate them and lashed himself severely when he failed. His heroes were soldiers and statesmen, sometimes both, who found their private joy in public service and placed cause and country above self. Their gods were *civitas* and honor—intense pride in private excellence and absolute devotion to the state. There was the implicit embrace of danger: few of his heroes had died quietly in bed. There was also the acceptance of a deadly bargain: life was the coin with which to purchase fame. In this as in much else he was again like that hero of whom Plutarch had written:

Caesar was born to do great things, and had a passion after honour; and the many noble things he had done did not now serve as an impediment to him to sit still and reap the fruits of his past labours, but were incentives and encouragements to go on, and raised in him ideas of greater glory, as if the present were all spent. It was in fact a sort of emoluous struggle with himself, as it had been with another, how he might outdo his past.[16]

37

I I I

SURPRISINGLY LITTLE is known of the exact nature of the relationship between George Washington and Alexander Hamilton, save for its strength and its tenacity, for the freedom with which these two guarded men habitually addressed each other and for the fact that much of their later correspondence has the quality of interrupted thought. With the exception of Hamilton's explosion in the heat of their one quarrel, they seldom wrote about each other to third parties, and there their language was understated and restrained. Of these, the most revealing are Hamilton's note to Tobias Lear, Washington's last secretary, that Washington was "an *Aegis,* very essential to me,"[1] and Washington's to John Adams, that Hamilton "possess[ed] the Commander's Soul."[2] "Possess the . . . Soul" is an odd expression, suggesting an intuitive and almost mystic knot. An *"Aegis"* is a shield or emblem; its function, the protection from hostile elements of a vulnerable being who would otherwise be naked and alone. There is a suggestion also of the supernatural, of powers almost godlike in their scope.

Washington ran his staff like a large household, treating his intimates as kin. He called his staff "the family"; his generals, like Anthony Wayne, Nathanael Greene and Henry Knox, my brothers"; and the younger men, "my child," or "my boy." The aides lived very much like children in a nursery, bunking together six or seven to the room, writing

38

at their desks all day like schoolchildren and joining their elders—generals, diplomats and visiting Congressmen—in the common dining room for meals. If this filled Washington's longings for the family that fate had denied him, it also came quite close to Hamilton's fantasies. His new life was a parody of the one he had missed in his childhood, with the special addition of the potent father. He was drawn to it, but he feared it too. If his new life tapped feelings he had always yearned for, it stirred resentments he had hidden and may also have repressed. As he told Philip Schuyler later, he had joined the staff only with some doubts: he did not want to be dependent, and he viewed older men (as he would also view some women) with misgivings, for he associated them with betrayal and with loss.

George Washington when Hamilton met him was forty-five years old. He was not yet the hero he would become some years later, but several of his achievements, with his striking looks, his physical power and his already awesome courage, had begun to clothe him in the raiments of a myth. It is hard now to look back through the mists of history to see him as he appeared to a young soldier: a strapping figure six feet two (an immense height in those days, especially to the slight and fragile Hamilton) with the musculature of the born athlete and the fluid movements of a man who had followed Indians through countless mountain miles in his youth. His skin was fair, flushing easily in weather or emotion, his eyes blue-gray, his hair a reddish chestnut brown. The face was long, full and symmetrical, with an impression of balance and harmony, though the painter Gilbert Stuart would note the visceral, almost primitive power in the broad bones of the nose and cheekbones, the depth of the sockets and the unusually wide spacing of the eyes. Force and sympathy are the traits of the born leader. They are the traits too of the ideal father, of whom all children dream.

Washington was an erratic general, by turns brilliant and hesitant, with a tendency to indecision coupled with a talent in extremities for the bold and daring stroke. Crisis alone could totally free him from the constraints of his paralyzing diffidence. Like all leaders, he was at his most effective under stress. But his genius in this war lay in his political mastery: his ability to grasp the core of a problem and hew to it through endless diversions, his instinctive talent for diplomacy and his genius at the art of using men. He understood from the beginning that independence alone was a partial and an incomplete solution, that the states must merge into a total union if they were to flourish or survive. Thus, through the war he would conduct himself as the leader of a united nation when

39

the opposite too often was the case, urging the flow of power to the national government, allowing himself to function as its symbol and its heart. This stewardship was the function of his paternal nature which, thwarted on the private level, reached out to embrace the army, the government and every aspect of national life.

The tragedy of Washington's life was that this man, whose every instinct was parental, had been denied his own children. He was sterile, perhaps from childhood infections, and the two surviving children of his wife's first marriage brought him only anguish and distress. Martha's daughter Patsy had died in her teens after years of suffering from epileptic seizures. Her son Jacky, an idle, indolent and spoiled creature, showed his hatred for his powerful stepfather by avoiding the army through six years of conflict, making a lone appearance only at the siege of Yorktown, literally in his own backyard. Deprived thus of children, Washington was cool to all but one of his surviving siblings, and his beloved half-brothers were long dead. The war, surrounding him as it did with quasi-brothers and a cluster of young aides who worshipped him, brought a secret pleasure of its own.

Most of his aides, whose backgrounds were less troubled, more traditional, responded easily to this overwhelming paternalism, sensing no danger to themselves. Hamilton did not. We have the word of Lafayette that his affection was tempered by an air of distance, almost consciously imposed. Yet these defenses were only partially effective and testified to the power of the spell. Of all the aides it was Hamilton who was to be drawn most completely into Washington's circle to become his ally, his intimate and, in a most important sense, his heir.

From the beginning of 1777, the lives of Washington and Hamilton were inextricably entwined. They remained so to Washington's death. Their mental accord was instantaneous. Washington, whose voluminous correspondence often touched on political subtleties, was delighted to find an aide who not only understood them but saw them from his viewpoint, and so could express his feelings with no instruction on his part. This accord, which flourished through the crucial period of nation building, grew into a remarkable duet. The story of the American government in the first years of its administration is also the tale of this alliance, founded here in the fires of the war.

The alliance also filled needs of a less tangible nature, whose subtleties today remain unclear. On Hamilton's part it was not completely without strain. He rebelled intermittently against Washington's power, rejecting the dependency he craved. This protection, extending into his mid forties, did him a practical disservice: shielded by Washington's mystique and power, he developed no skills at compromise or at negotiation, learned nothing about caution or restraint. In the end the price exacted was substantial. Outside the realm of Washington's sheltering presence, he was helpless and adrift. The relationship produced one of the ironies of a dramatically marked existence. Hamilton, the deserted child, forced into maturity too early, was oversheltered in his mature years. Treated by Washington as the favored child to be indulged and protected, he has come down to history in the role of the eternal protégé.

What Hamilton himself thought of the relationship is revealed obliquely in his choice of the pseudonym "Phocion" for a series of essays signed in 1784, just after the formal ending of the war. Phocion in Plutarch is described as a stranger, a young man from another country, whose parentage is shameful and obscure. Early in life he became an aide to a general, Chabrias. If it is possible to see Hamilton in Phocion, this proud, self-conscious and painfully defensive young man, it is possible also to see Washington in this general of temper, courage, kindness and caprice. The parallels are striking. Chabrias is described as moody and prone to attacks of indecision, but he is also ferocious in battle, his courage so marked that he throws himself into battle without caution or restraint. Washington rode point-blank into enemy fire and frightened his officers by walks amid a rain of shells. Chabrias was kindly, generous in spirit, but with an "unequal and capricious humor," prone to blasts of fury that could terrify his aides. Thomas Jefferson called Washington "high-toned and irritable." His outbursts later in Cabinet meetings made strong men pale. Between the two, Plutarch reported, grew a rapport so marked that they could read each other's minds. If this was Hamilton's assessment, it was a poignant and a graceful one, as well as a quiet nod of thanks. For Chabrias, Plutarch says, used Phocion less as an assistant than another self, "used his assistance in all affairs of moment . . . loved him much, and procured him commands and opportunities for action, giving him means to make himself known in Greece."[3]

Hamilton's role as captain of artillery kept him isolated in authority, above and distant from his men. On the contrary, staff life was a forging bed of intimacy with its elements of daily contact and of shared, consistent stress. Hamilton became close to Wayne, Knox and Greene among the generals, and among the aides to Tench Tilghman, Richard Henry Harison, John Fitzgerald, James McHenry and Richard Kidder Meade.

41

There was a special friendship with Baron von Steuben, a German émigré many years his senior who had come from Prussia via Paris and spoke only the most broken English, but whose incessant drilling did much to instill discipline and form into the troops. Later Hamilton "adopted" the Baron when both lived in New York, pressing Congress to grant him pensions and stipends, feeding him at his own table and bringing him into his family as something of a ward. He was awed by Steuben's courage, impressed by his dedication and touched by his innocence, for off the battlefield the Baron was as simple as a child and required care in keeping out of debt. There were also two other friendships—both with young aristocrats, one French and one American—that had a special meaning for his life.

Marie Joseph Paul Yves Roche Gilbert du Motier, Marquis de Lafayette, came from one of the great families of the French nobility. In September 1777, when Hamilton first met him, he was just twenty years old. His background in itself was glamorous. He was descended from ten generations of distinguished soldiers; his father had died in battle without having seen his infant son. This history had an inflammatory effect on Lafayette's imagination. "You ask me when I first longed for glory and liberty," he wrote in a memoir. "I can recall no time when I did not love stories of glorious deeds, or have dreams of travelling the world in search of fame."[4]

He was married at sixteen in an attempt to quiet him, but it did not have a domesticating effect upon his nature, and he was consumed with a desire to escape. "Republican anecdotes delighted me," he remembered, "and when my wife's family obtained a place for me at court, I did not hesitate to be disagreeable to preserve my independence. It was while I was in that frame of mind that I first learned of the troubles in America."[5] He now had a daughter, his wife was again pregnant and his family was appalled by his designs. "Some circumstances which it is not necessary to relate," he recounted, "taught me to expect from my family only obstacles to the attainment of my goal."[6] One wonders if this opposition was part of the allure.

Secretly, he secured a vessel and sailed for America without informing his relatives about his plans. "You will be astonished, my dear Papa, by what I am about to tell you," he had written his father-in-law from London, adding importantly, "I have found a unique opportunity to distinguish myself." He vowed to blow up his ship rather than surrender if captured by the British, and when he first set foot on American soil, his first words were "an oath to conquer, or perish in the cause."[7] Wending his way north through the Carolinas, he joined the army outside Philadelphia in the late summer of 1777. At the battle of Brandywine on September 11 he managed to fulfill at least one of his ambitions by being dramatically wounded in the leg. His ardor and simplicity endeared him at once to Washington, as did his usefulness. He became invaluable as the unofficial liaison between America and the French government, to extract supplies and troops from France. He had also become a friend to Hamilton, who served as his interpreter until he had learned English, and both became close to John Laurens.

Laurens was taller than Hamilton and sturdier than the reedy Lafayette; his handsome face, with its prominent nose and expression of somber melancholy, had the aspect of a Roman coin. The child of privilege and power, he came from an immensely rich family in the plantation country of South Carolina. His father, an early proponent of colonial independence, was a president of the Continental Congress and Washington's close friend. Laurens had been expensively educated in Switzerland, had married Martha Manning, a daughter of a director of the Bank of England, and was living in London when the war broke out. Here his story parallels Lafayette's: rumors say his desperate in-laws tried to bribe him to remain in England, but that he eluded them and their agents and boarded a ship for the United States. He never saw his daughter, born in France in 1777, and he never saw his wife again.

Gifted, charming, dramatically brave, Laurens was the golden boy of the rebellion. But there was an undertow beneath his glamour, a current of anger and despair. He stormed ceaselessly against injustices; he could not come to terms with life. He flung himself into forlorn causes with desperate fervor, as if it were the very hopelessness he loved. At the battle of Germantown on October 4, he had dashed up to a stone mansion in which part of the British army had barricaded itself, hacking at its door with his sword, clutching a torch in his other hand with which he tried to set it on fire, while bullets from the upper windows rained on him from above. He turned against slavery, the source of his own private fortune, devising with Hamilton a plan to draft slaves into the army and release them as free men. He made frequent trips to Charleston to plead his case to the state legislature, which treated the idea of armed blacks with horror and Laurens himself with contempt. Sent to France on diplomatic missions, he returned when the war was all but over and insisted upon volunteering to clear out pockets of enemy resistance in the south. On August 27, 1782, he left a sickbed to face a British party that had come out from occupied Charleston for supplies. Ignoring their pleas that they had come for barter, he attacked them and fell mortally wounded on the first fire, finding the death he longed for at the age of twenty-nine.

43

What drove John Laurens to his early doom? Some clues appear in the first edition of a life of Hamilton, published in the 1850s by Alexander's son John Church. Drawing upon unknown sources, the younger Hamilton found Laurens "infected with a self-distrust, a confiding weakness of temper," trapped in a longing for "ideal perfection" that led him to despise his life. What produced this inner bleakness is unknown. John Church added one more sentence, the meaning of which is obscure: "His friends knew of the deep wound he had received at an early period," and "that there was that upon his memory"[8] that made his last moment the most desired of his life. There are no further explanations of this trouble. In the revised edition the passage is entirely expunged.

Laurens's melancholy touched a special note in Hamilton's own nature, as Hamilton seemed to be the only one to sense the dark rivers running underneath the surface of the Revolution's perfect knight. In no way were they more alike than in their disregard of danger. Hamilton appalled onlookers by parading with his troops atop an open parapet in full range of enemy fire in the siege of Yorktown in 1781.

There was a sinister undercurrent to these friendships, for they were in a competition literally to the death. Whether to fulfill a brilliant heritage like Lafayette, to deny a bad one like Hamilton or to assuage whatever demons haunted John Laurens, the three young men were in search of a definition of themselves that could find expression only in their willing sacrifice—a fact that did not escape an acute observer of the battle of Monmouth, who noted that the younger members of the family appeared to be in a race among each other as to who should be the first to die. It was a grisly sport that they engaged in, and it was to take its toll. Two of the three died before old age in conditions suggestive of suicide, while Lafayette, the survivor, was in great danger throughout the French Revolution and almost died in an Austrian jail. His son managed to visit America in 1796, where he called on Hamilton, but Lafayette, confined to Europe, did not return till 1824. He was then sixty-seven years old. He had an enchanted visit with Thomas Jefferson, whom he had known as governor of Virginia when he was a young soldier in the war. The two old men strolled through the exquisite grounds of Monticello as they reminisced about the past. The ex-President, wary, unmartial and instinctively self-protective, was alert though frail at eighty-four. He was the only old friend Lafayette could visit. Washington, Hamilton and Laurens, his companions of the war, were dead.

Hamilton not only made friends, he made enemies, and he pursued his quarrels with intensity and rage. His aversions, as his affections, were intense. He did not fear power, for two of his quarrels were with major generals. In at least two cases, there were threats of violence, though these came to nothing in the end. Each of these people represented traits that he found threatening—cowardice, slyness or treachery—as courage, "honor," and a certain reckless daring were characteristic of the people whom he loved. He was sensitive to attacks on Washington's authority and attacks on his own honor, and when he learned in 1778 that he was rumored to have urged the people to dismiss Congress and make Washington dictator, he flew into a rage. After much effort, he traced the tale to William Gordon, a man already connected to several plots against Washington, and harried him for a retraction of his words. Though Gordon was over sixty, Hamilton threatened him with a duel and was infuriated when the old man backed down.

Eventually he succeeded in extracting an apology—forcing Gordon to admit to Washington that his evidence was fourth-hand and oblique. The charge in fact might have done great damage. Washington as military leader in a country that distrusted power was vulnerable to charges of ambition, and reports that Hamilton favored a dictatorship might have laid his plans for a career in politics in shreds. But it was the exaggerated nature of his reaction that revealed his developing character. He had a streak of contentiousness, a passionate concern for his reputation and a fatal sensitivity to slights. He was in a constant battle to control his own emotions, a battle that he often lost.

The Gordon episode was in part a private quarrel, but there were others that were not. Since the winter victories at Trenton and Princeton, the war had not gone well. Cliques in Congress and in some parts of the army had begun to turn on Washington as the army under his direction, battling to keep a larger British force out of Philadelphia, suffered a series of defeats. At Brandywine on September 11 the Americans were outmaneuvered and outnumbered; an attack on Germantown on October 4 had ended in a stalemate when an intricately planned maneuver involving the converging at once of four separate columns foundered, as they lost direction in an unexpected heavy morning fog. Some blamed Washington for what they saw as a dangerous concentration of power in the army; others for inexperience, indecision and the failure to achieve a knockout blow. There was some truth in the early charges. Washington could waver badly through his fear of failure, and his decisions in the New York campaign of 1776 were wrong. But the rebels were threatened mainly by organizational weaknesses—a lack of coordination that slowed supplies to a trickle, a lack of power to draft and discipline the army—and by Washington's need to lie about the strength of his own army, to keep the British from descending upon him and from overwhelming his undermanned and underfurnished troops. Lying to the enemy meant also lying to the public, raising expectations he was unable to fulfill. Through the first years of the war Washington was the victim of his own skillful propaganda, forging with his deftly leaked false estimates sharp weapons for his enemies to use. As he moved into winter quarters at Valley Forge late in 1777, with Philadelphia in the hands of the British, movements rose to replace him and his favorites, among them Wayne, Greene, Laurens, Lafayette and Hamilton, and to replace them with a man more acceptable to Congress who could promise more in the way of military success.

Horatio Gates was a major general and in charge of the armies of the north. In September he had won a dazzling victory capturing a British army under John Burgoyne at Saratoga while Washington was losing Philadelphia to the British, a contrast Washington's enemies did not scruple to exploit. Whether it was in fact his victory had been disputed: he was rumored to have hidden in a farmhouse, arguing with a wounded British soldier, while Benedict Arnold, who suffered a shattered leg in the encounter, led the forces in the field. Philip Schuyler claimed with great hatred that Gates "never saw an enemy, except at a good distance, and from places of perfect security."[9] Hamilton's own comment was concealed in a note of praise for Washington: "He did not hug himself at a distance and allow an Arnold to win his victories for him, but by his own presence brought order out of confusion, animated his troops, and led them to success."[10] Earned or not, Gates's victory at Saratoga added new luster to his name, nurturing hopes in a clique in Congress and the army that they had now found their savior, who could reverse the currents of the war.

A foretaste of Gates's power had come earlier in the year, when his allies in Congress had maneuvered him into the command once held by Washington's friend Philip Schuyler, a warning of his political guile and of the skill and resource of his friends. Gates was now the pet of Washington's enemies, and in particular of Thomas Conway. Conway was an Irish adventurer who had himself made a general by Congress. Having floated into camp on a tide of insults, he made himself cordially hated by Washington's friends. Gates in Albany, Conway at Valley Forge and Congress at Trenton now became the three arms of a triangular plot, however rudely connected, to displace Washington, make Gates commander and assume all power for themselves.

In late November Hamilton was sent to Gates at Albany with orders to extract one thousand soldiers, no longer needed in the northern sector, to reinforce the small and harried army in the south. The errand itself was an indication of Washington's trust in Hamilton. The task was delicate, requiring ingenuity and skill. It was also considered most critical: reinforcements were needed if the army was to survive the winter, to continue harassing British outposts and to stave off enemy attack. But on the way north Hamilton had found the generals under Gates hostile and Gates himself slippery. He promised Hamilton troops, then recalled his promise and then tried to dispatch him with a weakened squadron that was inexperienced and undermanned. Their differences were compounded by personal antagonism. Hamilton found it difficult to keep his emotions in control. To Washington he sent off a flood of angry letters. He claimed that Gates was withholding the troops to embarrass Washington and keep him weak and vulnerable; there were other things, too delicate to entrust to the postal system, that he would tell Washington when they were face to face. Fearful of Gates's political power, he could not challenge him directly, and their sessions became tense and strained. He was forced to check his temper, an unaccustomed act, and on the return trip became violently ill. The tension of the errand was a contributing factor, as was his physical exertion, straining as he was to reach Washington with the troops and promises before Gates could once more change his mind.

When Hamilton was able to rejoin the army one month later, the crisis was already past. Gates had been discovered in an incriminating correspondence with Conway and others that he had been unable to adequately explain. In his defense Gates had tried to implicate Hamilton by telling Washington his aide had rifled Gates's papers at Albany and that he had then leaked them to Gates's enemies himself. As the plot unraveled the conspirators were revealed as inept and devious, and their support in Congress melted away. Conway was forced to resign his commission and Gates was posted to Boston, out of the main theaters of the war. There he continued to rage against the family with undiminished venom. Robert Troup, his aide-de-camp, complained to John Jay of "hearing nothing but invective uttered against deserving characters . . . my reverence for certain persons, who had done me infinite and repeated favors, being the most heinous of all my crimes."[11]

In 1780 Gates was sent to North Carolina to repel a British invasion of the South. There at Camden on August 20 he suffered an utter and humiliating defeat. With untrained militia placed at the forefront to take the onslaught of the British regulars, his army had shattered at the first charge of the enemy, and Gates himself had taken flight. "Was there ever an instance of a general running away, as Gates has done, from his whole army?" Hamilton inquired acidly. "One hundred and eighty miles in three days and a half. It does admirable credit to the activity of a man at his time of life."[12] Though it was a catastrophe for the Continental army, which was not repaired until Greene arrived months later, it was typical of Hamilton's continued fury that he could not contain his glee.

Gates had been silly, weak, a bad general and potentially if not actually subversive, but in Charles Lee the family faced an adversary of a very different sort. Brilliant and literate, with an impressive past in a number of European armies, he was also slovenly and foul-mouthed, and filthy in his manner and his dress. He also was trailed by a pack of dogs, some of which he sat with him at table and insisted upon feeding with his guests. He did not regard this conduct as exceptional. "Until the common routine of mankind is somewhat mended," he had told John Adams, "I think the strongest proof of a good heart is to love dogs and dislike mankind."[13] This behavior only added to his reputation. It was believed that such eccentricity bespoke great genius and talents not bestowed on ordinary men.

Evidence of more bizarre behavior soon started to appear. At the end of 1776, during the desperate retreat through New Jersey, Lee withheld his troops along the Hudson from Washington, under the pretense of not having understood his orders at the time. Concurrently, he wrote long letters to Congressmen and other officers that Washington's mistakes were ruining the army and that the only hope of a successful outcome was to dismiss Washington and install Lee himself at once. But there was little time to promote this program of self-advancement. In late December, on his way at last to join Washington, Lee was captured, apart from his army, in a tavern four miles behind his lines. Sixteen months of incarceration in a British prison did nothing to improve his state of mind. When Elias Boudinot, then commissioner in charge of prisoner exchanges, visited him in jail on Long Island in January 1778, Lee took him aside into a corner and whispered there his secret plan. The war, he said, was over. America could not prevail against the Empire's united strength. To prepare for this, Congress must build a fort at Pittsburgh, stock it with gold, and equip it with three hundred boats. When the rebellion collapsed, which in the course of things must happen quickly, the government must flee, sail down the Ohio and Mississippi rivers to New Orleans and petition the Spanish government for relief. So stunned was Boudinot that he made a lengthy entry in his journal, saying he thought Lee had lost his mind.

Lee was exchanged soon after and returned to the army in May. Though Washington received him with great courtesy, Lee continued to berate him in private. He wrote to Boudinot that he "found the army in a worse case than he expected . . . and that General Washington was not fit to command a sergeant's guard."[14] In February the Americans had signed a treaty of alliance with the French government that was in fact to rescue them, supplying in addition to men and money the vitally important naval arm. This accretion of power made Philadelphia untenable for the British, who pulled out in April and headed northward to their stronghold in New York. Through May and June the Americans trailed them through New Jersey, harrying their rear in a series of guerrilla movements and debating the cost of an attack. Hamilton, Lafayette, Wayne and Greene urged battle. Lee alone held back among the senior officers, insisting the British were too strong to be contested and that a strike would end in terrible defeat. When Washington at last decided on a dawn attack on June 28 near Monmouth County Courthouse, Lee refused to lead the advance guard. He said the plan was unworkable and that he would take no part in the attack. When Washington gave the command to Lafayette, Lee reversed himself, saying he outranked the younger general and that that assignment would be wounding to his pride. Washington, in the interests of harmony, deferred to Lee and reinstated him. It was a decision he would soon regret.

No one knows if the British had indeed bought Lee in prison, or if what happened afterwards was a simple matter of disintegration under stress. When Hamilton rode up with Washington in the early hours of June 28, expecting to find the advance driving holes into the British rear guard, they found the corps fleeing with the entire British army at its heels. Lee was discovered at the rear of his retreating troops. He appeared distracted and made no effort to rally or control his men. He appeared rational, but became confused when Washington confronted him, acting as if he had not heard his questions and repeating "What? . . . what? . . ." several times.

Washington saved the day at the last moment, forming the troops seconds before the British onslaught and saving them from shattering defeat. But it was too late for the victory they dreamed of, and the surprise attack turned into a grueling day-long battle in excruciating ninety-nine degree heat. The battle ended at nightfall, when the field was littered with the dead and wounded and the survivors had collapsed exhausted on the ground. Before dawn of the next morning, the British, fatigued and worn, had drawn off. The Americans claimed a triumph in that they had held an army of regulars to a standstill for twelve hours, but they were cheated of the victory they longed for, and the fury of the army was intense. The feelings of the younger soldiers were particularly violent. Hamilton called Lee a "driveller" at the business of soldiership, or, ominously, "something much worse."

Lee was court-martialed for disobedience, found guilty and dismissed. It was decided he had ignored Washington's orders to attack the British and then had failed to press the fight. Hamilton testified against him as did John Laurens. There were curt exchanges as they were cross-examined in the box. The trial and sentencing dragged on through the winter with Lee still at camp, continuing to rage against Washington's officers and against the general himself. Hamilton challenged him to a duel but was forced instead to serve as second to John Laurens, who had made *his* challenge first. There was one fire in which Laurens nicked Lee's shoulder, after which Hamilton intervened to have the duel stopped.

When Lee retired, he slipped more and more into psychosis, nursing fantasies of an elaborate revenge. He spoke of the Revolution as doomed, of Washington as a tyrant and of his "earwigs" as parasites, "corrupt as those of any sceptered calf, wolf, hog or ass." He claimed at times to have won the battle of Monmouth, which he said Washington had nearly lost. He died at last in 1782, one year before the final peace with Britain, attended only by the dogs that constantly surrounded him, in squalor and despair.

Sometime in the middle of 1779, Hamilton's nerves had started to give way. There had been no major battles since Monmouth one year earlier, and the focus of the war had shifted to the south. The addition of the French fleet and army to the American forces produced a stalemate with the British in which both sides were locked in static combat, each too weak to decimate the other and too strong to be destroyed. Speculation was rampant, the army suffered greatly from shortages and there was a devastating crisis of morale. Hamilton raged in print against the speculators, but this proved no more than an outlet for his turbulent emotions, as did his letters to John Laurens, then on duty in the south.

His letters to Laurens breathe a special anguish, born of disillusion, frustration and despair. His language is extreme and bitter. The country, corrupted by greed and indolence, was in a "galloping consumption," ill almost to the death. Selfishness, "interest" and the dead hand of local influence, enemies worse than the King's army, were draining the blood from the war effort and eating at the nation's soul. No one would listen to his suggestions that Congress consolidate power, reform the currency and break the crippling power of the states. He was ill of the world and everything in it, except for Laurens himself "and a *very* few more honest fellows," and wished for nothing more than to make a "brilliant exit"— whether from the army or the world he did not say.

> Indeed my friend [he wrote from Morristown in the course of one winter] you cannot conceive in how dreadful a situation we are. The army in the course of the present month has received only four or five days ration of meal, and we really know not of any adequate relief. . . . The distress at this stage of the campaign sours the soldiery . . . The officers are out of humor, and the *worst* of all evils seems to be coming upon us—*a loss of our virtue.* 'Tis in vain you attempt to appease, you are almost detested as an accomplice of the administration. . . . I say this to you because you know it, and will not charge me with vanity. . . . I hate Congress—I hate the army—I hate the world—I hate myself.[15]

Part of his anguish was rage at his own role. What was he doing languishing at headquarters, while the war, his war, went on? Sometime in autumn he approached Washington for a talk.

> I explained to you [he later wrote plaintively] my feelings with regard to military reputation, and how much it was my object to act a conspicuous part by some enterprise that might raise my character as a soldier above mediocrity. You were so good as to say you would be glad to furnish me an occasion. . . .[16]

Washington, he thought, had promised to help him if an opportunity came up. One seemed to, in a proposed attack. "When the expedition to Staten Island was on foot, a favorable one seemed to offer," Hamilton wrote. "There was a battalion without a field officer, the command of

51

which I thought might be given me."[17] He applied through Lafayette, who brought him Washington's rejection, this time on three counts. As an aide, he was attached to no company. The rank of field officer was above his own rank of lieutenant colonel, and his elevation above the line officers might cause a riot in the ranks. And, his gifts with his pen and his rapport with Washington had made his services too valuable—if he had an "accident," what would the commander do? Hamilton said, or at least wrote, nothing of this incident, but his disappointment was deep.

Next, John Laurens, nominated as secretary to the American mission at Paris, asked Congress to send Hamilton instead. "I am sorry you are not better known to Congress,"[18] he wrote Hamilton. Despite his pleading, Laurens was named instead. Hamilton once more was frustrated, but his annoyance, which he did not hide, was softened by his pleasure for his friend. "I hope it will ultimately engage you to accept the appointment," he wrote stoically, but he let drop a forlorn note. "I am a stranger here. . . . I have no property, no connexions. If I have talents and integrity (which you say I have), these are deemed very spurious titles in these enlightened days."[19]

Finally, he begged Washington to let him join Nathanael Greene, who had gone in the aftermath of Gates's disaster to check the British in the south. This too came to nothing.

> I have strongly solicited leave to go to the southward [he later wrote Laurens]. It could not be denied, but arguments have been used to dissuade me . . . which, however little weight they have had in my judgment, gave law to my feelings. I am chagrined and unhappy, but I submit.[20]

He did not say who spoke to him, but it was doubtless Washington, who must have spoken softly, with much deferential charm. Doubtless too he used arguments he knew would be irrefutable: duty to country, duty to the army and the special duty Hamilton owed to him. If so, it was a manipulative tactic, for it turned the burden of Hamilton's rage upon himself. He could have gone into Greene's army, but at the cost of dreadful guilt. Remaining as aide had been his own decision, a fact he would recall with great resentment. New strains had begun to infuse his feelings about Washington. The "Commander's Soul" could be a heavy burden to possess.

Everything he had done in the family now worked against him: he was unconnected to a regiment, and he had not advanced in rank. His very skills appeared to shackle him. As the right hand of the general, his service was too vital to be risked. His abilities and dedication worked against him; each step forward set him further behind. How could he escape his shadows, shackled as he was to his desk? He was stalled, surely as the Revolution, still a humble aide-de-camp.

I V

In 1780, after a career of dalliance that was at once gallant, predatory and oddly guarded, Hamilton fell in love for the first and last time in his life. She was Elizabeth Schuyler, the daughter of a general in the Continental army. They agreed to marry after a courtship of little more than one month. She had come to visit an aunt who lived near Washington's camp at Morristown. They had met through Kitty Livingston, who was her cousin and his friend.

Eliza was dark, with black hair and skin that was described as "Indian," a warm complexion with an apricot and tawny tone. She was not considered beautiful, but everyone who met her was struck by her eyes—large, black, deep set and liquid, which dominated her thin and fine-boned face. Tench Tilghman, who had met her in 1775, described her as "a Brunette, with the most good-natured, lively dark eyes that ever I saw, which threw a beam of good temper and benevolence over her entire countenance. Mr. Livingston told me I was not mistaken. . . . She was the finest Tempered Girl in the World."[1]

Her charm lay in her sweetness, allied to a nerveless energy, an immense store of animal vitality that sustained her in full vigor to her ninety-seventh year. "Hers was a strong character," wrote James McHenry, warm and deep, controlled in feeling, "glowing underneath, bursting through at times in some emphatic expression"[2] of affection or distaste. Tilghman also called her good-natured and agreeable, but she had a stubborn, independent streak. He recalled a picnic at Cohoes Falls where she "disdained all assistance and made herself merry at the distress of the other Ladyes,"[3] laughing at their awkwardness as she scrambled over the craggy faces of the rocks.

Her father was Philip Schuyler, one of Washington's favorite generals, who had held the command of the northern army before he was displaced by Gates. A great landowner by birth and marriage, he lived in ducal splendor in two mansions in the Mohawk Valley: the Pastures, at the head of Schuyler Street in Albany, and a smaller house at Saratoga, burned in 1777 by Burgoyne. He had known Hamilton for three years as an aide to Washington and was pleased to welcome him as a son. The family was pleased by the match, and the Washingtons, who were fond of both of them, were glad to encourage this romance between an aide whom they had come to see as special and a girl whom they regarded as a pet. There was a fairy tale element to the match. The Schuylers were as close as Americans could come to an entrenched nobility, and the climb, for an orphaned alien, was very great. There were murmurs that Hamilton had been attracted by her money, but the stories were unfair. Touchily proud, he refused to take her money and insisted on living on the salary he made. But their political power was an attraction, as was their substantial status. The Schuylers were supremely legitimate, as had been the Scottish Hamiltons, and as firmly rooted in the land. A more poignant pull was the nature of the family, for the Schuyler clan, large, close-knit, fiercely protective and intensely loyal, was all that he had grown up without. But it was Elizabeth herself, his dark Eliza, who drew him with her strength and innocence, and in so doing revealed many of his hidden conflicts and his complex emotions touching sex.

In 1771, at the age of sixteen, Hamilton had sent a poem to the editors of the *Royal Danish American Gazette*. It was a love poem, outwardly conventional, and for the first four stanzas it stayed closely to its genre. A young man was discovered strolling on a hill. The setting was pastoral, but it was a gentle landscape that bore no resemblance to the island mountains with their fierce colors and their haze of torrid heat. He saw a shepherdess sleeping by a river, and woke her with a kiss. Though ardent, she was also innocent, for Hamilton called her "artless" and recorded her blush. Almost immediately the pair are married: Hamilton, who knew firsthand the perils of unlicensed pleasure, was not about to celebrate its joys. ("Believe me, love is doubly sweet/In wedlock's holy bands.") His concept was mannered and perhaps too idyllic. It was a dream world that he was describing. No worldly cares intruded on his lovers, who inhabited a country of their own.

At the fifth stanza the poem shifted, both in its content and its tone. His heroine changed without warning, and with her, his own voice. He is no longer speaking of a wife, but of a different kind of woman—"Coelia," a conniving temptress whose pleasure is to harry and destroy:

> Coelia's an artful little slut;
> Be fond, she'll kiss, *et cetera,*—but
> She must have all her will;
> For, do but rub her 'gainst the grain
> Behold, a storm, blow winds and rain,
> Go bid the waves be still.
>
> So, stroking puss's velvet paws,
> How well the jade conceals her claws
> And purs; but if at last,
> You hap to squeeze her extra hard,
> She spits—her back up—*prenez-garde;*
> Good faith, she has you fast.[4]

This is the language of intense suspicion, of betrayal in a silken sheath. No one knows what young affair had caused this outburst, yet this idea of the dual nature of woman echoed through his life. There is a dream of fidelity and innocence, and its appeal is strong. But behind this is another vision: the seductress, carnal and glittering, who will ensnare and then betray. The image of woman as temptress and destroyer had become imprinted in his mind. The confusion spilled over to his own behavior, for he too would play a dual role. The rake and the devoted husband would do battle in him for much of his own life. There is some reason to believe that his own adventures were themselves defensive and undertaken in a spirit of revenge. His background, if not his own experience, had taught him that men and women were deceptive and unreliable in their sexual relationships and that it was the nature of each gender to betray.

For some time, the roué in his nature seemed to hold the upper hand. In the army he was known as a rake, a name which seemed to please him, and he was widely popular with the young women and the officers' daughters who came each winter to the camp. At once courteous and

56

somewhat devilish, with his fresh looks and vivid coloring, he spouted classical poetry and sonnets of his own devising in a sprightly manner that enhanced his potent physical appeal. His friends envied him good-naturedly, for he seemed to garner conquests while remaining uninvolved himself. In early January, before he met Eliza, he was seeing two women, one an otherwise unknown "Polly," the other the daughter of an army officer, named Cornelia Lott. He could also be unscrupulous. When he became engaged to Eliza, he did not tell Polly, and he let her leave the camp believing he still cared for her.

By 1779 his reputation had gone beyond the bounds of his own army, for there was a suggestive reference printed in a Tory paper, *Rivington's Gazette:* "Mrs Washington has a tom-cat (which she calls in a complimentary way, Hamilton), with thirteen stripes around the tail, and its flaunting suggested the stripes for the flag."[5] "Tom-cat" is a suggestive idiom, and "flaunting" suggests the behavior of the dapper aide. His name for gallantry was becoming as well known as his reputation for battlefield courage, and perhaps as widely prized.

He enjoyed the game if in fact it was one, but it did not absorb him completely. In a letter to John Laurens in April 1779, he was thinking about something else. He asked his friend, on leave in the south, to find him a bride. While his tone was light-hearted, his instructions were serious, and his specifications were concrete. His wife must be handsome ("I lay most stress upon a good shape"), sensible ("A little learning will do"), "well-bred" but not snobbish, good-natured and generous ("she must love neither money nor scolding"), and pious without fanaticism ("she must love God and hate a saint").[6] She must be "chaste and tender," for his standards of love and loyalty were high. She must also have money, for he had little, and was not inclined to earn more for himself.

His phantom bride is a curious figure. Every trait she has is qualified as if he was disturbed and frightened by excess. It is looks and sophistication that seem most to threaten him, for it is these qualities that might draw other men to her and tempt her to stray. He has attempted to guard against this through a specification of character: though "tender," she must also be "chaste." It is the shepherdess of his poem that he has been describing, though endowed with fortune. He is too realistic to dwell in fantasy, and his reality does not encompass the simplicities of rural life. He is also describing Elizabeth Schuyler, whom he had not then met.

Yet even when he had met and won her, he remained at odds within himself. In February 1780 he wrote at her request to introduce himself to her sister Margarita (Peggy) Schuyler, and this letter has a fascination of its own.

> She is most unmercifully handsome [he wrote of Eliza] and so perverse that she has none of these petty affectations which are the prerogatives of beauty. Her good sense is destitute of that happy mixture of vanity and ostentation which would make it conspicuous to the whole tribe of fools and foplings, as well as to men of understanding, so that as the matter stands it is little known beyond the circle of these. She has good nature, affability and vivacity, unblemished with that charming frivolousness which is so justly deemed one of the accomplishments of the belle. In short, she is so strange a creature that she possesses all the beauties, virtues, and graces of her sex, without any of the amiable defects, which from their general prevalence are esteemed by connoisseurs the necessary shades in the character of a fine woman. . . . She has had the address to overturn all the wise resolutions I had been framing for more than four years past, and from a rational sort of being and a professed contemner of Cupid, has in a trice metamorphosed me into the veriest inamorato you ever saw.[7]

This letter is curious in many ways. He is instinctively flirtatious to his wife's sister, as he would be to women all his life. He is generous in his praise of Eliza, but the praise is qualified. There is a double meaning in his lines. The nouns say one thing, the qualifiers another, and it is in the adjectives that he betrays himself. It is a "happy" mixture of vanity and ostentation that she lacks; the defects she does not have are "amiable" ones; and it is a "charming" frivolousness (which Eliza misses) that is one of the flowers of the belle. This same attraction of conflicting qualities emerged in a letter to John Laurens, in which he says of Eliza, "though not a genius, she has the sense to be agreeable; and though not a beauty, she has fine black eyes."[8] There is a sleeping message in these letters: he is confessing that what she lacks attracts him greatly—and appalls him, with its power to destroy. Yet he reveals too what will bind him to her: she will not entice the "fools and foplings" and begin the intrigues that might lead her to betray. It is not known what Peggy made of this document, for Peggy herself, a "wild young flirt," was an example of the type of woman he was preparing (in marriage) to forswear. Yet such women

58

would continue to attract him. And in Eliza's family he would find another woman, more glamorous than Peggy, who would draw him into something only slightly short of an intrigue.

Angelica Church was Eliza's sister, the oldest of the Schuyler daughters and her senior by something over a year. In July 1777 she had slipped out a window at the Pastures to run away with John Barker Church (an Englishman traveling under the name John Carter), the first of four Schuyler sisters to elope. She lived with Church in Newport and Boston, where he worked in the commissary department of the American army and became extremely rich. Her portraits show a haunting beauty: her face a smooth and perfect oval, her features delicate, her eyes lustrous and dark. Cultured, witty and extremely feminine, exquisitely dressed in the newest and most costly fashions, she had a worldliness that was not possessed by her younger sisters and that captured her generation's greatest men. In 1785 she met Thomas Jefferson in Paris and began a friendship that lasted twenty years. Jefferson's letters to her are among his most appealing; until political differences made the idea impossible, they had planned to exchange visits to Monticello and to the Schuyler home. This tenderness shared for one lovely woman by two rivals of genius has gone down as one of history's ironies, and as the closest human bond of two embattled men.

Clever and literate, gifted with a fine political instinct that deepened her allure to the men her beauty had attracted, she was the coquette Eliza was not. Her correspondence with Hamilton bordered on a special intimacy, charged with an undertone that went beyond the brother-sister tie. She called him her *"amiable"* and her *"petit Fripon"*; she teased him about his ambition and about putting on too much weight. He in turn wrote to her of his political troubles and answered her provocations with a subtle teasing of his own. "Yours as much as you desire,"[9] he wrote in a postscript to one letter to her, implying that she might desire more than was conventional among the most attached of in-laws, and more than even he, if pressed, might be willing to provide. Her roving eye was forgiven as she was not his wife. The devotion of this enchanting woman, who openly confessed that she adored him, added a hidden measure of excitement to his life.

That he might have found her too exciting on a more intimate and more extended basis is suggested in the letters that he wrote Eliza in the months of separation in the first summer of their love. Over and over he wrote of her gentleness, her candid nature, the fierce devotion of her heart.

> I love you more and more every hour. The sweet softness
> and delicacy of your mind and manners . . . the real good-
> ness of your heart, its tenderness to me . . . your unpre-
> tending good sense and that innocence and simplicity and
> frankness which pervade your action . . . appear to me
> with increasing amiableness, and place you in my estima-
> tion above all the rest of your sex.[10]

The qualities that he selects to mention—simplicity, innocence and
frank good nature—are not those that distinguished his Angelica, and not
the hallmarks of the belle. In the end, the serenity and deep repose she
brought him were more seductive than the lure of the coquette. He would
write with truth of his reaction to the most dazzling among her rivals:

> I should only go in quest of disquiet, that would make me
> return to you with redoubled tenderness. You gain in every
> comparison I make, and the more I contrast you with oth-
> ers, the more amiable you appear.[11]

Through the spring, summer and fall they exchanged letters, teasing,
tender and intense. It was their one form of contact, for after Eliza had
left the camp in March they did not see each other until Hamilton arrived
in Albany four days before the wedding on December 10. She saved nearly all the letters he wrote her, but hers to him have all been lost. Clues to
their contents are given only fleetingly in his replies. He teased her about
other women. There was a Dutch girl at Tappan who was complaisant
and pretty, but he was not tempted, as "she has no soul." He urged her to
read more and improve her mind. He called her a sorceress, who had
seduced him from his duties and at night invaded all his dreams.

> You not only employ my mind all day, but you intrude
> upon my sleep. . . . I meet you in every dream, and when
> I wake I cannot close my eyes again. . . . 'Tis a pretty
> story indeed that I am thus to be monopolized by a little *nut
> brown maid*.[12]

He chided her for having sapped his ambition, reducing him from a
soldier to a "puny" lover and lessening his devotion to the war. If the
Revolution failed, he told her, in language reminiscent of the poem of the

60

shepherdess, they would live in Geneva and find happiness in each other's arms. Yet his concern with reputation had not totally been stilled. "I was once determined to let my existence and American liberty end together," he wrote in a revealing sentence. "My Betsey has given me motive to outlive my pride. I almost said my honor, but America must not be witness to my disgrace."[13] This sentence held a quiet warning. No attachments could supersede his need for honor or his inner terror of disgrace.

There were other letters in which he showed another side. The rake and soldier disappeared into the anxious child, afraid to lose something that he had not utterly secured. He worried when there were gaps between her letters and was seized by sudden fears: that he might lose her, to another or to illness, or to some sudden stroke of fate. Despite assurances, he was haunted by fears that she too might desert him, and his letters frequently expressed anxiety.

> It is an age, my dearest, since I have received a letter from you. The post is arrived, and not a line. I know not to what to impute your silence, so it is I am alarmed with an apprehension of your being ill. . . . Sometimes my anxiety accuses you of negligence, but I chide myself whenever it does. You know how precious your letters are to me and you know the tender, apprehensive, amiable nature of my love. You know the pleasure that hearing from you gives me. You know it is the only one that I am capable of enjoying. . . . Here I am immersed in business, yet every day or two I find leisure to write. . . . I do not say this to reproach you with unkindness. I cannot suppose you can in so short an absence have abated your affection; and if you have even found any change, I would have too good an opinion of your candour to imagine you would not instantly tell me.[14]

Then, he relented of even seeming to take issue and closed the letter with a plea:

> For god's sake my dear Betsey, try to write me oftener, and give me the picture of your heart in all its varieties of light and shade. Tell me whether it feels the same for me as it did

when we were together, or whether what seemed to be love was nothing more than a generous sympathy. The possibility of this frequently torments me.[15]

When three letters arrived, they eased his anxieties, but soon his letters showed another fear. If she did not leave him now, would she do so later, when the differences in their backgrounds became clear? He was not rich, like her father or Angelica's husband, and the provisions he could make for her were small. He knew how poverty could strain a marriage (or a relationship very like one), and she would have the added burden of being poorer than her family or friends. Relentlessly he examined her on the particulars of their future life. It was a test of his candor and of her devotion, and he staked their futures upon the result:

> Have you made up your mind on the subject of housekeeping? Do you soberly relish the pleasure of being a poor man's wife? Have you learned to think a homespun preferable to a brocade, and the rumbling of a waggon wheel to the musical rattling of a coach and six? Will you be able to see with perfect composure your old acquaintances flaunting it along in elegance and splendor, while you hold a humble station and have no other enjoyments than the sober comforts of a good wife? Can you in short be an Aquileia and cheerfully plant turnips with me, if fortune should so order it? If you cannot my Dear we are playing a comedy of all in the wrong, and you should correct the mistake before we begin to act the tragedy of the unhappy couple. I propose you a new set of questions . . . but though they are asked with an air of levity, they merit a very serious consideration, for on their being answered in the affirmative our happiness may absolutely depend.[16]

Carefully he described his narrow resource and the lean condition of his purse. "I have not concealed my circumstances . . . they are far from splendid; they may possibly be worse than I expect." He told her also that he was "indifferent" to property, implying that he would not amass a fortune of his own. He described a life bereft of all but the necessities and issued a grim warning. She, a child of riches, must not romanticize a poverty that he knew from experience to be squalid, humbling and mean.

I cannot forbear entreating you to realize our union on the dark side and satisfy, without deceiving yourself, how far your affection for me can make you happy in a privation of those elegancies to which you have become accustomed. If fortune should smile upon us, it will do no harm to have been prepared for adversity; if she frowns . . . by being prepared, we shall encounter it without the chagrin of disappointment. Your future rank in life is a perfect lottery: you may move in a very humble sphere. The last is most probable; examine well your heart. . . . Don't figure to yourself a cottage in romance. These are pretty dreams, and very apt to enter into the heads of lovers when they think of a connection without the advantages of fortune. But they must not be indulged. You must apply your situation to real life, and think how you should feel in the scenes of which you may find an example every day.[17]

His candor touched her, and he was reassured. Perhaps to break the tension, she answered in a poem, which unfortunately has been lost. He was contrite and embarrassed at having as he said "examined" her and called himself "presumptuous" for his doubts. He excused this with an explanation of his pessimism, which he had perhaps expressed to her before:

It is not a diffidence of my Betsey's heart, but of a *female* heart that dictated the questions. I am ready to believe everything in favour of yours, but am restrained by the experience I have had of human nature, and of the softer part of it. Some of your sex possess every requisite to please, delight, and inspire esteem, friendship and affection, but there are too few of this description . . . though I am satisfied, when I trust my senses and my judgments that you are one of the exceptions, I cannot forbear having moments when I feel a disposition to make a more perfect discovery of your temper and character. In one of those moments I wrote the letter in question. Do not however I entreat you suppose that I entertain an ill opinion of your sex. I have a much worse one of my own.[18]

He stressed again her difference from the common run of women:

I have seen more of yours that meritted esteem and love, but the truth is, my Dear Girl, that there are very few of either that are not very worthless. . . . I think that I have found a perfect jewel.[19]

But the reassurances were not lasting, and his anxieties revived. He wrote another troubled letter on October 13:

Do you find yourself more or less anxious for the moment to arrive as it approaches? . . . Do you begin to repent or not? Remember, you are going to do a very serious thing. Though our sex has generously given up a part of its prerogatives . . . yet we still retain the power of happiness and misery; and if you are prudent you will not trust the felicity of your future life to one in whom you have not good reason for implicit confidence. I give you warning; don't blame me if you make an injudicious choice; and if you should be disposed to retract, don't give me the trouble of a journey to Albany, and then do as a certain lady I have mentioned to you, find out the day before we are to be married that you "can't like the man." But of all things I pray you don't make the discovery afterwards, for that would be worse than all.[20]

The reply he received did not soothe him, or perhaps he received no letter, for on October 21 he sent an anxious note:

It is now a fortnight since I received a letter. . . . I wish you would write by the post, which would assure me a letter once a week at least; for though I am convinced there is no neglect on your part, yet I cannot help being uneasy when I have been longer than usual without hearing from you.[21]

Longingly he spoke of the day that they would marry. Legality remained most precious, the symbol of security and faith. He ended with a passage that gave expression to his mixed anxieties and hopes:

I had a charming dream two or three nights ago. I thought I had just arrived at Albany and found you asleep on a green near the house, and beside you in an inclined posture stood a gentleman I did not know. He had one of your hands in his, and seemed fixed in silent admiration. As you may imagine, I reproached him with his presumption, and asserted my claim. He insisted on a prior right, and the dispute grew heated. This I fancied awoke you, when . . . you flew into my arms and decided the contention with a kiss. I was so delighted that I immediately waked, and lay the rest of the night exulting in my good fortune. Tell me I pray you who is this rival of mine. Dreams you know are the messengers of Jove.[22]

Hamilton and Eliza were married in the great hall of the Pastures at noon on December 14. The wedding was impressive by wartime standards for the house was filled with company, much of it her kin. For Hamilton it was the end of his loneliness. It was not only a marriage, but an induction into the center of a clan. The Schuyler family henceforth closed ranks around him. A political family with many girls and few male heirs of his generation, it would consider him the brightest diamond in its crown. Hamilton was now protected both by Washington's favor and by the most powerful family in New York. He may have allowed himself to marvel at how his circumstances had changed.

What had not altered was his drive. Once he had pushed himself to gain recognition and escape the obscurity that had seemed to be his fate. Now he was driven to prove that he deserved what been given him; that he was something other than a rich man's "son." More than ever he had to make his reputation. And the way to do that was in war.

V

HAMILTON RETURNED to winter quarters in January 1781, unhappy and depressed. Despite the security his marriage brought him, he continued under stress. Several things contributed to his frustration: he was unhappy with his work at headquarters, under pressure to impress the Schuyler family and disturbed at what he saw increasingly as Washington's indifference to his plight. And in late fall he had been shaken by a human tragedy that had nearly shattered him and added new strains to the growing tensions between the commander and himself.

On the morning of September 24 Hamilton had breakfasted with Benedict Arnold, then a brigadier general in the American army and commander of the vital river fortress of West Point. In the course of the meal a message had been brought to Arnold that scouts had captured a British soldier thirty miles north of New York City and had discovered plans of West Point in Arnold's writing in his boot. Arnold had excused himself and left the table, ostensibly on business, in reality to be rowed downriver to the British warship *Vulture*, which would bring him into occupied New York. Chance alone had kept Washington from being at the table with them: he had been returning with Lafayette and Hamilton from a meeting with the French at Hartford and had at the last minute decided to cross the river to inspect the fortress for himself. As details came in through the succeeding hours, the outlines of the plot emerged.

Since 1779 the hero of Saratoga had conspired to sell West Point to the British for £10,000 sterling, a high rank in the British army and lifetime annuities for his children and his wife.

Arnold was unhappy with his rank in the American army and thought himself undervalued and ill-used. But it was his wife, a small, fragile blonde of social ambition and of Tory sympathies, who had begun the intrigue, starting a correspondence with John Andre, an aide to the British general Sir Henry Clinton, and her friend. The plot was carried on in letters to New York in cipher, and then in secret meetings between Arnold and Andre, who was smuggled up from Manhattan, in a farmhouse halfway between West Point and New York. The negotiations were protracted, for there was incessant haggling over price. Arnold's character had coarsened in the process, and a streak of callousness emerged. Though Washington had befriended him, trying to get him favors and promotions, he had planned to give him to the British as a captive. He turned over the Americans who had rowed him to the *Vulture* to the British as prisoners of war.

Margaret Shippen (Peggy) Arnold had been left behind by her husband when he made his hurried boat ride to New York. He had calculated she could extricate herself from trouble, and he was right. She played a tableau of devastated innocence, feigning distraction and then madness, screaming at Washington that he planned to kill her child as tears streamed down her enchantingly sweet face. All the officers were touched by this performance, but Hamilton was especially moved.

> It was the most affecting scene I was ever witness to [he wrote Eliza]. She for a considerable time entirely lost her senses . . . One moment she raved; another she melted into tears. . . . All the sweetness of beauty, all the tenderness of a wife . . . and all the fondness of a mother showed themselves in her appearance and conduct. We have every reason to believe she was unacquainted with the plan.[1]

Eight days later his angelic Peggy maliciously told the story of her masquerade to the British fiancée of Aaron Burr. Hamilton was not alone in his peculiar innocence, but he was particularly vulnerable to her appeal. Peggy's story of the deserted wife held echoes of his mother's history. It was not the last time he would be deceived by a lovely woman using the weapons of pathos and physical appeal.

Peggy followed her husband to Manhattan, and then to exile in 1783.

Betrayal did not bring them the fortune or esteem they longed for. British society did not welcome them, and they passed their later years in loneliness and need. As Hamilton knew nothing of her deception, it is likely he knew nothing of her sufferings. She died alone in London in 1806, her husband having died before her of cancer at the age of forty-six.

The other "victim" of intrigue was still less fortunate: the discovery that blasted the Arnolds' dreams of vengeful glory meant death for the British soldier, John Andre. Andre was twenty-seven, a naturalized Briton of Swiss ancestry, much loved in the army for his gallantry and charm. Hamilton, who was sent to interview him in prison, found him a tragic figure, as he wrote to John Laurens:

> There was something particularly interesting in the character and fortunes of Andre. To an excellent understanding well improved by education and travel, he united a pleasing elegance of mind and manner, and the advantage of a pleasing person. . . . His knowledge appeared with ostentation, and embellished by a diffidence that rarely accompanies so many talents, which led you to suppose more than appeared. His sentiments were elevated, and inspired esteem. They had a softness that conciliated affection. His elocution was handsome, his address easy, polite and insinuating. By his merit he had acquired the unlimited confidence of his general, and was making a rapid progress in military rank. . . . But at the height of his career, flushed with new hopes from the execution of a project most beneficial to his party, he was at once precipitated from the summit of prosperity, and saw all the expectation of his ambition blasted, and himself ruined.[2]

Unfortunately for everyone, Andre was the victim of a particularly vicious trick of fate. Unable to return by ship from his last rendezvous with Arnold, he had been forced to travel over land to New York City, and Arnold had insisted that he change from his uniform into civilian clothes. It was this act, taken against his will, that doomed him, for it changed his status from a soldier to a spy. The penalty for spying was hanging by the neck. Andre found this prospect untenable and sent a letter to Washington himself. He said that he accepted his fate and was prepared to meet it as part of the fortunes of war. He did not fear death since his life had been without dishonor, and he had taken no action that

had given him occasion for remorse. But he was tormented by one prospect: the idea of ending his life upon the gallows, which was the death not
of a man of honor but of a thief. He said that he had been a courier, not a
spy, among the Americans, and that the change of clothes, which had
been his undoing, had been Arnold's idea, not his. If Washington could
feel sympathy for a soldier, esteem for his courage or pity for his situation, he begged him to use his powers to annul the sentence and allow him
to perish by the gun.

Hamilton pleaded with Washington, first for Andre's life and then for
his last pleasure—to die as he was living, as an honorable man. Washington, who admired Andre, was sick at heart but adamant; hanging was
the universal penalty for spying, and the rebel nation, whose status was
still questionable, could not afford to breach a code of war. It was a
legitimate position for Washington to take, and perhaps the only one
possible. But Hamilton, who identified with Andre, saw it as a rejection
of himself.

In the following days Andre conducted himself with a pathetic dignity
that struck the Americans with awe. He staged his death almost as a play,
by which he rose above his brutal destiny and transformed it into an act of
grace. Not a false move or gesture marred the tableau of his last days. He
was gallant in interviews, weeping only at the thought of Clinton, who
had been a father to him and was shattered by his approaching death. He
spent his time in prison sketching, leaving among other tokens a delicate
line drawing of himself. He walked calmly to his execution, nodding to
his anguished captors, a small and quiet smile on his face. He halted as if
struck at the sight of the gibbet (no one had told him his request had not
been granted), then sprung on the gallows cart and fastened the noose
around his neck. His last words were to linger in Hamilton's memory:
"You will witness to the world that I die like a brave man."[3]

Hamilton was haunted by Andre's composure and by his radiant
embrace of death. He was also stunned by what he took as Washington's
callousness in refusing him a soldier's end. Washington kept Andre from
a death of honor as he kept Hamilton from an honorable occupation, and
the thoughts may have dovetailed in his mind. He wrote an agitated letter
to Eliza on October 2:

> Poor Andre suffers today. All that is admirable in virtue, in
> fortitude, in delicate sentiment and accomplished manners
> pleads for him, but hard-hearted policy calls for a sacri-
> fice. . . . I urged a compliance with Andre's request to be

shot, and I do not think it would have had an ill-effect, but some people are only sensitive to motives of policy, and . . . from a narrow disposition, mistake it.[4]

"Some people . . . hard-hearted . . . narrow . . . cold." For the first time his hostility to Washington had spilled over into print. Was he thinking of Andre, or himself? He had pled for an honorable assignment, and "policy" had kept him anchored at his desk. His relations with Washington, always troubled, were entering their darkest phase.

He made desperate new efforts to escape. There was a scheme to attack upper Manhattan with a small force of mixed companies in which he thought he might take part. On November 22 he appealed to Washington, but this time he wrote and did not speak to him, and the reasons he gave for this departure foreshadowed the extension of the rift. "I take this method to avoid the embarrassment of a personal explanation,"[5] he wrote near the end of the letter, suggesting that he now found confrontations with Washington particularly difficult, and in some ways too painful to endure.

His tone throughout the letter was supplicating and shy. He reminded Washington of his many requests for action, of Washington's promises and of the many times he had been refused. He recounted the explanations Washington had given him and countered them with reasons why they did not apply in this instance. He would lead a mixed corps in a position commensurate with his own rank. He would displace no field officer from his position. It would be a one-time effort, at a moment when demands upon the staff were few. "Bayard's Hill would be the pretext for my being employed," he admitted, "on the supposition of my knowing the grounds, which is partly true."[6] He ended on a plaintive note, with his old affection and the deference he only rarely lost:

> I wish your Excellency entirely to consult your own inclination, and not from a disposition to oblige me, to do anything that may be disagreeable. . . . It will, nevertheless, make me singularly happy if your wishes correspond with mine.[7]

British movements caused the measure to be scuttled before the gesture could be made. If he had had his taste of glory, could the damage have been healed? He was frustrated, but there remained another hope. Alexander Scammell was resigning as adjutant general, and there was a chance that he might have the post. It seemed ideal, for it was connected to headquarters but held more scope for independence and command. This time he did not speak or even write to Washington but approached him via Lafayette. He asked Lafayette not to approach Washington directly, but to write him a letter. And through shyness, diffidence or a sense of his own futility, when Washington asked his advice on the appointment, Hamilton suggested Edward Hand.

Lafayette was troubled by the distance he saw growing between these two men whom he knew depended on each other, and whom he loved as friends. Unsuccessfully, he tried to heal the breach. He begged Hamilton to let him speak to Washington directly and was disturbed when Hamilton demurred. Days later he was forced to write to Hamilton that their approach had failed. Before his letter could reach Washington, the general met Hand by accident and offered him the post. Lafayette stressed that Washington's action had been "innocent" and had been taken upon Hamilton's advice. He closed on a conciliatory note:

I know the general's friendship and gratitude for you, my Dear Hamilton, and both are greater than you perhaps imagine. I am sure that he needs only to be told that something will suit you, and when he thinks he can do it, he will.[8]

Hamilton's frustration was compounded now by self-reproach. Desperate, he pursued another exit: the nomination for an embassy to France. Someone had to go, to beg munitions for what might be the last campaign. Laurens and Lafayette, who had themselves been nominated, lobbied on his behalf. They wanted commands in the southern states, to which they had access and Hamilton did not. They also knew of his extreme unhappiness. Lafayette sent letters from Philadelphia exuding confidence and hope. "I think you ought to keep yourself in readiness," he wrote after a day of lobbying, "and in case you are Call'd for, come with all possible speed."[9] He promised him access to a realm of power: "I shall give you all the public and private knowledge I am possessed of," he had written, "besides many letters that may introduce you to my friends . . . any thing in my power shall be entirely yours." Despite their efforts, the attempt fell short. Hamilton, as Laurens told Washington, was still too unknown to Congress to procure the needed votes. Laurens himself was elected minister on December 11, 1780.

71

Hamilton had now been frustrated three times in one month. Before leaving for Albany, he made another effort. Without informing Washington, he applied to friends in Congress for consideration as a "financier." Washington, when he heard of this, sent a generous recommendation. But this too was turned down.

The efforts of his friends had come to nothing. He was chained to his desk, dreaming of war to release him, much as he had done when very young. The fact that Washington had been central in his repeated disappointments had no doubt often crossed his mind. The ascent of his friends was also irritating. Lafayette was leaving for Virginia where he would see constant action; Laurens was en route to France. Where was he? Back full circle, as at his desk at Cruger's warehouse, in the "grovelling condition" of a clerk.

On February 14 Hamilton and Washington had an encounter on the stairs. Washington asked to see him immediately. Hamilton demurred, saying he had a letter to deliver to Tench Tilghman but would rapidly return. On his way back, however, he was detained by Lafayette. The two stood chatting for a minute, then Hamilton broke away. Running up the stairs again, he was confronted by Washington, who loomed above him at the top of the steps. Washington's words (in Hamilton's account) were harsh:

"Colonel Hamilton. . . . You have kept me waiting at the head of these stairs ten minutes. . . . You treat me with disrespect."

Hamilton's answer was equally abrupt.

"I am not conscious of it, Sir, but since you have thought it necessary to tell me so, we part."[10]

One hour later, Washington sent Tilghman to Hamilton's room. He had not meant to hurt his feelings, and he wished to make amends. Hamilton was adamant. His decision to leave was irrevocable. Since he did not wish to hurt the army, he would not leave while Washington was understaffed. For similar reasons he would not make their quarrel public but would act as if nothing had occurred. He would stay until the other aides had returned from their assignments. He did not want to speak to Washington, as there was nothing more to say.

The one full account of the altercation is in a letter written by Hamilton to Philip Schuyler on February 16. Though two days had passed since the quarrel, the letter shows signs of intense stress. Portions are crossed out and rewritten, there are numerous interpolations and deletions and the whole reveals a turbulence that has not calmed. There are attempts at structure, but it remains digressive. Cool analyses are undercut with outbreaks of vituperation and of almost infantile rage.

He began with an account of the quarrel, which he described in great detail. His defense of his innocence was insistent and agitated. His message to Tilghman had been urgent and pressing. He had met Lafayette on a matter of business, and then his manner had been hasty and abrupt. Washington had "accosted" him in an "angry" manner, and then his accusation had been wrong. He could swear that the wait Washington said had lasted ten minutes had in reality been less than two.

He outlined his other grievances, which were more complex. He had not wanted to become an aide-de-camp. He disliked the office and had consented only through a sense of duty and a false idea of what Washington was like. The commander was not what he appeared to be on first impression: he was moody, with an uneven temper, given to outbursts at his aides. He was also selfish, thinking only of his own convenience, and this self-interest had kept Hamilton, who had served him devotedly, chained to desk work he detested despite repeated entreaties to escape. For some time he had determined on a severing; the quarrel provided the excuse he sought. He would never forgive Washington or return to his service. The wounds exchanged on both sides were too deep.

It was almost too neat a symmetry that the one long account he wrote was to Philip Schuyler. Having cut loose from one "father," he was compelled to explain his actions to the next. It was vital that Schuyler approve of him. "I have given you so particular a detail . . . from the desire I have to justify myself in your opinion," he had written. "I wish what I have said to make no other impression than to satisfy you that I have not been in the wrong."

The outburst did not purge his rage. Though he had sworn to Washington that he would keep a stolid front in public, he sent off a string of angry letters, not only to his friends but to men who were also friends of Washington and dependent on him for their careers. He asked Nathanael Greene to find a job for him in the southern army, as he no longer was employed. To James McHenry he sent a longer letter, bursting with rage at the "Great Man." "I pledge to you that he will find me inflexible," he wrote to this man who also was an aide of Washington. "He shall for once repent his ill-humour. Without a shadow of reason and on the slightest ground, he charged me in the most affrontive manner with disrespect."[11] Though he performed in public with an impassive countenance, he could not stop himself from talking, and his behavior assumed a manic edge. When Washington learned from Lafayette in April that he and others had full knowledge of their quarrel, he was moved to his own display of pique. He said he found Hamilton's conduct "a little extraordinary" in swearing him to silence while talking openly himself. When Lafayette approached them in an effort at reconciliation, he found "each disposed to believe the other was not sorry for the separation,"[12] and each convinced it was the other's fault.

What had caused it? Not the calculation some have charged. It was calculation of an odd variety for Hamilton to put his own career at peril, and then compound that peril by writing wildly unguarded letters that could have been used against him with devastating effect. There was an accumulation of intense frustration, an eddy of guilt and anger that whirled for months, and then erupted upon insult in a storm. Lafayette testified more than forty-five years later that the quarrel "was neither new nor sudden," that "Hamilton had pressed Washington for another position; that Washington had refused his request, as in the case of the adjutant generalship, and that they had had two or three more disagreements growing out of this wish of Hamilton's before the final breach."[13]

There was also a sense of private outrage, of injury beyond the nature of the cause. Hamilton had told Philip Schuyler that he had been lured from his command in the artillery by "an opinion of the General's character, which experience soon taught me to be false."[14] What this opinion was is not difficult to guess. It is not hard to imagine the feelings that the hero-general, so conveniently the "father" of his country, aroused in the bastard alien, whose parents had disappointed him. The problem with this was that it diverged from reality. It was impossible for any human being to be as stalwart, stoic and selfless as Hamilton demanded; under pressure his disappointment would explode. The store of undischarged anger at his own parents added fuel to his anger and to his predilection to feel himself abused. This time, however, *he* would not be deserted—"I had determined that if a break came it should be final"—and he had snapped the bonds himself.

What he could not break so easily were Washington's power and the hold that he had taken on his life. For all his temper, Washington remained his rock, his shelter, his "*Aegis*," upon which he could consistently depend. Through Hamilton's anger ran the secret knowledge of one given fact: that Washington, provoked as he was, would not betray him, that he would understand, and continue to protect him, even as need be against himself. Weeks after the quarrel, Hamilton pressed him for special favors. Less than one year later, their letters had regained a confidential tone.

In 1787, under attack from his political enemies, Hamilton was secure enough to apply to Washington with a request. "They have had recourse to an insinuation that I *palmed* myself on you, and that you *dismissed* me from your family," he had written. "This I confess hurts my feelings, and will require a contradiction."[15] Washington replied immediately with a statement that both charges were untrue. His emotions on receipt of this letter are unknown. If Hamilton sensed there was a danger in resurrecting the memory of their old quarrel, the thought did not deter him. It may not have even crossed his mind.

In March Hamilton had left headquarters in a fury, swearing contact between himself and Washington was forever at an end. In April he had written Washington two letters saying that as he was no longer in the "family," he saw no obstacles to obtaining a commission in the field. He advanced the arguments he had used previously: his former command in the artillery, his long and distinguished service, his special knowledge of the war. Washington replied gently that many of the obstacles remained. The troops were sensitive and had rioted when given outside officers; if a new corps were formed, it would consist largely of troops from New England, who would insist on being led by their own men. Two things emerged from this correspondence: that Hamilton still relied on Washington to do special favors for him, and that Washington was trying to oblige.

By July he had received no answer, and his anxieties increased. French and American troops had gathered at Dobbs Ferry to mass for their final effort against Cornwallis in Virginia or Clinton in New York. Desperate, he arrived in person and made his final try. He sent Washington a letter enclosing his commission—an offer, or a threat, to resign. The tactic worked. Tench Tilghman came to him the same morning, returning the commission and bringing Washington's promise of a command.

His reward came on July 31. An announcement was made at the morning reveille that two light companies would be joined to two companies of New York levies, to form a battalion under the command of Hamilton and Nicholas Fish. In August he wrote to Eliza:

A part of the army my dear Girl, is going to Virginia, and I must of necessity be separated from my beloved wife. . . . It is ten to one that our views will be disap-

75

pointed, by Cornwallis retiring to South Carolina. . . . At all events, our operations will be over by the latter end of October, and I will fly to my home.[16]

At Yorktown he was in a mood of manic elation, happy to be inside his war at last. John Trumbull sketched him standing in the trenches in profile, at an angle that accented the strong lines of his nose and jaw. His arms are folded at his chest and he is staring down at something in front of him. A strange expression, intense, indrawn and oddly happy, is upon his face.

On October 14 came the moment he had awaited all his life. At eight P.M. two companies stormed the British redoubts at the far end of the lines. Hamilton led one company, Lafayette the other, which was composed mainly of French troops. Jumping on the shoulders of a taller soldier, Hamilton hopped over the barricade into the fort. Seconds later the others followed, hacking at the abatis with axes. The entire action took eight minutes to complete. His spirit of warfare—dash and chivalry—is reflected in the account that he sent Lafayette:

> Inclosed is a return of the prisoners. The killed and wounded did not exceed eight. Incapable of imitating examples of barbarity, and forgetting recent provocations, the soldiery spared every man who ceased to fight.[17]

His part at Yorktown appeared to placate him. Trumbull painted him again at the surrender of Corwallis, next to John Laurens in the front row of soldiers, slight and fragile as ever, but his features now tranquil and composed. He could now live more calmly—studying law, which he intended to practice, dipping his toes into the stream of public life. He left the army almost immediately, keeping his commission in reserve until he resigned the next September. He returned to Albany almost immediately—Eliza was expecting a child—and began to study law. He wrote to Washington frequently on public business. Their letters contained the same tone of candor and utter openness that had always marked their correspondence. Each seemed eager to forget the incident. They did not meet again until two years later at Fraunces Tavern when the British evacuated Manhattan in November 1783. Hamilton was seen with the others, weeping copiously at the farewell embrace. Save for the brief note in Hamilton's letter four years later, no mention of the falling out was ever made by either man again.

76

V I

AN INDEPENDENT America did not end Hamilton's active involvement. He insisted that it be not only a free nation but a strong and great one, and its present weakness filled him with anger and disgust. Disunited during the war, which was almost lost through its ineffectiveness, it was now unable to keep domestic order or to pay its debts. Hamilton had personal experience of its impotence: in 1782, as collector of Continental taxes, he was unable to raise a single dollar in New York. He called his country "embarrassed" and "despicable" and was profoundly anguished by its state. Excerpts from his essays written between 1782 and 1787 reflect his anger:

> There is something noble and magnificent in the perspective of a great federal republic, closely linked in the pursuit of a common interest, tranquil and prosperous at home, respectable abroad; but there is something proportionally diminutive and contemptible in the prospect of a number of petty states, with the appearance only of union, jarring, jealous and perverse.[1]

Hidden here are images of the broken family, doubtless recollected from his youth. These would be a potent factor in his political theory, but another impulse was at work:

States like individuals who observe their engagements are respected and trusted, while the reverse is true of those who pursue an opposite conduct. . . . The former, as well as the latter, are bound to keep their promises. . . . Without this, there is an end to all distinct ideas of right and wrong.[2]

It was not only his pride that was affronted, but his sense of ethics. The combination of the two would drive him on.

In June 1782, still ailing from the campaign at Yorktown, he was named to the New York delegation to the Continental Congress for the term running from November to July. He went to Philadelphia with one burning purpose: to push a plan for a national financial system that would both function as a cement to the union and enable the government to pay off its outstanding debts. Money was owed to foreign governments and to domestic creditors, among them the army, then at Newburgh with Washington, waiting the conclusion of the peace treaty with Britain in a state of poverty, suspicion and unrest.

Hamilton's hopes for the tax and the army had already received a heavy blow. In January 1782 the defection of two states had defeated a plan for a federal impost that would have raised enough money to allow Congress to pay the army its back salary, and allow it to disband in peace. Hamilton had gone to Congress hoping it would pressure the state legislatures to reverse their decision, but this it seemed unable or indisposed to do. Delegations meanwhile had arrived from the army pleading the sufferings of the soldiers, their impatience and their growing fears. This aroused all of Hamilton's impatience and all of his old fury. On February 7, 1783, he sent a letter to Washington at Newburgh suggesting that both he and the army play a role:

It appears to be a prevailing opinion in the army that the disposition to recompense their services will cease with the necessity for them, and that if they once lay down their arms, they part with the means of obtaining justice. It is to be lamented that present appearances afford too much ground for their distrust.

He urged that the army retain its weapons after the conclusion of the peace:

78

The claims of the army, urged with moderation, but with firmness, may operate on those weak minds which are influenced by their apprehensions more than their judgments, so as to produce a concurrence in the measures which the exigencies of affairs demand. They may add weight to the applications of Congress to the several states. So far an useful turn may be given to them.

It was at this point that he wished Washington to act:

> . . . the difficulty will be to keep a *complaining* and *suffering* army within the bounds of moderation. This Your Excellency's influence must effect. . . . It will be advisable not to discountenance their endeavours to procure redress, but rather . . . *to take the direction of them* . . . this will enable you to guide the torrent, and to bring order, even good, out of confusion. . . . The great *desideratum* at present is the establishment of federal funds, which alone can do justice to the creditors of the United States (of whom the army is the most meritorious class), restore public credit, and supply the future wants of government. This is the object of all men of sense.[3]

Hamilton was doing his own part in Congress, speaking to other members of the dangers of mutiny, and perhaps urging friends from the army to encourage a show of moderate resistance there. What he had not realized was how rapidly the situation could ignite. On March 10 a flood of pamphlets inundated the camp at Newburgh, calling for immediate revolt. The army must retain its arms after the surrender of the British, displace Washington and all commanders who counseled moderation, march on Congress, take the members captive and hold them hostage for their pay. A meeting of the officers was called. Washington derailed the rebellion in an improvised appeal to conscience, but the menace had been frighteningly real. "I was forced to arrest on the spot the foot that stood wavering on a tremendous precipice," Washington wrote later. "If the officers had met . . . resolutions might have been taken, the consequences of which might be more easily conceived than described."[4]

Hamilton explained his own role in the near-mutiny to Washington on March 17:

> Your Excellency mentions that it has been surmised that the plan . . . was formed in Philadelphia, that combinations have been talked of between the public creditors and the army, and that members of Congress had encouraged the idea. . . . This is partly true. I myself have urged in Congress the propriety of uniting the influence of the public creditors and the army . . . to prevail upon the States to enter into their views. I have expressed the same sentiments out of doors. Several other members of Congress have done the same. The meaning of all this however was simply that Congress should adopt such a plan as would embrace the relief of all the public creditors . . . in order that the personal influence of some, the connections of others . . . as well as the apprehensions of ill consequences, might form a mass of influence in each State in favor of the measures of Congress. . . . In this view, as I mentioned . . . I thought the discontents of the army might be turned to a good account.[5]

Hamilton had hoped that the threat of mutiny, controlled by men of reason, would impress and terrorize the states. His intentions had not been violent, but he had not understood the effect of his statements or how easily a tense situation could become inflamed. His powers of calculation had proved unreliable. As he admitted, he had been pushed by emotion into positions he might not have taken if reason alone held sway. "I often feel a mortification, which it would be impolitic to express, that sets my passions at variance with my reason," he admitted to Washington. "I confess, could force avail, I should almost wish to see it employed." Some of this had doubtless come through in his speech.[6]

Washington, to whom he confessed everything, absolved him of malign intent. But he did hold him guilty of indiscretion, and of a naiveté dangerous in the extreme. In three separate letters written in the weeks following the abortive mutiny he warned him against trafficking in forces that he could not fathom and whose consequences he could not control. He also warned him gently that he had expected far too much of him.

The plot recoiled, scattering his projects at his feet. The states were now more frightened than ever of central power. The army, suspecting it had been toyed with in a plot to establish central funding, was in a fury at its friends in Congress and was about to turn upon them in a rage. He was forced to drop his scheme for Continental funds. When Congress did pass a plan on May 20 to pay the soldiers, it was at the irreducible minimum: a month's pay in cash, three months' pay in nearly worthless government certificates and an instant furlough by which the troops would be released at once. "Furlough" was a euphemism for disbanding them without admitting it at the barest fraction of their wage. Some of these men had served eight years in the army with no other source of income; they were now released into the need and poverty that Washington had foreseen and feared. To him, and to Hamilton, it was a tactical defeat and a corrosive human tragedy that made the Treaty of Paris little more than an appalling farce. To Hamilton, who saw the state as part of his own person, it was something more—a catalogue of the things he held most horrible in nature; a state corrupt and damaged at its very outset—ungrateful, ungenerous, untrustworthy and unjust.

Congress had become unendurable, a memory of error and reproach. To Nathanael Greene he wrote that he had "no motive" to "lose his time" in the affairs of state. The words underline his disillusion. He pelted the governor with pleas to let him go home.

> *14 May:* I wish the two other Gentlemen . . . may appear as soon as possible, for it would be very injurious for me to remain much longer here. Having no future view in public life, I owe it to myself without delay to enter upon my private concerns.[7]

> *1 June:* I wish your Excellency would urge a couple of Gentlemen to come on, as it becomes highly inconvenient for me to remain . . .[8]

> *11 June:* In two or three letters . . . I mentioned the necessity of a representation of the state here and at the same time of my returning to my private occupations. I am obliged to inform your Excellency that I cannot remain here above ten days.[9]

On the tenth day after this cry for release came a terrible humiliation. On June 21 four hundred soldiers from the Lancaster barracks surrounded Congress as it sat in the State House and beseiged it for four days. Pleas to the government of Pennsylvania to call out the militia were unavailing, and Congress was forced to leave the city for Princeton on June 24. It was a grim experience for all the members, but for Hamilton

81

the sight of the national government imprisoned, helpless and then fleeing was a nightmare vision that struck at the center of his fears.

Compounding his anger were rumors that he, as head of the committee negotiating with the state authorities, had plotted to get Congress out of Philadelphia to enrich Manhattan, and then that he had fled the city out of fear. So hurt was he by these stories that in the summer and fall he wrote three lengthy pieces, which he did not publish, in defense of Congress and, indirectly, of himself. He sent a letter to James Madison asking him to write an "impartial account" of Hamilton's actions that would wipe this latest blemish from his name. "Did I appear to hasten it, or did I not rather show a strong disposition to procrastinate?" he asked about the flight of Congress. "I should be obliged to you in answering, to do it fully. . . . I do not intend to make any public use of it, but through my friends to vindicate myself."[10]

At Princeton he drew up a twelve-point indictment of the confederation, with a plan for a remodeled government and a plea that a convention must be called. If he had believed this last disaster could activate Congress, he had erred. He showed his paper to Madison and perhaps to two or three others, but their response was so tepid that he did not even bring it to the floor. On the back of the sketch is a sad note in his writing: "Plan for a government, presented at Princeton, but abandoned for lack of support." His scheme included a Supreme Court and an executive power, both independent of the legislature, whose influence pervaded all the states. It also envisioned an active role for government which would make it an innovative and creative factor, a fountainhead of power and of wealth. The disparity between his vision and the reality of America in 1783 was enormous, reflecting the chasm between the majority of his countrymen and himself. His disillusion with the government was now all but complete. To the previous indictments of "ungrateful," "unjust" and "ungenerous" had been added the most dreaded of all conditions— "weak." More and more he brooded on a final remedy. More and more he hated the confederation, the architect of disorder, the author of debt and ruin, which had brought disgrace upon his country and himself.

Abashed and temporarily defeated, Hamilton returned from Princeton into an almost private life. He was living now in a small cottage near the Pastures, which he, Eliza and their small son Philip shared with Robert Troup. Troup was tutoring Hamilton in law, which he had decided to make his profession and which he had never studied in his truncated career at King's. Studying hard, with his usual intensity (and his full quota of pacing and muttering) he passed the bar in September 1783. In November he moved Philip and Eliza to Manhattan to set up his law practice and his household in New York.

Hamilton was now just under twenty-nine years old. He had reached the appearance he would maintain through maturity with only the slightest variations, such as the gradual dimming of his reddish hair. His appearance had altered little since his youth. An air of adolescence clung to him, and would do so to the end of his life. He retained a boyish pliancy in his five-foot-seven frame. His face too possessed a youthful quality in the pink and white freshness of his coloring, which persisted into middle age. The slight fleshiness of his cheeks and chin would sometimes give his face an added plumped-up youthfulness. In other portraits or from other angles, his face is angular and sharp. The mouth is long, thin, curving and sensitive; the nose high-bridged and prominent: some portraits show an upward tilt. His eyes were deep blue and had a penetrating quality. Moreau St. Mery, who did not like him, described his eyes as small.

Impressions from other sources are remarkably alike. James Parton, Aaron Burr's biographer, has described "a slight, undersized, elegant figure, with a bright, rosy face,"[11] and Alexander Graydon quoted an observer, who knew Hamilton in life:

> He was under middle size, thin in person, but remarkably erect and dignified. . . . His hair was turned back from his forehead, powdered, and collected in a club behind. His complexion was exceedingly fair, varying only in the almost feminine rosiness of his cheeks. His might be considered, as to figure and colour, an almost uncommonly handsome face. When at rest it had a severe and thoughtful expression; but when engaged in conversation . . . became gentle and animated. . . . Those who could speak of his manners . . . concurred in pronouncing him to be a frank, amiable, high-minded, open-hearted gentleman. He was capable of inspiring the most affectionate attachment, but he could make those whom he opposed hate and fear him cordially.[12]

He dressed well, always at the height of fashion; he liked brightly colored waistcoats and touches of lace about his cuffs. His energy, almost palpable, created a charismatic quality that came across to men as leadership and to women as a powerful sexual current that few could successfully resist. His quick and lively charm and his magnetic quality created his immense appeal. As Alexander Macdonald would later tell John Church Hamilton, "There was a fascination in his manner by which one was led captive unawares."[13]

To 1802, the Hamiltons lived in a series of rented houses in which they did not seem to put down roots. Save for the years between the end of 1790, when the capital moved to Philadelphia, and the beginning of 1795, when Hamilton retired from the Treasury, their focus always was New York. Their houses were modest and near his place of work. Something of his taste in dwellings is shown in a letter written as he was about to move to Philadelphia: he wanted large rooms, a garden and some sun. There were frequent visits to the Schuyler house at Albany—often at the insistence of Philip Schuyler—to escape the stifling city summers and the plagues of yellow fever in the fall. It remained a place of refuge for them: Hamilton and Eliza went there to convalesce after their near-fatal bouts of fever in the fall of 1792. He would not take money from the Schuyler family. But he did accept the barges, filled with game and produce, sent down river from their farms upstate.

The Hamilton family continued to grow. In all there were eight children (with at least one miscarriage) in a span of more than twenty years. Philip, born in 1782, was followed by the first daughter, Angelica, in September 1784; then by James Alexander, Alexander, John Church, William Stephen, Eliza, and the youngest, the second Philip, in July 1802. There was an adopted daughter, Fanny Antil, child of a veteran of the Revolution, whom the Hamiltons raised as their own. By all accounts the elder Philip was the favorite, adored of the younger children and his father's pet. His portrait shows a thin, triangular, sweet face, with his father's features and his mother's coloring, dark eyes, and a halo of dark curls around his head. Angelica, the oldest daughter, appears to have been frail and gentle, with a musical talent that her family went to some effort to indulge. She was sent a pianoforte from London by her aunt Angelica, which she played often, with her father singing at her side.

Hamilton had wed Eliza as a loyal helpmeet, and here she did not let him down. There was an obsessive quality to her absorption in him; he became the soul and center of her life. Her letters have been lost, but her actions showed an intense passion. In later years she considered it an extraordinary hardship to be parted from him for a portion of the week. He was not faithful, but he was devoted, and his dependency appeared to grow with age. As he would write in 1802 while on a business journey, "I am a solitary lost being without you all."[14]

As he had warned her in their courtship, he was not able to provide her with the living standard enjoyed by her friends and sisters. She had chores and worries that did not fall to their lot. Her son James has preserved a record of her activities: "She was a skillful housewife, expert at making sweetmeats and pastry; she made all the undergarments for her children, was a great economist, and a most excellent manager . . . her mind and body never rested, for both were constantly employed."[15]He has given us a picture of the morning routine at their house at Broadway. Eliza sat at the head of the table cutting bread for the smaller children while one of them, standing beside her, read aloud from the Bible or Goldsmith's *History of Rome*. Lessons over, the older boys came down to breakfast, after which all were sent to school. Hamilton always read all of his addresses to her, both for comments and to judge their impact on the ear. When he wrote his report on the Bank of the United States, one of the greatest of state papers, she was one of those, among his office assistants, who sat up nights writing and revising drafts. In the long years of her widowhood, she would recall this involvement with pride.

Hamilton was a compulsive toiler. His interests outside his work were few. The outdoors or exercise did not appeal to him, and there are no records of his fondness for a sport. Angelica would chide him for this, saying he would grow fat and lose his glamour. Philip Schuyler, brooding as usual over the health of the entire family, fretted over the effect of too much mental, sedentary effort and begged Eliza to get him out to ride. None of this had much effect upon him. Perhaps it was the memory of what strain had done to his frail body in the Revolution that made him shun exertion for its own sake. Perhaps too, not having been raised in a climate of leisure, forced to spend each waking moment in the pursuit of advancement or sustenance, he saw no reason to spend time or effort on pastimes that did little to improve his reputation, and nothing whatever for the cause of the United States.

His pleasures were urban, domestic and confined to the indoors. Like Washington, he liked the theater; he went to concerts of the Philharmonic when it played at Snow's Hotel. There are signs of an interest in drawing and an eye for color and for line. According to his grandson, he did some weekend painting and advised Martha Washington on her purchases of works of art. He could not afford to purchase paintings, but he did buy copper and wood engravings (including a Dürer and Mantegna's *Tri-*

umph of Caesar) and other lesser prints. By far the largest personal expense was for his library, which ranged from philosophy and history to novels, and from the classics to current works. An inventory of his books taken at his death revealed volumes of letters by Pliny and Socrates, Cicero's *Morals* and Plutarch's *Lives*, the orations of Demosthenes, essays by Montaigne and Bacon, Lord Chesterfield's *Letters*, biographies of Charles V and Frederick the Great, the works of St. Anselm, assorted works on history, finance and government, *Gil Blas*, and the works of Laurence Sterne. There were volumes in French, which he continued to read and study, including sets of Diderot, Molière and Voltaire. He continued to perfect his knowledge of the language, studying in 1794 with a French tutor. His friend and client William Constable later willed him an entire library in French. He was an early patron of the Public Library, taking out romantic novels (perhaps on the pretext that they were for his wife or daughter) which he is believed to have read himself.

A less likely interest was his passion for medicine, begun in his days at school. David Hosack, his friend, physician and a noted botanist, whose private gardens once covered much of what is now Rockefeller Center, considered his knowledge remarkable. "In every important case of sickness that occurred in his family," Hosack told Hamilton's children, "he was not only the skilled nurse, he was also the skillful physician, for few men knew more of the structure of the human frame, and its functions, or possessed a surer knowledge of the principles upon which human diseases are to be countered or relieved."[16] It was not a minor or a passing interest. He had planned to be a doctor before the Revolution supervened. Hamilton's letters home in times of family illness are filled with detailed instructions as to remedies. To the last, he was prescribing treatments for his friends. At the very end, through a haze of pain and disorientation, he was able to diagnose as mortal his bullet wound from Aaron Burr.

Many of his strongest character traits had an air of paradox. His grandson Allan MacLane Hamilton wrote of his "almost feminine" concern for the welfare of others, a nurturing and careful strain. "He endeared the soldiers of his company to him by sharing their hardships," he related. "When New York and Philadelphia were crowded with refugees, he would hunt up the neediest"[17] and send them gifts of money and of food. His life was marked by many small acts of kindness. When the painter Ralph Earle was jailed for debt, he sent Eliza to sit for him in prison. Her friends followed her and through commissions Earle was soon released.

He cared little for money. Robert Troup defined his legal fees as "moderate," adding, "It was not uncommon for him to advocate the cases of persons too poor to remunerate his services, when such persons had manifest justice on their side."[18] He took cases for the deserving poor, for Loyalists whom he thought had been unfairly deprived of rights or property, for freed blacks resisting deportation to the South. When offered high retainers, he frequently refused them, saying the money was not justified by work. No doubt it was this that caused a friend to comment, "I hear . . . you will not even pick up money when it lies at your feet."[19] Friends were frequently obliged to remind him that he could not make a living on charity cases. When he astounded Troup by asking a client for money owed him, Troup took this as a sign (mistaken as it happened) that his friends would not have to pay to bury him.

He possessed a devastating candor, which damaged his political career. No man was ever more transparent: he said what he thought, which was often unnecessary, since one could read his meaning in his face. "On most occasions," said Alexander Macdonald, "when animated with the subject on which he was engaged, you could see the very workings of his soul."[20] He was without discretion, without "skin," without the self-protective coloring that politicians require to survive. He spoke openly of his own ambition, considering it a normal quality, and was puzzled when it was taken as a threat. He also said openly what appeared to him evident— that men were selfish, cruel and often silly, their own worst enemies, misleading others and themselves. He was as hurt and as surprised as a child when his words were used against him in ways, utterly predictable, that he did not intend. It was perhaps for this reason that his friend James Kent, one of the greatest of New York jurists, recorded, "He had the most guileless simplicity of any man I ever knew."[21]

With this characteristic went its corollary: open himself, he was distressingly credulous, given to taking others at their word. "He was too sudden in bestowing his confidence,"[22] ran an otherwise laudatory piece in the *Boston Repertory*, and the worldly Gouverneur Morris recorded, "This generous indiscretion subjected him to censure. . . . His unsuspecting confidence in professions which he believed to be sincere, led him to trust too much."[23] Some men are humanitarians on principle, despising mankind in the flesh. Hamilton was their polar opposite—his cynicism was on paper only, applied to mankind in general, not to people he knew. He was seduced by a beautiful woman pleading passion and helplessness, who extorted many thousands from him, and by a friend and cousin by marriage whose lethal thirst for fiscal speculation badly shook the state. The first experience nearly wrecked his marriage; the second, his political career. His wife and friends, who knew his unexpected and remorseless innocence, forgave him. The public, ignorant of his guileless-ness, did not.

The most disturbing thing about his character was a constriction in his point of view. The web of his loyalties of understanding and affection ran the length of the eastern seaboard, and stopped cold. His knowledge of the rest of the country was sharply circumscribed. New York was his own friends and his Schuyler relatives. Virginia was George Washington; the South, John Laurens—and later Charles Cotesworth Pinckney, from a background very similar to Laurens's; New England, save for some tem-porary political allies, was unknown country; he did not know the West at all. He was alienated to a large degree from much of the country he lived in and to which he intended to devote his life. His alien birth, though it would later come to seem symbolic, had little influence. The difference was internal, in his temperament, worked on by his experience, in his imagination and his mind.

If his friends agreed with his priorities, most of his countrymen did not. He equated freedom with security and order; they equated it with a relaxation of governmental ties. They saw the states as a line of defense against governmental excess; he saw them as strongholds of prejudice and mean-spirited local interests, seedbeds of a potential civil war. He saw a strong leader as essential; they equated one with tyranny, and saw therein the shadow of a king. They did not agree with him about the states or power, and especially, as time would show, they did not agree with him about the future of the country as an urban, industrialized power, turning away from the small farm and the land. Most of all they did not agree with him about their own essential nature, as succinctly quoted by James Kent, that

> all plans of government founded on any new and extraordi-
> nary reform in the morals of mankind were plainly uto-
> pian . . . that mankind were exceedingly prone to error:
> that they were likely to be duped by flattery . . . inflamed
> by jealousies and bad passions . . . seduced by artful and
> designing men.[24]

No wonder that he was called a "non-American," a child of Europe in his soul. James Parton called him "the shining example of a class of characters which Great Britain produces in numbers."[25] Samuel Eliot Morison compared him to the younger William Pitt, "the least American of his generation,"[26] a man whose "love of order and system" was fired by the lack of it among his fellow men. Thus, as Parton says, Hamilton had no hold on the people "except as the man trusted and preferred by Washington."[27] As such, his grasp on power was artificial, fragile and fine-spun.

The war between Alexander Hamilton and America as it was in his lifetime raged on for twenty years. Eventually, with the help of Washington, he changed it into something a little closer to his vision. Ultimately, it was to break his heart.

In the fall of 1785 Hamilton ran for a seat in the New York state Assembly from the city of New York. His interest was not in local politics; he had decided that the push for a strong central government must come this time from the states. He planned to resurrect the old revenue plan of 1783, and if that was rejected, to push on to bolder means. Even then, these were not his real objectives. "He had no idea that the legislature could be prevailed upon to adopt the system," Robert Troup wrote later. "Neither had he any partiality for a commercial convention, otherwise than as a stepping-stone."[28] He got nowhere with his pleas to the Assembly. But he did get himself and his friend Egbert Benson named as commissioners to the convention on commercial union, held in Annapolis in September 1786.

The convention was authorized to discuss only economic matters. Only twelve members from five states had arrived. There were rumors later of a prearrangement, but of this one cannot be sure. Hamilton was rumored to have written the first draft of the call for a general convention, but it was too inflammatory and was given for revision to a New Jersey delegate, Abraham Clark. This draft was accepted by the delegates on September 12, and they adjourned the next day. When they left, they had committed the United States to a convention to revise the American government, to be held in Philadelphia in May.

Back in the Assembly he was especially active, and his speeches had a spacious tone. Believing now that his country might yet become powerful, he was at pains to keep it generous and just. He objected to plans to restrict the franchise, calling them "successive innovations destructive of liberty" that could end in a despotic state.

If once we depart from this rule, there is no saying where it may end. Today a majority . . . disqualify one description. . . . A future legislature . . . disqualify another

89

set. One precedent is the pretext of another, till we narrow the ground to a degree subversive of the Constitution. . . . Why should we abridge the rights of any class of citizens? If we once break the ground . . . it may lead us farther than we now intend.[29]

He objected to an amendment allowing interpreters to "explain" the ballot to illiterates: they would "explain" things to their own advantage, and deprive the unlettered of a sacred right. He opposed a scheme to force loyalty oaths on native-born citizens, a proposal with an anti-Catholic bias. One sees here, beyond his tolerance, another deep concern. There must be no stepchildren in the American family, none disinherited or shunned.

Other speeches have a different timbre, reaching farther back into his past. There is his comment on a motion to take the vote from merchants in the New York area who had been pressured by the British army into carrying cargo for their troops. Hamilton said the merchants had been "weak," not criminal, and his memories of his own flawed parents may have colored his appeal.

It may be said they were guilty of a culpable want of firmness. But if there are any of us who are conscious of a greater fortitude, such persons should not on that account be too severe on the weaknesses of others. They should thank nature for its bounty to them, and should be indulgent to human frailty. How few are there who would have had strength enough?[30]

On February 8, 1787, he responded to a bill proposing that mothers of children who had died at birth appear within the month before a magistrate with a witness to testify that the children had not perished at their hands. The implication was that the children were bastards, murdered by their mothers for fear of public censure and disgrace. What memories this brought Hamilton of his own bastardy or of his mother's torments are unknown. What is known is the nature of his speech.

Mr. Hamilton observed that the clause was neither politic nor just; he wished it obliterated from the bill. . . . He expiated feelingly on the delicate situation it placed on an unfortunate woman . . . who might by accident be delivered still-born. From the concealment of her loss of honor, her punishment might be mitigated, and her misfortune end there. She might reform, and be again admitted in virtuous society. The operation of this law compelled her to publish her shame to the world. It was to be expected that she would prefer the danger of punishment . . . to the avowal of her guilt. He thought it would involve courts in a delicate dilemma; the law would have no good effect as it would be generally evaded. Such circumstances should be viewed leniently.[31]

V I I

THE CONSTITUTIONAL CONVENTION was Hamilton's child. No one had wanted it more than he did, or had fought for it so long. It was his hope for the transformation of his country from its state of disgrace and impotence into the great and mighty nation of his dreams. The idea had gone back to army days. In 1780 he had told a friend that a convention ought to meet that winter to revise the government and give Congress sovereignty in all affairs of state:

> The sooner the better [he had written]. Our disorders are too violent to admit of a common or lingering remedy. . . . The measure of a Convention would revive the hopes of the people, and give a new direction to their passions. . . . There are epochs in human affairs when *novelty* even is useful. . . . This is exactly the case now.[1]

No one underestimated the problems involved in making a nation of the suspicious and divergent states. Few areas so extensive had ever been brought under the control of one government, and there were problems of organization that were unique. Of the many arms of government, only the state assemblies existed, having evolved from the colonial legislatures, and Congress, which had come into being as a league of resistance to the

British Empire and developed into a league to run the war. Substitutes had to be created to fill the functions once handled by the Empire. An executive and a national judiciary had to be created. Also needing to be clarified was the relationship between the states and central government, which was at present ill-defined.

Hamilton's staunchest ally was James Madison, the sober young Virginian he had first met in Congress in 1782. Four years older than Hamilton, Madison was three inches shorter and even more frail physically. He had had a breakdown from overwork while a student at Princeton, and he suffered also from an illness akin to epilepsy, causing convulsions and coma, which caused him great embarrassment and fear. Madison's two terms as President in the early nineteenth century would prove that he lacked the executive temperament, but he had a genius for political organization, which his experience in Congress and in the Virginia legislature had refined. An increasingly powerful and respected figure, he had also won the friendship of Washington, and of Thomas Jefferson, then American minister to Paris, whom he kept advised of developments at home by mail. Madison's mind was clearer than Hamilton's, more detailed, controlled and more objective, if less capable of innovative leaps; and his illnesses, with their periods of forced inactivity, had given him an opportunity for research and reflection that Hamilton had lacked. Though both were small and serious, the two were fundamentally divergent personalities; Hamilton's glamour, drive and forceful manner contrasted with the dry reserve of Madison, who dressed consistently in somber colors and never seemed to raise his voice. For the rational Madison, the Convention was to be his finest hour, the apex of a lengthy and remarkable career. For Hamilton, whose mind fought with, and never mastered, his own tempestuous emotions, it contained a series of hidden traps to which he increasingly fell victim and in which he became finally enmeshed.

Hamilton's first indication that the Convention might mean trouble for him came with the selection of the delegation from his state. George Clinton, the governer, was hostile to the idea of the Convention and made no secret of his hopes that it would fail. Though Schuyler's power had forced Hamilton on to the New York delegation, Clinton had balanced him there with two friends of his, Robert Yates and John Lansing, who were suspicious of federal power and of all efforts to augment it and whom Hamilton believed had been placed there largely to spy on him. Both were distrustful of the Convention, attached to state sovereignty and pleased with the confederation as it stood. At Philadelphia they would outvote Hamilton consistently and reduce him to a state of unendurable frustration. His son John Church has described his feelings graphically. "The policy of Clinton had sent him to be a cypher and a sacrifice. He felt the cold palsy of his state upon his vote."[2]

Hamilton had hoped that Washington, whose influence in the country was unrivaled, would give him backing and support. But Washington, who knew himself to be the certain choice to lead the country under its new government, was in an agony of self-consciousness throughout the Convention, and through fear of seeming to vote himself more power, was silent on the floor. Named president of the Convention on the first full day of its meeting, he took that as an added reason for diffidence and confined his participation to rulings and to formal votes. Hamilton in his political career was seldom able to function effectively without the presence of Washington as a guide and reference. That guidance and restraint were missing here.

The Convention opened at the end of May. The first weeks were spent discussing fundamental plans. As Hamilton listened to the debate around him, he became increasingly restless and depressed. He was unhappy with the plan presented by Virginia on May 29, endorsed by the seven members of the delegation and drafted by Madison himself. He liked some things about it—the bicameral legislature, and the grant of power it gave the central over the state governments—but he disliked its plan to let the states elect the members of the Senate, and the provisions for the presidency dismayed him. It pictured an executive (whether in one man or three was left unspecified) elected by Congress, serving a limited period and ineligible for election to another term. But if this disheartened him, he was appalled by the New Jersey plan presented on June 15, which was little more than a series of amendments to the confederation calling for additional powers to regulate commerce, a one-house legislature, and a plural executive elected by Congress, ineligible for reelection and liable to be removed at any moment on a majority vote of the state governors. Both plans impressed him as weak and woefully inadequate, unable to control the "passions" or ensure the union of the states. Early on he had begun to brood that the convention he had longed for was a futile and unproductive gesture.

His desperation was compounded by his position in his state. Hemmed in by Yates and Lansing, he was unable to make his presence felt. Under the rules adopted by the Convention, the states voted as a unit, and he was forced to watch in silence as New York's vote went consistently for measures he despised. Impatient and restless, he decided on a bold stroke of his own: to present a *"solid plan*, without regard to temporary *opinion. . . .* a model which we ought to approach as near as possible . . . not as a thing attainable by us."[3]

Hamilton made his one address to the Convention on June 18. He spoke haltingly, and his manner was shy. According to the copious notes Madison took of the Convention's proceedings, he explained that he had been "hitherto silent" partly from his "delicate situation" in regard to his own delegation and partly from "respect to others, whose superior age & experience rendered him unwilling to bring forward ideas dissimilar to theirs." He confessed that his ideas were radical, but said he had been driven to them by extraordinary means. He viewed the state of the country as critical, requiring extraordinary measures, and hoped the people might be brought in time to shed their prejudices and see the justice of his views. "He did not mean to offer the paper he had sketched as a proposition to the Committee," Madison recorded. "It was meant only to give a more correct idea of his views."[4]

Much of what Hamilton said that morning was to delight his enemies and startle and confound his friends. He established himself as the staunchest of nationalists, devoted to the union and jealous of its rights. He also gave the impression of himself, through the repeated use of ill-chosen phrases, as an Anglophile, a devotee of the British constitution, and as a potential monarchist—an image that was to damage his career.

He was afraid of the states, believing they had too much hold on men's affections and loyalties and might undermine the federal government. To avert this he proposed a series of measures that took many of his listeners aback. He wanted national laws to supersede state laws on all occasions. He wanted state governors appointed by the federal government, and to have an absolute veto over all laws passed. He called the states "not necessary" to the "great purposes of commerce, revenue, or agriculture" and spoke of the benefits if they could be destroyed.

> If they were extinguished, he was persuaded that a great economy might be obtained. . . . He did not mean to shock the public opinion by proposing such a measure. On the other hand, he saw no *other* reason for declining it.[5]

95

He admitted that "subordinate authorities" would be necessary: "district tribunals . . . corporations for local purposes," to enact the measures the central government decreed. Hamilton was later to insist at the New York ratifying convention and elsewhere that he had not meant to suggest their annihilation. But that was his purpose, as his words revealed.

He wanted a Congress of two houses, with their differences carefully defined. The lower house was to be elected directly by the people, out of their own numbers, and the members were to serve for three-year terms. The upper house, or Senate, was to be elected by "electors chosen for that purpose by the people" from among the rich and learned, and to serve for good behavior during life. Each house was designed to protect its class from the incursions of the other, and the Senate was to play a special role. Secure in office and beyond temptation, it was to stand between the Constitution and the people, likely to be swayed by "passions," or the executive, likely to be tempted to seize unlawful powers for himself. The comparison to the House of Lords was inescapable, and one that he did not try to step around.

> To the proper adjustment. . . . the British owe the excellence of their Constitution. Their House of Lords is a most noble institution. Having nothing to hope for by a change, and a sufficient interest by means of their property, in being faithful to the national interest, they form a permanent barrier agst. every pernicious innovation, whether attempted on the part of the Crown or of the Commons.[6]

His view of the Senate was not as a body wielding power, but as one acting as a check and a restraint. In his eyes, therefore, it was not menacing. But in comparing it to the House of Lords and speaking of the latter favorably, he had made an error that would haunt him all his life.

The President, who in his notes he called the "monarch," was to be elected by electors chosen by the people, and to serve for good behavior during his life. As with the Senate, security, riches and immunity from the passing gusts of passion were supposed to induce fidelity to the common weal. He denied that this plan approached the evils of a monarchy, since the President was elected by the people on his merits and could be removed upon proof of misconduct. But he then went on to make some extremely indiscreet comments on the nature of presidents and kings.

The English model was the only good one on this subject. The Hereditary interest of the King was so interwoven with that of the Nation, and the personal emoluments so great, that he was placed above the danger of being corrupted from abroad.[7]

The specter of corruption haunted him, even in the highest places of the government. It was not a love of power but a fear of "interest" that controlled him, and Madison revealed in his notes:

On the plan of appointing him for 7 years, he thought the Executive ought to have but little power. He would be ambitious, with the means of making creatures; and as the object of his ambition would be to *prolong* his power, it is probable that in case of a war, he would avail himself of the emergence to evade or refuse a degradation from his place.[8]

It was very like the arguments he had made in his first papers, before the Revolution, arguing the comparative dangers of tyranny by parliaments or kings. As Gouverneur Morris explained years later:

It was not. . . . because he thought the executive too feeble to carry on the business of the state, that he wished him to have more authority, but because he thought that threre was not enough power to carry on the business honestly. He apprehended a corrupt understanding between the executive and a dominating party. . . . which would destroy the president's responsibility, and he was not to be taught what everyone knows, that where responsibility ends, fraud, injustice, tyranny and treachery begin.[9]

Hamilton believed that all men were subject to temptations. He could see no way to keep them loyal to the trust reposed in them than by giving them in the beginning more than they could hope to buy. By advocating the life term, he seemed to feel that he was placing them above temptation. But the proposition could be taken differently, and was.

In his speech, and in his treatment of the President in general, some distinct oddities emerged. He could not reconcile his conscious mind with his emotions and some curious discrepancies emerged. Never in his polit-

97

ical life did Hamilton make one move to extend the powers of the President beyond what he believed to be its legal limits, much less to change its nature from an elective to an hereditary base. There is thus no real reason to doubt the words of this letter, written in 1792 to Edward Carrington:

> I am *affectionately* attached to the republican theory. I desire *above all things* to see the equality of political rights, exclusive of all *hereditary* distinction, firmly established. . . . This is the real language of my heart.[10]

Yet in his notes for the speech, though not in the speech itself, he referred to the executive as the "Monarch," and the words "He ought to be hereditary"[11] appeared at one point in the text. Countless flattering references to Britain, the British government and the hereditary principle were scattered through his speech. The British model was "the only good one," the British House of Lords "most noble," and the British constitution (in its theoretical construction) an excellent thing. Hidden here is his inescapable longing not for power and oppression, but for the symbols of legitimacy, continuity and order, the need for which he never managed to outgrow. The image and the symbols of the monarchy, as detached from its application in practical politics, touched certain chords in his own life. The monarchy was the symbol of unbroken lineage, reaching back through eight centuries of time. Hamilton by contrast had seen breakage ravage all levels of his family. James Hamilton, who had been turned out by his Scots family, had deserted his own family before Hamilton was in his teens. Rachel Faucette, herself torn from her own father at age eleven, had deserted her own child by Levein.

The monarchy, irrespective of the merits of the King as a personality, was symbolic of the father, itself an image of protection and of strength. Hamilton's own search for fatherly protection had led him to George Washington and Philip Schuyler, both men of imperial demeanor and strong parental instincts, who were also the lordly rulers of immense land holdings which they ran like minor kings. The monarch was the symbol of patrimony, of the kingdom itself as the supreme inheritance, passed on from parent to son. Hamilton was familiar with the theme of lost inheritance. He knew that the slaves willed him by his mother had been taken by her lawful husband. And he knew too from his father of the estates, riches and prestige in Scotland from which his descendants were cut off forever. The monarchy was also the symbol of legitimacy, the lack of which still haunted Hamilton. In 1802 he was to tell the pathetic lie to James McHenry that his parents had been married, but that through technicalities resulting from the divorce of his mother, the marriage was declared void.

Predilections for the symbols of monarchy, as distinct from their political application, ran strongly through Hamilton's life. The Convention, concerned with fundamental principles of society and government, was an invitation to soul searching on the part of all its members, awakening reactions to symbols of law, freedom and authority that may have been deeply buried or suppressed. In the case of Alexander Hamilton, they roused yearnings from his troubled childhood that impinged upon his rational thoughts about government and caused a sensation when exposed. It was his misfortune that he could not control them, and that they surfaced here.

Hamilton's ambivalence on this touchy issue pursued him to the end of his career. Uneasy with his feelings, unable to admit or understand them, he came to give a series of differing versions of his proposals, and in time to deny that he had given them at all. His stories are confusing and would have a darker connotation, save for the presence of three things: the unmistakable signs of lifelong conflict, the persistence with which he upheld his version of things that could be easily verified, and the testimony of all who knew him, among them James Madison, that he was incapable of a conscious lie.

He claimed at one point that the speech had been a series of speculations, and not a concrete plan. "Neither the propositions thrown out in debate, or even those voted on in the early stages, were considered as evidence of a definite opinion," he said plaintively. "It appeared to me in some sort understood."[12]

He told Thomas Howe, his military aide from 1799 to 1800, that he had made the speech in concert with Washington and Madison, who had urged him to bring a strongly federal proposal to the floor.

THEY WERE COMPLETELY UP TO THE SCHEME [Howe quotes him as saying]. No one of the three thought it could possibly carry. It was thought. . . . adviseable to sketch a plan of sufficient stability, and in defending it, bring forward those sound principles which could endure the test of time.[13]

It is possible such a scheme existed, though Hamilton may have exaggerated its meaning. If such talks took place, they are mentioned nowhere else. Strangest of all were his recollections of what he actually proposed. Sometime near the end of the century he appears to have convinced himself that a plan for a constitution that he drew up in New York over the summer and showed in September to Madison contained a provision for a chief executive to serve a limited number of years. In an article he wrote in the third person for the *New York Post* in 1802 he mentioned his

> more deliberate and final opinion, [which] adopted a more moderate term of years for the duration of the office. . . . as also appears in a plan of a Constitution in writing, now in this city, drawn up by that Gentleman in detail.[14]

He told Howe he had changed his mind, from a fear that the "passions" surrounding the selection of a permanent President might be too much for the system to endure. And in 1803 he wrote to Timothy Pickering that "in the plan of a Constitution which I drew up while the Convention was sitting. . . . the office of President has no greater duration than for three years."[15]

When word of this letter reached Madison years later, the then ex-President was stunned. "Now the fact is that in that plan," he wrote to J. K. Paulding,

> the tenure of office is not *three years, but during good behavior*. The error is the more remarkable, in that the letter apologizes for it not having been a prompt one, and as it is so much at variance with the known cast of Mr. Hamilton's political tenets, that it must have astonished his political, and most of all, his personal friends.

But Madison had been a friend, and he closed with a sentence absolving Hamilton of purposeful intention to mislead:

> I would do injustice. . . . to myself as well as to Mr. Hamilton, if I did not express my perfect confidence that his misstatement was involuntary, and that he was incapable of any that was not so.[16]

In the eleven days that passed between Hamilton's speech and his departure, his behavior altered, but it did not improve. If he was now more vocal, he also was more indiscreet. The reception of his speech may have altered his intentions, for he had said he wished to offer amendments to the plan submitted but no amendments were made. He did say that he wanted a broad representation for the lower house of Congress, and he urged that federal elections not be channeled through the states. He shocked some people with what was widely taken as an attack on the state governments, suggesting they might at some future time fade out of existence, and that he would not be sorry if they did. He startled others by saying at another point (in Madison's version) that "he did not think well of republican government. . . . but addressed himself to those who did."[17] It was one of the inexplicable statements that he made in the course of the summer that did great harm to his career.

He confessed also that he had "found it difficult to convince persons who had been in a certain habit of thinking"[18] of the innocence of his designs. This was candid, but an understatement of events. There was an air of strain and tension, and a growing sense that he was laboring in vain. With no explanation beyond some oblique notes in a letter to George Washington, he left Philadelphia for New York on June 30. He said no more about it than what he told the New York State Ratifying Convention one year later: "Some private business calling me to New York, I left the Convention for a few days."[19] But it was not a few days, it was weeks together, and when he finally returned to Philadelphia, it was just to sign his name.

Hamilton had left the Convention in the middle of its greatest crisis and at the lowest point in its career. He no longer felt his presence useful, and the strains had become too great for him to bear. As if to prove the worst of his suspicions, Yates and Lansing returned to New York days later and cosigned a letter to George Clinton that called the Convention a conspiracy to install monolithic government in America and destroy the powers of the states. Lansing later called the Constitution a "triple-headed monster" and a "wicked conspiracy" against the liberties of the United States.

"Yates and Lansing never voted in *one single instance* with Hamilton," George Mason wrote to Thomas Jefferson, adding that "Hamilton was so much mortified at it that he went home."[20]

In a letter written to Washington halfway between Philadelphia and

New York, Hamilton expressed his worries that the Convention would not go far enough. He thought the result would be a "motley. . . . feeble measure" that would humiliate the assembly and reflect badly upon all concerned. He said he would remain ten to twelve days in New York, returning only if given reason to believe his presence would not be a waste of time. His words recall his letters when he left Congress four years earlier, when he also believed himself outvoted in a body doomed to failure and disgrace.

In New York he plunged into private business, little of it pressing, and none urgent enough to justify his absence from a convention he had worked seven years to bring about. He took several cases concerning debts and payments and attended the circuit court at Albany on July 16. He wrote a long letter to the press attacking Governor Clinton, and he tracked down with some urgency a rumor that the Convention planned to ask a younger son of George III to serve as King. He thus edged around the fringes of involvement in the Convention, while staying remote from the outcome of the case. He seemed to have made an inner commitment to support the Convention's product while isolating himself from its development. He had decided to do his best for what he had concluded was bound to be an insufficient thing. He showed no curiosity about events in Philadelphia and, aside from the note to Washington, wrote only two letters, both to his new friend Rufus King. In the first he said that he had asked Yates and Lansing to return with him to Philadelphia but had gotten no reply. In the second he inquired as to rumors that late changes had given the Constitution a "higher tone." He also asked to be notified when the Convention would conclude its business, as he wished to be present at the end.

One event of that summer was genuinely important, and cast long and colored shadows on his life. In July he stopped a duel between his client, a New York City merchant, and a delegate to the Convention from Georgia, Major William Pierce. He wrote to Nathaniel Mitchell, his friend and Pierce's lawyer, urging Pierce to moderation, and sent a gentle note to Pierce himself. The offense, he said, stemmed from a misunderstanding, which he begged the major to forgive. "I can never consent to take the character of a second in a duel," he had written, "till I have tried in vain that of a mediator. Be content with *enough*, for *more* ought not to be expected. I remain, with sincere attachment, your friend."[21]

When the duel had been averted, he wrote again to Mitchell, happy that it had been stopped. He stressed the obligation of men of honor to do everything to prevent bloodshed, until it became "an absolutely necessary sacrifice"[22] to the demands of public opinion. It was a humane and moving statement, and no one could doubt his compassion or his pleasure at having saved these people's lives. There was only one thing troubling in his exposition. What he meant by a "necessary sacrifice" he had not bothered to explain.

Hamilton returned to the Convention briefly on August 13 and again on September 6. This last time he stayed for good. He had missed meanwhile the major debates of the Convention, the shaping of the offices and arms of government, but this did not seem to bother him. He brought with him the plan for a Constitution that he had worked on between cases in New York. His plans for this remain unclear. His new plan differed in some particulars from what the Convention had drafted. The Constitution now had a President elected for four years, and an upper house for six; he still wished them both to serve for life. He also wanted a larger and more inclusive lower house.

The most extraordinary feature of his new proposal was his plan to elect the President, which was intricate in structure and incredibly contrived. The propertied voters of each state would vote for electors, who could not hold other office, equal in number to the number of senators and representatives combined. These electors would vote for two secondary electors and would also cast a ballot for President. None of the secondary electors could be among the presidential candidates or among the electors chosen first.

The secondary electors would meet at the seat of government on a preappointed date. There they would open the ballots from the states. If one candidate had a majority, he would become President. If not, the electors would ballot among themselves. If *they* found a majority, their choice would be President. If they failed, the election would go to the candidate with the highest number of votes. This system, so complex, baroque and intricate, is the final measure of his distrust of human nature. Each step is a screen to filter out corruption, to sieve the dangers of corrosive influence, to stand between man's interests and his treacherous misleading soul.

He made no secret of his dislike of the Constitution or his belief that it was not strong enough. His remarks were sullen, and he made no effort to temper his distaste. Madison's notes for September 6 quote him as saying that "he had been restrained from entering into the discussion from his dislike of the Scheme in general, but as he meant to support the plan. . . . as better than nothing, he wished to offer a few remarks."[23]

His remarks were that he wished Congress to have no say whatever in the election of the President. He said it could be bought or influenced, or party interests could subvert the rightful choice. He did not know the extent of his prescience, or its dreadful application to his future. The plot of the Federalist House to control the election of 1800 would have a crucial bearing on his life.

Hamilton signed the Constitution with thirty-seven others on September 17, 1787. He asked in the end that everyone sign, since rumors of dissension would impede its chances of acceptance in the states. Even his endorsement held a note of condescension. "No man's ideas were more remote from the plan than his were known to be," he is quoted as saying, "but is it possible to deliberate between anarchy and convulsion on the one hand, and the chance of good."[24] He had not lost his pessimism, or his fear. "Gentlemen differ in their opinions concerning the necessary checks," he had told the Convention earlier, "from the different estimation they form of the human passions."[25] Because he so distrusted men's passions, his concept of the checks was fierce. If others complained, as they did often, that his fears were exaggerated, he would respond, as he did frequently, that they were unaware of the furies within human nature; that they did not know them as he did.

His fears would influence the rest of his career. He would give his life in government to propping up "the frail and worthless fabric," giving it the sinew that he feared it lacked. Nothing would ever be strong enough to still his fears. Was there a chance ever that men could control their passions, resist the pulls of greed and interest and unite without coercion for the common good? The answer, indubitably, was no. It was James Kent, the young lawyer who met him the year after and became his lifelong friend and his devoted disciple, who detailed his creed to Daniel Webster thirty years after Hamilton was dead:

> Hamilton said in the Federalist, and in his speeches, and a hundred times to me, that factions would ruin us, and our Government had not sufficient balance to control their tyranny. . . . All theories of government that suppose the mass of people virtuous, and able and willing to act virtuously, are plainly Utopian, and will remain so until the Saturnian age.[26]

VIII

THE FEDERALIST is Hamilton's testament. Few public figures have expressed their theories so comprehensively or at such length. He had collaborators, but writing it was his decision, and the impetus was utterly his own. Once begun, the project mushroomed. From a projected thirty it grew to eighty-five papers, and from one book of 250 pages to two volumes of 200 pages each. Of the essays that compose the work, Hamilton wrote thirty-seven, Madison, thirty, and John Jay, who was incapacitated soon after he began by a crippling attack of rheumatism, five. There are fifteen others of disputed authorship, which may have been written jointly in the early winter when Madison was in New York.

The initial intention was to produce a series of arguments to convince the delegates to the New York Ratifying Convention, whose assent was considered both crucial and unlikely, that the Constitution was conformable to republican principles and that the Confederation would be in great danger if it failed to pass. The papers did all of this, but they also turned into a discourse on government that is now a classic. Within months it had attained a wide, though secret, following. Though the authors made a show of keeping their names secret, they did send copies to their friends. Hamilton sent Washington the first paper soon after it had appeared in the *New York Journal;* Madison sent copies to Edmund Randolph, who had been a member of the Virginia delegation at Philadelphia, and he passed them on to others of their friends. Thomas Jefferson in Paris also knew the secret, though through another source. His copy, now in the Library of Congress, is inscribed "to Mrs. Church, from her *Sister*," in Elizabeth Hamilton's hand.

Hamilton's portion of the papers are his political creed. In them can be traced his philosophy and the basic structure of his thought. Not all are of equal value to the modern reader, for some concern problems that have been long since resolved by time. Others concern predictions since resolved as erroneous—such as Hamilton's theory that the system of electing presidents was so nearly perfect as to permit the election of only wise and able men to office (an opinion he would shortly alter), and his belief that the lower classes, bowing to the superior experience and education of those above them, would be content to place their futures in their hands. Others are of enduring value, for they changed the destinies of the United States. Here Hamilton explained for the first time in public his concern for finance and revenue as the sine qua non of national security, which he would translate into policy as Secretary of the Treasury under Washington, and in three remarkable reports that he was to make to Congress in 1790 and 1791. These theories, which form the essence of his work in office, will be considered later on. *The Federalist* is the forecast of these policies, which were later to divide the nation, to horrify some of his friends, Madison among them, and to create a rift between Madison and Hamilton that was unhealed at Hamilton's death. The papers function on another level: as the first definitive exposition of Hamilton's deepest feelings concerning the functions and purpose of government, among them three pervasive themes: the need for strong figures at the head of government, combining the principles of order and energy; his sense of the uses and the limits of power, and his very great fear of disunion and faction, personified in the existence of the states. Without an understanding of these themes, his future acts are incomprehensible. Taken together, they form the moral background for his actions and give color and direction to his life.

The first theme to surface is his terror of the states. It is clear that he sees them not only as inefficient, but as evil, repositories of greed and interest in which small-minded men, amassing vast powers through appeals to prejudice, use their positions to further their own ends. In the fifteenth *Federalist*, he explains the perils of leaving great decisions in their hands:

> The rulers of the respective members . . . will undertake
> to judge of the propriety of the measures themselves. They
> will consider the thing proposed . . . to their immediate
> interests or aims. All this will be done, and in a spirit of
> interested and suspicious scrutiny without that knowledge
> of national circumstances and reasons of state, which is
> essential to a right judgment, and with that strong predilec-
> tion in favor of local objects, which can hardly fail to mis-
> lead the decision. . . . The execution of the plans, framed
> by the councils of the whole, will always fluctuate on the
> direction of the ill-informed and prejudiced opinion of every
> part.[1]

He considered the members of the central government more wise, more judicious and more liberal than the members of the state government, less enslaved by local prejudices, and hence more concerned with the general welfare. As he said in the twenty-seventh paper, "circumstances promise greater knowledge, and more comprehensive information" on the great issues of the state.

> They will be less apt to be tainted by the spirit of faction,
> and more out of the reach of those occasional ill-humors, or
> temporary prejudices and propensities, which in smaller
> societies frequently contaminate the public deliberations,
> beget injustices and oppression of a part of the community,
> and engender schemes which, though they gratify a
> momentary inclination or desire, terminate in general dis-
> tress, dissatisfaction and disgust.[2]

He feared the states not only for their evil, but for their power. He feared an "eccentric tendency . . . a perpetual effort . . . to fly off from the common center," abetted by the lust for power of the local governors and the sentimental attachment of the people to their local governments, which were close and tangible, as opposed to the central government, which was distant and remote. To counter this, he wanted the powers of the central government to cut through the states to the people directly—"We must extend the authority of the Union to the persons of the citizens . . . the only proper object of government"—and in the twenty-second *Federalist* he expounded on this theme:

107

It has not a little contributed to the infirmities of the present existing system. . . . that it never had a ratification by the PEOPLE. Resting on no better foundation than the consent of the several legislatures, it has been exposed to frequent and intricate questions concerning the validity of its powers. . . . The possibility of a question of this nature, proves the necessity of laying the foundations of our national government deeper than in the mere sanction of delegated authority. The fabric of the American empire ought to rest on the solid basis of the CONSENT OF THE PEOPLE. The streams of national power ought to flow immediately from that pure, original, fountain of all legitimate authority.[3]

There was an added reason for his distrust of state power. If the Union was a contract entered into by the states, then the states, one by one, could nullify the contract and withdraw. If, on the contrary, it was the act of the people, such secession was impossible on moral and on legal grounds. On this, he was most prescient. Disputes on this matter were to continue for decades after and culminate in the disaster of the Civil War.

Hamilton had a complex aversion to the states that bordered on hatred. Much of it stemmed from his war experience, when state pride, state power and state resentment of the "tyrannical encroachments" of federal power had effectively blocked the flow of supplies to the army. He had seen state suspicion of central power result in soldiers without bread for six days running, in soldiers in the winter without shoes. He remembered that it was state resentment of the federal impost in 1783 that had dismissed the soldiers, many after eight years of service, into penury and need. He equated state power with human suffering and national weakness, both of which he found intolerable and a menace. But his distaste had a cause that ran still deeper in his character, concerning his sense of moral order, and of the legitimate roots of power in the state.

Hamilton believed the enemies of proper government were "interest" and "passion," and that governments were moral as they made efforts to contain them and immoral as they allowed them sway. He believed the states to be the strongholds of "interest" on the part of the people and their governors, and as such, unfit repositories of the public trust. The very extent of the American republic was the surest safeguard against corruption by interest or prejudice: opposed by conflicting interests, they were purged of their power and lost their ability to mislead. What emerged from this process, like nectar distilled, was the legitimate "voice of the people," the national interest and the true public will.

Unlike some of his contemporaries, Hamilton did not believe in the wisdom of the people as unalterably and consistently correct. But he did believe that the public welfare was the only legitimate end of government, and that a system that did not try to serve the people was tyrannical and unjust. He believed that public officials must often temper the opinion of the public, serving its permanent interests at the expense of its transient will. But he thought a just government must spring from the people, refer to its wishes and rest on its consent. It was this dialogue between the people and the national government that he suspected the states of corrupting. This was an offense he was not ready to forgive.

Hamilton believed in power for two reasons—that crises were unpredictable and incalculable in their nature, and that human nature, often rapacious, vicious and self-interested, required regulation and control. Frequently these reasons intertwined: crises on the foreign and domestic levels stemmed from the desire of men to war, to enslave one another and to profit unreasonably at one another's expense. He said that men by nature were not peaceful, that frequent attacks on justice and the public welfare were to be constantly expected and that men who thought otherwise were "visionaries," trapped by delusions and living in an unreal world. "Why has government been instituted at all?" he queried. "Because the passions of men will not conform to the dictates of reason and justice, without constraint."[4] He mocked the claims of others who insisted that men could be trusted to act on a reasonable estimate of their own best interests, or that rapacious conduct was the province of monarchies alone:

> Is it not . . . the true interest of all nations to cultivate the same benevolent and philosophic spirit? If this be their true interest, have they in fact pursued it? Has it not, on the contrary, invariably been found that momentary passions and immediate interests have a more active and imperious control over human conduct than general or remote considerations of policy, utility, or justice? Have republics in practice been less addicted to war than monarchies? Are not the former administered by men? . . . Are not popular assemblies frequently subject to the impulses of rage,

109

resentment, jealousy, avarice, and other irregular and violent propensities . . . Has commerce hitherto done anything more than change the object of war?[5]

In the thirty-fourth *Federalist* he argued that the government, to preserve its safety, must base its calculations on the grim view of human
nature that came so naturally to him:

> To judge by the history of mankind, we shall be compelled
> to conclude that the fiery and destructive passions of war
> reign in the human breast with much more powerful sway
> than the mild and beneficent sentiments of peace: and that
> to model our political systems upon speculations of lasting
> tranquillity would be to calculate upon the weaker springs
> of human nature.[6]

A government must base its powers on the lowest estimate of human
nature, and on the worst that can be expected to occur:

> . . . we are not to confine our view to the present period,
> but to look forward to remote futurity. Constitutions of civil
> government are not to be framed upon a calculation of exist-
> ing exigencies, but upon a combination of these with the
> probable exigencies of ages, according to the natural and
> tried course of human affairs. Nothing . . . can be more
> fallacious than to infer the extent of any power . . . from
> an estimate of its immediate necessities. There ought to be a
> CAPACITY to provide for future contingencies as they
> happen, and as they are illimitable in their nature, so it is
> impossible safely to limit that capacity.[7]

In the twenty-third *Federalist,* he expounds on this again:

> The circumstances that endanger the safety of nations are
> infinite, and for this reason no constitutional shackles can
> wisely be imposed . . . This power ought to be coexten-
> sive with all the possible combinations of such circum-
> stances, and ought to be under the direction of the same
> councils. . . . The *means* ought to be apportioned to the
> *end*: the persons from whose agency the attainment of any

110

end is expected ought to possess the *means* by which it is to be attained.[8]

Hamilton's experience had taught him that life was full of unpleasant surprises. He did not want his country to be caught unprepared.

He based the safeguards against oppressive power upon three things: the restrictions already built into the Constitution; the relationship of means to ends, by which any power used toward a proscribed purpose is itself unlawful; and accountability of men in office, wherein each was held responsible for his activities, and liable upon proof of maladministration to be censured or removed. All other "remedies" he mockingly dismissed:

> The moment we launch into conjectures about the usurpations of the federal government, we get into an unfathomable abyss and fairly put ourselves out of the reach of all reasoning. Imagination may range at pleasure till it gets bewildered among the labyrinths of an enchanted castle, and knows not on which side to turn from the apparitions which itself has raised. Whatever may be the limits or modifications of the powers of the Union, it is easy to imagine an endless train of possible dangers and by indulging an excess of jealousy and timidity, we may bring ourselves into a state of absolute skepticism and irresolution. I repeat here what I have observed in substance . . . that all observations founded upon the danger of usurpation ought to be referred to the composition and structure of the government, and not to the nature or extent of its powers.[9]

Hamilton regarded the national defense and the pursuit of the general welfare as legitimate objects of national power. All measures to procure these that did not curtail civil liberties or infringe otherwise upon specific reservations within the Constitution were lawful in his eyes.

To Hamilton, the true enemy of liberty was not power but secrecy, and he urged every possible measure to keep the latter force from gaining ground. In secrecy, he thought, small groups of men could plot to gain unlawful power and to further their interests at the expense of the common good. His answer to this was to have all public officials watched closely while in office, held closely accountable for all their actions, censured for corrupt or maladministration and, if possible, removed. "In a

111

republic," he insisted, "every magistrate ought to be personally responsible for his behavior in office,"[10] and this was one of his reasons for wanting the executive powers concentrated in one man. "It is far more safe that there should be a single object for the jealousy and watchfulness of the people . . . from the very circumstance of his being alone, [he] will be more narrowly watched and more readily suspected."[11] He compared this favorably with the system then prevailing in New York.

> The council of appointment consists of from three to five persons, of whom the governor is always one. This small body, shut up in a private apartment, impenetrable to the public eye, proceed to the execution of the trust committed to them. It is known that the governor claims the right of nomination . . . but it is not known to what extent or in what manner he exercises it; nor upon what occasions he is contradicted or opposed. The censure of a bad appointment, on account of the uncertainty of its author, and for want of a determinate object, has neither poignancy nor duration. And while an unbounded field for cabal and intrigue lies open, all idea of responsibility is lost.[12]

To Hamilton, power is embodied in the central government and in the branches of which it is composed. It was James Madison who wrote the portions of the work concerning the House and Senate, so Hamilton's views on Congress remain undetailed. It is likely that he was suspicious of it, as it represented the people in either states or districts, and responded thus to local pressures as opposed to the national will. It is the executive and the judiciary, the two branches that are truly national, that he discusses. It is these to which he is the most truly sympathetic, and with which he is the most emotionally in tune.

The Supreme Court is treated in the final essays of the work. It is a figure of reverence, solid, forbidding and remote. It is static, where the other branches have the capacity of innovation. It cannot initiate measures, it can only react. But it is in this capacity that it is most impressive. It stands for the timeless and eternal values: for the basic nature of the Constitution, for the enduring interest of the people against their transient passions, for their safety against the excess or error of the President or of either house.

> In a monarchy, it is an excellent barrier to the despotism of the prince: in a republic, it is a no less excellent barrier to

112

the despotism of the prince, to the encroachments and repressions of the representative body . . . [it is] the best expedient . . . to secure a steady, upright, and impartial administration of the laws.[13]

In the seventy-eighth *Federalist*, he details the doctrine of judicial review, which gives the Court its power—the right to override an act of Congress which it believes to contravene the Constitution's basic sense:

The Constitution ought to be preferred to the statute, the intention of the people to the intention of their agents. . . . It only supposes that the will of the people is superior to both, and that where the will of the legislature . . . stands in opposition to that of the people declared in the Constitution, the judges ought to be governed by the latter over the former. They ought to regulate their decisions by the fundamental laws.[14]

Hamilton believed order essential to the maintenance of freedom and justice. As such, he tended to revere the Court. For the rest of his life he would work to strengthen it, to bolster its independence and prestige. Abstract justice, standing against the tides of human error, could not be overvalued.

Considerate men of every description ought to prize whatever will tend to fortify that temper. . . . As no man can be sure that he may not be tomorrow the victim of a spirit of injustice, from which he may be a gainer today. And every man must now feel that the inevitable tendency of such a spirit is to sap the foundations of public and private confidence, and to introduce in its stead universal distrust and distress.[15]

If Hamilton reveres the Court, he is still more reverent toward the office of the presidency, which he examines in a series of eleven essays near the conclusion of the work. This care is both deliberate and meaningful, for the President is a figure of special interest to him, in his political theories as well as in his emotional life. The presidency stands in his mind (as did the monarchy) for strength, union and fatherly protection, as well as encompassing the republican virtue of merit, for the President is chosen on his talents by his peers.

The presidency is the center of the government. It is the symbol of union, and it has a legitimacy that the other branches lack. It is the only one that is both elected and truly national in outlook. Unlike the Court, it is not removed from appointment by the people. Unlike the members of Congress, it has no local interests or obligations by which it is shackled, and which interrupt its larger duty to the state. It is an amalgamation of the best parts of the other branches, for it combines stability and energy. Thus, Hamilton saw it as the one arm of the government that was truly legitimate and morally authorized to wield power. As he explained in the seventieth *Federalist*, he regarded it as the driving force in government, without which the government itself must fail.

> Energy in the executive is a leading character in the definition of good government. It is essential to the protection of the community against foreign attacks: it is not less essential to the steady administration of the laws: to the protection of property against those irregular and high handed combinations which sometimes interrupt the ordinary course of justice; to the security of liberty against the enterprises and assaults of ambition, of faction, and of anarchy. . . . A feeble executive implies a feeble execution of the government. A feeble execution is but another phrase for a bad execution: and a government ill executed, whatever it may be in theory, must be, in practice, a bad government.[16]

Hamilton's insistence that the President must be something other than the passive executor of laws passed on by Congress took on the force of a crusade. He fought, as he had fought in the Convention, for extensive presidential powers—for duration in office, for independence from Congress, for the right to appoint officers, for the right to veto laws. And in the seventy-first *Federalist*, he struck out firmly for another power: the power of resistance and restraint:

> There are some who would be inclined to regard the servile pliancy of the executive to the prevailing current, either in the community or in the legislature, as its best recommendation. . . . The republican principle demands that the deliberate sense of the community should govern the conduct of those to whom they trust the management of their affairs, but it does not require an unqualified complaisance

114

to every sudden breeze of passion, or to every transient impulse which the people may receive from the arts of men, who flatter their prejudices to betray their interests. It is a just observation that the people commonly *intend* the PUBLIC GOOD. This is applicable to their very errors. But their good sense would despise the adulator who should pretend that they always *reason right* about the *means* of promoting it. They know from experience that they sometimes err; and the wonder is that they so seldom err as they do, beset as they continually are by the wiles of parasites and sychophants, by the snares of the ambitious, the avaricious, the desperate, by the artifices of men who possess their confidence more than they deserve it, and of those who seek to possess rather than deserve it. When occasions present themselves in which the interests of the people are at variance with their inclinations, it is the duty of the persons whom they have appointed to be the guardians of those interests to withstand the temporary delusion in order to give them time and opportunity for more cool and sedate reflection. Instances might be cited in which a conduct of this kind has saved the people from the very fatal consequences of their own mistakes, and has produced lasting monuments of their gratitude to the men who had courage and magnanimity enough to serve them at the peril of their own displeasure.[17]

The resemblance to the parent-child relationship is unmistakable. The President, a wise and loving father, guards his children from the consequences of their own misjudgment. It is the role Hamilton expected the President to play in relation to the people, and the role also that Washington played in relation to himself. Hamilton knew, as did all Americans, that Washington would be the first President, and would hold that office as long as he wished. Inevitably, Hamilton's feelings about Washington colored his approach. How much this influenced his concept of the office, how he would have written of it with the thought in mind of another man as President, is impossible to know.

Despite the glimmers of hope that flicker through these papers, the prevailing note is gloom. He is pessimistic as regards the government, and in relation to himself. He had continuing doubts about the ability of the republic to prevail against the tides of faction and the intrigues and ambitions of designing men. For those who believed that a republican system would bring out the best in human nature, he had nothing but contempt.

> What reason can we have to confide in those reveries which would seduce us into an expectation of peace and cordiality? [he asked in the sixth paper] . . . Have we not already seen enough of the fallacy and extravagance of those idle theories which have amused us with promises of an exemption from the imperfections, the weaknesses, and the evils incident to society in every shape? Is it not time to awake from the deceitful dream of a golden age, and to adopt as a practical maxim for the direction of our political conduct that we, as well as the other inhabitants of the globe, are yet remote from the happy empire of perfect wisdom and perfect virtue?[18]

As the bearer of these tidings and as the advocate of power, he knew he was regarded as dangerous and felt himself destined to be censured and misunderstood. It is not remarkable that it was in the very first paper that he had tried to explain and extricate himself:

> It will be forgotten that the vigor of government is essential to the security of liberty . . . their interests never can be separated, and that a dangerous ambition more often lurks under the specious mask of a zeal for the rights of the people, than the forbidding appearance of zeal for the firmness and efficiency of government. History will teach us that the former has been found a much more certain road to the introduction of despotism than the latter, and that of those men who have overturned the liberty of republics, the greatest number have begun their careers by playing an obsequious court to the people, commencing demagogues, and ending tyrants.[19]

Four years later, in a letter to his friend Edward Carrington protesting his innocence against opponents who charged him with trying to introduce a dictatorship, he would strike much the same note:

> If I were disposed to promote Monarchy . . . I would mount the hobby horse of popularity . . . cry out usurpa-

116

tion . . . prostrate the national government . . . raise a ferment . . . then "ride in the whirlwind, and direct the Storm."[20]

It is evident from his reiterations that Hamilton believed firmly that power and cynicism on the part of the ruling bodies were the only ways to guarantee the survival of liberty. It is also evident from his own use of the word "forbidding" to describe his program that he did not expect to be believed.

I X

FROM THE TIME the Convention adjourned in September to the completion of the Cabinet when Thomas Jefferson took office in the spring of 1790, the American government was in the process of formation. Its first problem was the passage of the Constitution through the states. Nine states of thirteen were required to pass it. Resistance was strong in New York and Virginia, which were both regarded as crucial, and in which Hamilton and Madison both faced a struggle—Madison with George Mason and Patrick Henry, Hamilton with the Clinton faction and with his old enemies Lansing and Yates.

The New York State Ratifying Convention was held at Poughkeepsie between June 17 and July 28. Hamilton was attacked as a monarchist, a man "unattached to the feelings of the people," and a man of exceptional ambition who wanted a new government to gather power to himself. He defended himself against the last charge in a rather poignant passage:

> The changes in the human condition are many and frequent. Many on whom fortune has bestowed her favors, may trace their family to a more unprosperous station. . . . If today I am among the favored few, my children, tomorrow, may at a future day be suffering the severe distresses to which my ambition has reduced them.[1]

118

The Clintonians opposed him fiercely, including Yates and Lansing, who remained in bitter opposition, and were among the holdouts to the last. It was not until other states had ratified that New York was pushed into a grudging accommodation, spurred by news of what was largely Madison's victory in Virginia at the end of June. This, with the threat of secession by the southern counties, which would have left the north land-locked and isolated, produced a narrow victory at last. At the end, fearing that his speech had been too vehement, Hamilton made an apology to his erstwhile foes:

> If such has been my language, it was from the habit of using strong phrases to express my ideas. . . . I have ever con-demned those cold, unfeeling hearts, which no object can animate. I condemn those indifferent mortals, who can neither form opinions, nor ever make them known.[2]

Neither condition was likely to apply to him.

Hamilton returned to New York City as the hero of the day. On July 23 there had been a parade in the city, with a scale-model flagship, the *Alexander Hamilton*, pulled in triumph through the streets. The city was preparing for its own brief glory as the first capital and seat of govern-ment, an honor it would hold to 1790. If the new government was not royal, it was still to be impressive, and there was an outpouring of social activity around the "Federalist Court." The famous, the familied, the gifted and the merely rich would vie for the honor of entertaining the President, Congressmen, and other officers of government at a series of lavish and glittering soirees. In New York the social burden was taken on by the Livingstons, Jays and Schuylers among others, some of whom held weekly gatherings. In 1791, when the capital moved to Philadelphia, the role was assumed by the William Binghams, who maintained a salon at Mansion House, their palatial estate presided over by the exquisite queen of society, the chestnut-haired Anne.

Washington was uncertain as to the social tone of his administration and sent his friends queries as to the proper posture to adopt. It was finally decided, on Hamilton's advice among others', to hold weekly receptions to which the public was invited which the officers of govern-ment would attend. In addition there were dinners for Congressmen and other dignitaries, and other functions, including a dinner for Washington, his Vice-President and Cabinet officers at his old headquarters at Har-lem Heights and a three-day excursion when the President and his officers of government went fishing off Sandy Hook. Some republicans found this an unseemly display of European manners, as did Senator William Maclay, who entered in his diary a stream of critical remarks. But it was largely an effort to find a structure for power, to erect a form of ceremony around a government whose construction was radical and whose stability was still untried.

George Washington was sworn in as first President on April 30, 1789, on the balcony of Federal Hall. Two weeks later he sent a message to Hamilton inviting him to become Secretary of the Treasury in the new regime. The post was the most powerful, as well as the most arduous, in government, since it involved the most crucial problem facing the republic—the settlement of the $80-million debt. It was a demanding challenge, but Hamilton had seen fiscal stability as the key to national union since his days in the army when he had seen the debilitating effects of a weak economy upon the political structure. As he told Lafayette, he had no doubts as to his capacity. He had been forming his program for the past eight years.

As expected, Hamilton was pleased with Washington's election. He had his friend and his protector in power, and a willing ally in his plans. He was pleased also with the other men in government: with the election of Philip Schuyler as one of New York's senators, and of James Madison as Speaker of the House. He was also happy with the composition of the Cabinet. Henry Knox, in the War Department, was an old friend of his and of Washington's and was expected to follow the President's lead. He knew less of Edmund Randolph, who had been in the Virginia delegation to the Constitutional Convention, and who had been named Attorney General largely for reasons of geographical balance. It is likely that he was pleased by the appointment to the State Department of Thomas Jefferson, whom he knew by reputation to be able, brilliant and talented and one of Madison's close friends.

The one development that did not please him was the election of John Adams as Vice-President. Hamilton was hostile to Adams, partly because he did not know or trust him, and partly because his office, though it was in fact to come to very little, seemed at the time too close to the presidency. In the fall of 1788 Hamilton began to write a series of letters to his friends around the country, intended to isolate Adams within the new administration and remove him as a threat. "I believe Mr. Adams will have the votes of this state," he wrote to Theodore Sedgwick in October. "He is certainly, I think, to be preferred to the other Gentleman, yet *certainly* is perhaps too strong a word." Since the "other Gentleman" was George Clinton, his reservation is strong indeed. He went on to cultivate new doubts in Sedgwick, adding rumors of "a suggestion . . . that he is unfriendly in his sentiments to General Washington. . . . The Lees and Adamses have been in the habit of uniting, and hence may spring up a Cabal."[3]

To James Madison he wrote on November 23, "I have concluded to support Adams, though I am not without apprehensions on the score we conversed about," leaving the source of their discomfort unrevealed. But his conversion was the result not of enthusiasm but of fear. If not elected, he said, Adams "must be nominated to some important office for which he is less proper, or will become a malcontent."[4] Adams under the heel of Washington was less threatening than Adams in the Cabinet, or as the leader of a faction of his own.

Hamilton also mentioned for the first time another source of his disquiet: under the provisions of the Constitution, the candidates for the presidency and vice-presidency were voted on together, with no distinctions made between them, and he feared they might be interchanged. He did not want to take the chance of Adams supplanting Washington, nor did he wish him to approximate his vote. "It would be disagreeable to have a man treading close upon the heels of the man we wish as president," he told Madison in a statement not completely political. He began to tell his friends to waste their votes.

> I conclude it might be prudent to throw away a few votes, say seven or eight [he told James Wilson]. . . . I have proposed to friends in Connecticut to throw away two, to others in Jersey to throw away an equal number, & I submit it to you whether it would not be well to lose three of four in Philadelphia. . . . Your advices from the South will be your best guide.[5]

Evidence that his strictures were followed was shown in a letter from a friend in New Haven the next month:

> Our votes were given favorably to your wishes. Washington 7—Adams 5. Governor Huntington 2. . . . I hear that Clinton is the anti-federal Vice President, but I think we have nothing to fear.[6]

How far Hamilton's stated reasons were the true source of his uneasiness is now impossible to know. Adams was jealous of Washington, and had been suspected in the war of sympathy to plots to supplant him or to reduce his power, which did not win him friends among the aides. It is also true that the election system held a sleeping danger, which would surface twelve years later in the election of Jefferson and Burr. There was cause on both counts for suspicion, but it was also likely that Hamilton was moving to diminish the power of a potential rival and to check the powers of a government official of whose ideas and loyalties he was not sure. Whatever its sources, its intrigue had made its point. Still outside the government, he had already altered its complexion. He had made Washington's triumph more assured and illustrious. And he had taken off Adams's smaller triumph and diminished him in the country's estimation and his own.

Another effort at manipulation misfired, with long-term damage. Hamilton was desperately anxious that the Senate from New York be "safe." One seat would go to Philip Schuyler, his alter ego in politics, who was genuinely family and who adored him as a son. But he was greedy for the second seat, and when Rufus King, whom he now counted as an adoring younger brother, moved to New York in 1788, Hamilton insisted that the seat be his. King was charming, and so gifted that he was kept on as ambassador to Britain in the administration of Thomas Jefferson, but he had no local following. He was resented by the Livingstons, cousins to the Schuyler family, who had counted on the seat as theirs. Affronted by this slight, they joined Clinton as allies. When Schuyler's term expired two years later, they took their revenge. Their new alliance swept the Federalists from office. Schuyler was replaced by Aaron Burr.

Angelica Church returned from London to America in April 1789, after an absence of almost five years. When she landed once more in her native country, she was an elegant woman of thirty-nine, her charm refined by maturity and experience, enchanced by money and honed by contact with Europe's political and literary elite. The Churches lived in a town house in London and at Down Place, their country house three miles down the Thames from Windsor. They entertained the Prince of Wales at dinner, and attended the theater in the company of Sheridan and Fox. A young American cousin left a dazzled record of his visit to her country mansion, where she gave a gala ball for the future George IV and other notables, and later took him to the Drury Lane Theater, where she had a private box.

Her new friends were William Smith, son-in-law of the Adamses, the artist John Trumbull, the French aristocrat Madame de Corny and Maria Cosway, the delicately beautiful artist who became romantically entangled with Thomas Jefferson in 1786. She had moved into a world infinitely richer and more dazzling than the somewhat provincial society the Schuylers represented in America, but there were signs that this had brought new tensions. She resented the move to Europe, which had been the idea of her husband. Her return to America without her husband or children may have been an act of defiance.

John Barker Church had left the Revolution an exceedingly rich man. Honestly or otherwise, he had reaped large fortunes in his roles as commissary to the northern army and then to the French. There is a note to Hamilton from a mildly resentful James McHenry that Church had enough money to last him through several lives. Church bought himself something of a place in London society, purchasing a place in Parliament and cementing his aquaintance by acting as a banker to his political associates, once lending £20,000 sterling to the improvident Charles James Fox. But Church also showed the first signs of what became a perilous addiction to gambling. He was coarsely materialistic, and many who found his wife enchanting thought him ponderous and dull. Angelica made frequent trips to Paris, often in the company of her new friends in the artistic and political communities. She often visited the convent school in Paris where her daughter Kitty boarded, her schoolmate being the daughter of Thomas Jefferson, then American minister to France.

Restive and homesick, Angelica began to run down her husband, making derisive comments to Eliza and to Hamilton himself. She compared him to Hamilton, always unfavorably. "Church's head is full of politics, he is desirous of making one in the House of Commons, where I should be happy to see him, if he had your eloquence,"[7] she wrote to Hamilton: and her letters to her sister were even more direct. "Ah, Bess! You were a lucky girl to get so good and so clever a companion."[8] she wrote in one letter, and in another, "Embrace your *master* for me, and tell him that I envy you the fame of so clever a husband, one who writes so well."[9]

She began to stake out a claim in Hamilton's reputation, and to enlarge her own role in his life. "I am really so proud of his merit and abilities that even you, Eliza, might envy my feelings,"[10] she wrote, and she ended another letter with an unusual request:

123

If you were as generous as the old Romans, you would lend him to me for a little while. . . . Do not be jealous, my dear Eliza, since I am more solicitous to promote his laudable ambition than any person in the world. . . . There is no summit of true glory that I do not desire that he may attain, provided that he pleases to give me a little chit chat, and sometimes to say, I wish our dear Angelica was here."[11]

Church had made Hamilton the executor for his financial interests when he moved to Europe. Hamilton's records show a pattern of continuous activity which sometimes interrupted his own professional and political affairs. There is some correspondence between Church and Hamilton, but it is largely about financial matters. Its tone is businesslike. Superficially this was a conventional relationship between two couples, but the reality was different. The dynamics were an interweaving of complex emotions under the guise of brotherly affections between one man and two women, one of them the sister of his wife.

The two families spent much time together while the Churches were in America, and written records of this time are few. But after the Churches moved to Europe, Hamilton and his sister-in-law embarked on what can only be termed a long-term, long-distance courtship. They acted within the parameters established by their formal relationship, dealing in subtleties and undertones, in the suggested and implied. Constraint added piquancy to their flirtation—as did the repeated use of the words "friend" and "brother" when they were charged, but never too directly, with hidden meanings of their own.

Their correspondence assumed a note of the conspiratorial. Emphasis became a language of its own:

You have, I fear, taken a final leave of America, and of those that love you [Hamilton wrote in August 1785]. I saw you depart from Philadelphia with a peculiar uneasiness, as if foreboding you were not to return. My apprehensions are confirmed, and unless I see you in Europe, I expect not to see you again. . . . Judge the bitterness it gives to those who love you with the *love of nature*, and to me, who feel an attachment for you not less lively. I confess for my part I see one great source of happiness snatched away.[12]

* * *

Amicable Angelica! [he wrote again] How much you are formed to endear yourself to every good heart! How deeply you have rooted yourself in the affections of your friends! . . . *Some* of us are and must continue to be inconsolable for your absence.[13]

Sometimes he showed the pique of a jealous suitor:

How do you manage to charm all who see you? While naughty tales are told to you of us, we hear nothing but of your kindness, amiableness, agreeableness. . . . Why must you be so lavish of these qualities upon those who forget them in six weeks, and withhold them from us, who retain all the impressions you make, indelibly?[14]

And there were constant urgings, as one would urge a lover, to return: "You know how much we all love you. 'Tis impossible you can be as well loved where you are."[15] The variations with which their code within a code was written are revealed at their most subtle in his answer to a letter of 1788:

There was a most critical *comma* in your last letter. It is in my interest that it should have been designed, but I presume it was accidental . . . Adieu my chère, soeur.[16]

Eliza's letters to her sister and her husband have been lost. Thus one must refer to Hamilton's letters for signs that she shared his attachment in degree, if not in kind. "Betsey and myself make you the last theme of our conversation at night, and the first in the morning,"[17]Hamilton told Angelica. In another letter he said, "The only rivalship we have is in our attachment to you."[18] Eliza adored Angelica for the wit and glamour she shared with Hamilton, and which Eliza herself did not possess. Angelica loved her younger sister, of whom she remained protective. "Soothe my poor Betsey," she wrote to Hamilton after she had gone to London. "Comfort her with assurances that I will certainly return to take care of her soon."[19]

While Angelica remained in Europe, remote and inaccessible, the three could live inside their fantasies. But her return in the flesh and without her husband set off a confrontation no one could avoid. It was doubtless a

125

crisis for Eliza, who had to face an idealized figure, and one quite unlike herself. At the balls and dinners that accompanied the installation of the new government, the brother and sister-in-law behaved like courting lovers, and their conduct gave rise to talk. There was a ball at which Hamilton retrieved a garter that Angelica had dropped. When she protested that he was not a Knight of the Garter, her sister Peggy let a sharp-tongued volley fly: He would be a Knight of the Bedchamber if he could.

If Eliza was aware of the rumors, as is likely, she ignored them, rose above them or simply pushed them from her mind. This was her pattern in all scandals concerning her husband: she attacked not the principals but the tale-bearers with great fury, and formed resentments she took with her to the grave. Her husband's role in these scandals was something she ignored. This was true of the rumors about him and her adored sister, whom she could not afford to turn against. It was also true of her conduct in the Reynolds scandal, when she turned her fury not on Hamilton, nor as it would seem, upon his mistress, but on the man she suspected as the bearer of the story, James Monroe. The reasons for this were twofold. She had made an emotional investment in Alexander Hamilton that she could not afford to jeopardize, and she shared the belief of the entire Schuyler family that Hamilton was a genius of rare luster and that those who knew him were privileged on any terms to share his life. Whether she ever took revenge in secret on him is unknown.

Angelica sailed for England on November 5, 1789. Her departure was sudden and may have been the result of a family quarrel. A letter that she sent to Hamilton while aboard ship contains references to a difference with her father, the details of which are not revealed. Eliza was ill with anxiety the night before the departure and did not accompany her husband and her sister to the ship the next morning.

> After taking leave of you aboard the Packet, I hastened home to soothe and console your sister [Hamilton wrote to Angelica]. I found her in bitter distress; though much recovered from the agony in which she had been.[20]

Eliza herself sent a postscript to "My Very Dear Beloved Angelica," which she added to Hamilton's note:

> I have seated myself to write to you, but my heart is so sadend by your absence that it can scarsly dictate, my Eyes

so filled with tears that I shall not be able to write. . . . *Remember, remember,* my dear Sister, the Assurances of your returning to us, and do all you can to make your Absence short.[21]

From the ship Angelica sent Hamilton a letter before the packet left New York. In it she sounded more like a woman torn from her closest attachments than one returning to her family after months abroad. She complained of being too disspirited to enjoy the company of her companions aboard ship.

How can I be content when I leave my best and most invaluable friends. Adieu my dear Hamilton, you said I was as dear to you as a sister keep your word, and let me have the consolation to believe that you will never forget the promise of friendship you have vowed. A thousand embraces to my poor Betsey, she will not have had as bad a night as the last, but *poor angelica, adieu* mine plus chèr.

Clearly her losses in the people she was leaving outweighed her gains in those that she was going to. "Adieu my dear Brother, may god bless and protect you, prays your ever affectionate Angelica, ever ever yours."[22]

X

HAMILTON'S QUARREL with Thomas Jefferson appeared to take him by surprise. Never had he imagined opposition from within the government, which he had seen as his stronghold and the symbol of national unity. It was with a mixture of hurt feelings and genuine astonishment that he was to write this sentence in a remarkable letter to his friend Edward Carrington in May 1792:

> It was not till the last session that I became unequivocally convinced of the following truth—"That Mr. Madison cooperating with Mr. Jefferson is at the head of a faction decidedly hostile to me and my administration, and actuated by views in my judgment subversive of the principles of good government and dangerous to the union, peace, and happiness of the Country."[1]

Perhaps naively, he had envisioned the easy passage of a program that would bring strength, power and domestic tranquillity to the country, and honor and reputation to himself. Instead, he was plunged almost at once into political quarrels and moral quandaries which he was not prepared for: into what he thought of as the "betrayal" of two men he had counted as his friends and allies, and into a scarring battle with a rival of

128

great resource, who matched him in genius and whose political talents far exceeded his.

Thomas Jefferson, when Hamilton first met him in the spring of 1790, was forty-seven years old. He was fair, with a square and open countenance, red hair, hazel eyes and a pale skin that peeled and freckled in the sun. He was as tall as Washington (and six inches taller than Hamilton), but his carriage and his dress were careless, and he often wore ill-fitting clothes. He had changed very little in appearance and manner when Augustus Foster, Secretary of the British Legation, left this portrait in 1804:

> He was a tall man, with a very red freckled face and grey neglected hair; his manners good-natured, frank and rather friendly, though he had something of a cynical expression. . . . He wore a blue coat, a thick grey-colored hairy waistcoat, with a red underwaistcoat lapped over it, green velveteen breeches with pearl buttons, yarn stockings, and slippers down at the heels—his appearance being very much like that of a tall, large boned farmer.[2]

His manner was shy, his voice low-pitched, almost a whisper. It was often noticed that he seldom looked men in the eye.

Jefferson was the son of a Virginia planter, a self-made émigré of Welsh extraction, and of the English-born Jane Randolph, a woman of high connections and of gentle birth. The dual identity thus imposed upon him colored and controlled his life. His refined tastes were aristocratic, including an interest in the arts that was the most catholic of his generation, a talent for architecture, an ear for music and an appreciation of good food and wine. But his imagination, colored by his father's memory, was focused on the future and the west. He believed in the people, in democracy as the highest form of political organization and in the small farm as the superior unit of social and of economic life. Unlike Hamilton, who thought of sin and error as firmly embedded in the human character, Jefferson saw them as transient qualities that could be corrected by education and good will.

A great sophisticate who mingled easily with the nobility of Europe, a scholar, and a political genius of great guile and subtlety, he cherished a fantasy of rural simplicity that was as compelling a part of his emotional makeup as Hamilton's dream of order was to him. His great house at Monticello, an exquisite mansion built on the best principles of European architecture, filled with books, art works, French furniture and expensive wines, built on a hilltop in a part of Virginia that was still wild and largely uninhabited, shows the infinite contradictions of this complicated man.

Jefferson had had an expensive education, and had gone with the other children of the rich into the Virginia House of Burgesses, where he had been caught at once in the passions of the revolutionary movement. He had gone as a delegate to the Continental Congress and served as war governor before being sent abroad to replace the ailing Benjamin Franklin as minister to France. In America he had conceived a hatred of entrenched authority and of traditional social structures, a feeling that found eloquent expression in the Declaration of Independence, which had been his work. But it was in Europe, in his service in France and in his tours of neighbor countries, that this sentiment became refined. He had been appalled at the luxury and self-indulgence of the nobility and the misery of the common people, condemned to lives of poverty and degradation. Hamilton may have heard from Madison of Jefferson's successes at the court of France and of his efforts at reform of the government—which were later to erupt in revolution—with Hamilton's old friend Lafayette. But Madison may not have told him of Jefferson's growing aversion to authority, his distrust of power, his increasing conviction that government was a pernicious influence, inimical to the interests of free men.

> There is not a crowned head in Europe whose talents or merit would entitle him to be elected a vestryman by the people in any parish in America [he had written to Washington]. There is scarcely an evil known in these countries which may not be traced to their king as its source.[3]

When news had reached him of Shay's Rebellion, the Massachusetts riot that had been a mighty spur to the Constitutional Convention, he had written Madison, "One rebellion in thirteen states in the course of eleven years is but one for each state in a century and a half. No country should be so long without one."[4] And he had written William Smith, the Adams's son-in-law:

> What signify a few lives lost in a century or two? The tree of liberty must be refreshed from time to time by the blood of patriots and tyrants. It is its natural manure.[5]

Hamilton and Jefferson were both moralists, concerned with the balance of freedom and order in the state. But their definitions of these things were most dissimilar, coming from temperaments fundamentally different and backgrounds that were totally opposed. The one's morality, at least at first impression, would seem the other's sin. Conflict between them would be inevitable. It was also inevitable that it would be fierce.

The quarrel between them first became serious in the beginning of 1791. Jefferson was disturbed by Hamilton's program, which (as detailed in three reports to Congress) involved the funding of the national debt as stock certificates held by private investors, the establishment of a National Bank which combined public and private money and a complex plan to involve the government in American industry through a complicated program of tax incentives and rewards. Hamilton's purpose in combining government and business was twofold: he wished to involve the rich and powerful with the national government and to make it in their interest to support it: and he wished to give the government the power to shape the economy in the interests of the state. But to Jefferson, already distrustful of commerce, it came to seem a plot to bribe the rich to support his policies and consolidate his power. Alarmed at Hamilton's interpretation of the Constitution, which gave great powers to Congress and the President, by reports of Hamilton's comments at the Constitutional Convention and by some favorable references to Julius Caesar and to the British constitution, Jefferson came to believe that Hamilton was plotting the transformation of the government from a republic to a monarchy with the installation of an hereditary Senate and a King. He believed that Hamilton was forming "an Anglican, monarchical, aristocratic party," based on the men he had corrupted by his financial programs, to change the character of the United States. As he wrote to Washington in a famous letter:

> His system flowed from principles adverse to liberty, and was calculated to undermine and demolish the Republic, by creating an influence of his department over the members of the Legislature . . . for the purpose of subverting, step by step, the principles of the Constitution, which he has so often declared to be a thing of nothing, which must be changed.[6]

He told friends in Europe (Lafayette among them) that Hamilton,

131

"puffed up by a tribe of Agiteurs . . . hatched in a bed of corruption,"[7] was plotting to install a king.

Hamilton was stunned in 1790 when Madison, whom he counted on as a friend and ally, led the opposition to his program in the House. Madison was a southerner, attached to his region and its agrarian culture, and his vision of Federalism—a balance between the state and central governments—had not anticipated the practical consequences of Hamilton's attack upon the states. With Jefferson he began to organize a group of men who called themselves Republicans (in contrast to Hamilton's presumed monarchist principles)—planters, farmers and the remnants of the anti-Federalist movement—in a program of opposition to government policy. In 1791 they made a trip to New York, forming a party of national dimensions and joining forces with the Livingstons and Aaron Burr. Hamilton, watching this with resentment and anger, suspected Jefferson of trying to destroy the government through an excess of frustrated ambition and of trying to become President himself.

Political differences were complicated by personal grievances and added depth and color to the feud. Hamilton blamed Jefferson for the defection of Madison and came to despise them both.

> I cannot persuade myself that Mr. Madison & I, whose politics had formerly so much of the same point of departure, should now diverge so widely [he told Edward Carrington]. The opinion I had entertained of the simplicity and fairness of Mr. Madison's character . . . has given way to a decided opinion that it is one of a *peculiarly artificial and complicated kind.*[8]

Jefferson believed that Washington had been seduced by Hamilton into an unwitting endorsement of sinister and pernicious schemes. When Washington told him in one interview that "he did not believe there were ten men in the United States, whose opinions were worth attention," who entertained thoughts of a monarchy, and that Hamilton's policies had saved the country's credit, Jefferson went home and wrote in his journal:

> He was not aware of the drift, nor of the effect, of Hamilton's schemes. Unversed in financial projects and calculations and budgets, his approbation of him was bottomed in his confidence in the man.[9]

132

One sees here Jefferson's resentment and jealousy—of the "confidence" he did not have. Each blamed the other for his growing distance from a man whose affections he once had cherished, and this undercurrent darkened the dispute.

John Fenno, a young printer, had been approached by Hamilton's friends to establish a press to promote the newly established government in 1789. It soon became a government organ, mirroring, and sometimes printing, Hamilton's views. In 1790, when the government moved to Philadelphia, Jefferson engaged the poet Philip Freneau as a translating clerk in the State Department, with the understanding that he would use his subsidy to establish an opposition press. As the feud in the Cabinet ripened, these presses became the vehicles of fury as the Secretaries—Hamilton directly and Jefferson through numerous surrogates, Madison among them—vilified each other without reservation in the press. The attacks, which included charges of corruption, sedition, treason and attempts to reduce the country to despotism or anarchy, grew ever more vehement. When Washington appealed to them for moderation, they replied with anguished accounts of their provocations and innocence and continued to berate each other. Each now found the presence of the other in the government intolerable and seemed driven to force the other out.

Working secretly through his friend Virginia Congressman William Branch Giles, Jefferson composed nine resolutions calling for Hamilton's dismissal on the grounds of speculation and mismanagement of government money, which were submitted to Congress on February 27, 1793. It was at the end of the session, and they hoped the charges would fester through the congressional recess, growing in impact until Congress reconvened. Working feverishly through two days of all-night sessions, Hamilton composed a defense and was acquitted, but he was as enraged at the tactics as at the charges leveled, and his fury grew. Lingering resentment showed itself in a letter he wrote John Marshall eight years later in which he called Jefferson a "contemptible hypocrite" and added, "He is not very careful of the truth." To John Jay he complained of "malicious intrigues . . . to stab me in the back."[10] As did Jefferson, he longed to retire, but each feared to leave the Cabinet in the possession of the other, and each feared withdrawal would be seen as a defeat. Jefferson had told Washington in a revealing letter:

> I will not suffer my retirement to be clouded by the slanders
> of a man, whose history, from the moment at which history
> can stoop to notice him, is a tissue of machinations against

133

the liberty of the country which has not only received and given him bread, but heaped its honors on his head."[11]

Nothing in their quarrel was so to embitter Hamilton as the charges of Jefferson and of his allies that he was morally corrupt. When he burst out angrily to Edward Carrington, "They have *even* whispered suspicions of the rectitude of my conduct,"[12] he was detailing not only his own priorities but the most grievous of their sins. For all his brave talk of his indifference to popular opinion, he longed for respect and affection, or failing that, for acknowledgment as an honorable man. He found assaults on his moral character hard to parry or accept.

> They assume to themselves, and to those who think with them, infallibility [he raged to Washington]. Take their words for it, they are the only honest men in the community . . . [they call] every man of a different opinion . . . an ambitious despot, or a corrupt knave.[13]

Jefferson's secret goading of his friends in Congress to mount campaigns against Hamilton infuriated Hamilton, and the sight of Jefferson claiming innocence from involvement in the press attacks, while paying Freneau to do so, drove him into helpless rage. He was jealous of Jefferson's ability to paint himself as a scholar, philosopher and idealist, while engaging meanwhile in political battles; and scathing references to republican "purity" began to appear in Hamilton's letters and his speech. Behind the anger was envy: he craved the public adulation that Jefferson could win so easily and that he himself could not. But there was another reason why he found these attacks unsettling: in the grand sweep of his programs there were flaws he did not care to think about, and about which he did not wish to hear.

When Hamilton complained to Washington about his innocence, he believed it of his quarrel with Jefferson, but it is not certain he believed it of himself. Among the things about his program that he did not care to dwell on was the inescapable conclusion that the veterans and poor had been betrayed. His system rested on a plan to pay the national debt by funding at par the government securities that had been devalued in the financial chaos of the postwar years, many of them held by veterans who had taken them in lieu of pay. Ideally, his plan would have profited these holders. But while its details were secret, known only to the few in Hamilton's office, speculators had descended on the back country, buying stock at debased prices, selling it at par months later and becoming very rich. In his journal, Jefferson penned a murderous description of the chase:

> Courier and relay horse by land, and swift sailing boats by sea, were flying in all directions. Active partners and agents were associated and employed in every State, town, and country neighborhood, and this paper was bought up at five shillings, and even as low as two shillings on the pound. . . . Immense sums were thus filched from the poor and ignorant, and fortunes accumulated by those who had been poor enough before.[14]

Hamilton could claim that the success of his plan had benefited everyone, the poor among them, by stabilizing the economy. But he could not argue with Madison's comment that the process had been "radically immoral," a "flagrant injustice" that enriched the country's least worthy men.

Hamilton's role in this transaction is the single glaring blot on his career. His reactions throughout were contradictory, suggesting hidden conflicts of his own. He himself remained remote from speculation, refusing to buy, sell or even talk of stocks. But the leaks did originate in his department, the source of this lucrative osmosis being William Duer, his assistant at the Treasury, whose role will be examined at a later point. When Madison proposed a compromise offering different rates of payment to primary and secondary holders of certificates, Hamilton dismissed it as too complex, too intricate and too difficult to be enforced. In his defense, which he detailed in a letter to Washington, he blamed the plight of the poor on his political opponents, whose refusal to pass a comprehensive financial program years earlier had led to the depressions and panics in which the value of the stock was lost. This was true, but it was a lame defense, as he seemed to be aware. That he harbored great hatred of the class he had enriched surfaced in 1792 in a letter to Philip Livingston, in which he complained at length of "certain characters" who sported with the market and with the "distresses" of their fellow men.

> 'Tis time there should be a separation between honest Men & Knaves, between respectable stockholders and dealers . . . and unprincipled Gamblers. . . . The relaxations in a just system of thinking, which have been produced by an excessive spirit of speculation, must be correct-

ed. . . . Contempt & Neglect must attend those who manifest that they have no principle but to get Money.[15]

Yet at some point he had to face the fact that the despised people "with
no principle but to get Money" were the bricks with which he built his
state.

Hamilton and Jefferson were both to soil their hands considerably in
the service of their visions, between things done themselves in temper and
things done in calculation through agents of whose precise doings they did
not always wish to be informed. The difference was that Jefferson's
vision, the world of small farms and scattered settlements, of loose social
bonds and pliant contracts, was in place and perfect as it stood. Hamilton's vision of discipline and intricate social arrangements required a
structure that did not come easily and implied a conscious forcing of
material. His excuse for the inequities created by his efforts was that the
crisis facing him was urgent, and that the smaller, temporary injustices
would be swallowed in the greater good. He had realized, as he said, that
men's greed and selfishness must be appealed to and used to create
national stability. But the fact that in the process he might end by encouraging and strengthening these greedy, vicious, evil passions was something he had not anticipated and which he did not want to admit.

Nothing illustrated Hamilton's moral problems as vividly as the career
of William Duer, his associate, his cousin by marriage and his friend.
Eight years older than Hamilton, he too had immigrated to America, and
had made his fortunes in wartime, serving the Continental Congress on
the Board of Treasury and ingratiating himself among the powerful with
displays of gallantry and wit. Like Hamilton, he had married into the
provincial gentry—George and Martha Washington had been guests at
his wedding to "Lady Kitty" Stirling, the daughter of a revolutionary
general and Eliza's cousin, and he had introduced Angelica to John
Barker Church. In his story there were many parallels to that of Hamilton, along with a superficial resemblance in their energy and grace. He
may have presented the younger man with a mirror image, in which
Hamilton imagined he saw something of himself.

Duer had manic charm and an engaging manner. What soon became
apparent was that he was also rapacious and unstable and had a gift for
attaching public money to himself. He had, it was discovered later,
retired from the Board of Treasury leaving a discrepancy of $200,000 on
the books. He owed money to many private creditors, whom he showed

136

no interest in repaying. He speculated constantly in government securities, and in 1788 with Jean-Pierre Brissot de Warville, another wartime friend of Hamilton, he had joined a French-American syndicate formed to speculate in the American national debt. On borrowed money he lived in New York in regal style, keeping house in a mansion staffed with fifteen servants, driving in a carriage emblazoned with his coat of arms and entertaining his friends at lavish dinners served in gold dishes and accompanied by eleven kinds of wine. Duer was still charming, but his lack of control was becoming noticeable, and had begun to worry many of his friends.

Whether it was calculation, innocence or a misplaced confidence in Duer's connections and experience, Hamilton took him into the Treasury as his assistant when he was appointed Secretary in September 1789. On October 20, one month after he took office, William Constable, a onetime partner of both Church and Duer, told Robert Morris that it was "common knowledge" that Duer was "working with John Hopkins at buying up the soldiers' pay. . . . He may not only incur censure, but be turned out."[16] On December 23, two weeks before the Report on Public Credit was made public, Duer and Constable signed a contract to purchase in North Carolina, to the extent of $16,000, "as many continental securities as can be obtained."

The next month Hamilton intervened, perhaps at Duer's urging, to avert a suit against him. For the first time Hamilton expressed in writing his worry over "the unsettled state of his affairs."

> The nature of our connection will apologize to you for my interference in a matter which is of purely private concern [he told the creditor, who also was his friend]. He assures me that he will do everything that impartial persons could say he ought to. . . . I feel intire confidence in the sincerity of a declaration of this sort *made to me*.[17]

There is the suggestion here of personal concern over Duer's lawlessness. Still, he issued no public censure, remaining silent when Duer was forced from office by the threat of a congressional investigation in April 1790. But he did not defend him, and though he closed his parting letter with a vow of friendship, there was implied censure in another sentence: that "*upon reflection*," it was proper for Duer to resign. He asked that his compliments be sent to Duer's wife.

Once out of the Treasury, Duer lost all vestiges of control. Constable described him as "making schemes every hour, and abandoning them simultaneously. . . . I have always known him better at marring a plot than furthering any project." Duer was behind a "bubble" in August 1791 when stock prices rose to terrifying heights. Hamilton sent him two sternly worded letters, mentioning rumors of "fictitious purchases, in order to take in the credulous and ignorant," and warning him against himself:

> You are sanguine, my friend. You ought to be aware of it yourself, & to be on your guard. . . . I feared lest it might carry you further than was consistent either with your safety, or with the public good. . . . If extensive mischiefs had ensued, you would certainly have had a large portion of the blame.[18]

Duer's response was an outraged defense of his operations and an impassioned acquittal of himself.

> I have scrupulously adhered to the most rigid principles of Candor and fair Dealing [he insisted]. I despise the malicious aspersions of those who Aim to destroy my Character in your, and in the public esteem. The Citizens amongst whom I live have I am persuaded too good an opinion of my head and heart to think me so weak and wicked to pursue that line of conduct which your letter intimates. I feel a Consciousness that it cannot have made an impression (even for a moment) in your mind.[19]

In December, four months after this indignant letter, Duer formed another partnership, this time with Alexander Macomb, to speculate again in American securities, using all his money and going more deeply than ever in debt. Stocks rose at first and he showed a profit, but in late January they began a steep five-week decline. His investments plummeted, and on March 8 he was $500,000 in debt. On March 9 he suspended payments, dragging hundreds of investors into ruin. On March 12 he received word from Philadelphia that Oliver Wolcott, his replacement as Hamilton's assistant, was about to bring suit against him for the $200,000 owed the United States.

Duer's reaction was to write an hysterical letter to Hamilton, mixing supplication with thinly veiled threats.

For Heaven's sake, *this once* use your influence to defer this . . . My public transactions are not mixed with my private affairs. Every farthing will be immediately accounted for. . . . If a suit should be brought on the part of the public, under my present distressed circumstances, my Ruin is complete.[20]

He issued vague and surly warnings—"Those who persue this Measure will in a short time lament the Consequences"—but whether he had the intention or the means to blackmail Hamilton remains unknown.

That Duer was incapable of making the account he promised became rapidly apparent as Hamilton was deluged with further letters from Manhattan, giving grim pictures of financial chaos and of Duer's mental and emotional decline.

The notes unpaid amount to about half a million [Robert Troup told Hamilton], & Duer has not a farthing of money or a particle of stock. . . . All the property he has in the world is land in the province of Maine, on which there is a heavy encumberance of purchase money due. You will ask what had become of his Money & Stock. His answer is & he calls God to Witness the truth of it, is that every iota . . . has been applied by him to the satisfaction of engagements personally made.[21]

Four days later Philip Schuyler found him at Baron von Steuben's, hiding from the fury of the mob. He was incoherent and rambling and spoke distractedly of betrayals and of plots.

[I] found him exceedingly distressed and agitated [Schuyler told Hamilton], not prepared to come forward with any specific propositions. . . . complained that some who had pretended friendship had deserted him. . . . assured me that he would be able to convince the candid that he had not acted dishonestly.

After a long argument Schuyler urged him to make a full accounting and place his remaining assets in the hands of his creditors, but "I found great reluctance. . . . he would rather go to Gaol than give up his Estate." To Schuyler's horror, he claimed that Hamilton had told him he was not responsible for some of the notes that he had signed. He refused once more to part with his remaining property. " 'By God, I will not give up my Estate,' " Schuyler quoted him as saying. " 'I cannot give it up. I have conveyed it.' I walked out, and have not seen him since."[22] Schuyler warned Hamilton not to write to Duer, and if appealed to, not to answer him.

Hamilton in Philadelphia was trying desperately to stabilize the economy, which he did at last on April 15, throwing more than $100,000 of government funds into the stocks. He was also concerned about the Society of Useful Manufactures, his corporation to stimulate industry, in which $10,000 under Duer's management had been lost. He wrote to Duer three times during the crisis, each time offering commiserations, and one time offering advice. He urged him to make a statement of his debts and assets, and to try to pay off public institutions and then the needy and the distressed.

> Be this as it may, act with *fortitude* and *honor*. . . . I have experienced all the bitterness of heart on your account, which a warm attachment can inspire. . . . God bless you.[23]

Duer was taken to debtors' prison on March 28. By then it was partly a safety measure, to remove him from the threat of lynching by the enraged crowds that milled around his lodging day and night. He stayed in prison, drifting more and more into insanity, for the remainder of his life. His correspondence with Hamilton broke off thereafter, save for three letters at the start of 1799. He complained of illness and of concern about his family.

> My days are sad beyond Description—My Nights miserable. . . . in the course of this year, I shall probably terminate a wretched existence. . . . the thought drives me to Distraction—and the Agony of my Mind Encreases that which is incident to my Complaint.[24]

He thanked Hamilton for intervening to transfer him to his family in the crisis of a serious illness. Now dying, he begged for one last interview.

> I wish to see you. . . . The sympathy which Mr. Morris informs me you feel for me and my miseries affords me

Consolation in the Depth of my Misery. My Affection for yourself and my sensibility for whatever interested your happiness has ever been sincere—and I have felt with Pain any Appearance of your Withdrawing from me. Whatever impressions have been made in your Mind I know not: whilst my Reason maintains its ascendancy I wish to remove them. . . . for this purpose I request on the ground of our ancient Friendship that you will see me soon.[25]

X I

HAMILTON'S FINANCIAL PROGRAM, presented to Congress in three remarkable papers between January 1790 and December 1791, is at once the fullest statement of his political philosophy and the greatest public act of his career. He was proud of the papers, and he defended them, in terms that were aggrieved and puzzled, for the remainder of his life. He was hurt and puzzled at the reaction to them. He could not understand why after funding the debt, restoring the nation's credit and breathing life into an economy he had found floundering, he should be denounced as a corruptor of his country and a betrayer of its dreams. As he aged he continued brooding, until this became synonymous with his other troubles and one with his sense of grievance and loss.

Nothing so outraged him as the fact that Thomas Jefferson, who opposed his plans in their inception, later inherited as President the financial system he had crafted, and went on to build an administration of unparalleled prosperity upon its base. He was not blind to the irony, and when Jefferson in his first inaugural stated that the government, which had to that date been Federalist, was in "the full tide of successful experiment," Hamilton took it as an "undesigned eulogy" of his administration and an unconscious tribute to his plans. He particularly resented the references of the deistic Jefferson to the role of "Providence" in securing American prosperity, which Hamilton attributed not to divine intervention but to his own. He claimed it was the product of the plans he adopted, in opposition to the ideas of politicians like Jefferson, "who now triumph in the success of their arts, and enjoy the benefits of a policy which they had neither the wisdom to plan, nor the spirit to adopt." Thus, his program was absorbed into the feud between them, which continued to consume their lives.

Part of Hamilton's problem was that he defied definition, with the eclectic quality that made him one of the most unclassifiable men of pronounced opinions in the history of American thought. He wanted government to help business and developed a complex system of incentives, but he also wanted government supervision, with heavy regulation and control. He proposed heavy taxes, anathema to the liberals of his generation, but he wanted the funds to come from what he called "luxuries" and fought all efforts to curtail the buying power of the poor. He sponsored a national bank, which did indeed aid the privileged, but he also proposed a program of massive (for his day) public spending, some of it for things that touched only tangentially upon the business interests, and that concerned what we would call "the public service sector," which he called the public weal. In much of this he was ahead of his time by years, if not by centuries, proposing concepts that his era thought bizarre. This too was part of his great trouble—for it distanced him even further from his countrymen, driving them more and more apart.

The reports were an act of defiance, a challenge flung in the face of a simple and pastoral society, and of a people who believed with Thomas Jefferson that the government was best that governed least. America in 1790 was a country of seven million people, most of them living on farms or in villages on a sustenance economy in which each unit provided for its needs. Many regarded the Constitution, passed only two years before, as having gone too far in the direction of consolidated power, and viewed it with misgivings and distrust. This revulsion from control was not parochial. Adam Smith in England had defined in *The Wealth of Nations* the laissez-faire doctrine that business flourished best when left alone. Hamilton had read the book, for Angelica sent it to him, but he did not take its counsel for his own.

In coming years Hamilton's ideas were adopted almost surreptitiously by his enemies, such as Madison and Jefferson, and others as diverse as Andrew Jackson, Abraham Lincoln and Henry Clay. In his own time, however, his stubborn insistence on his own vision compounded his sense of alienation. While he did in some sense push the country closer to the ideal that he held of it, his programs sowed divisions in the country that

143

never were joined, and first outlined and then fixed forever his tortured sense of difference from other men.

Much of this was evident in the Report Relative to the Public Credit, presented to Congress in January 1790, ostensibly to discharge the public debt. In it one sees the fruition of his thinking, the doctrines of the *Federalist* made live. He wanted the state debts absorbed by the central government, which would consolidate them and pay them off as one. He wanted the debt converted into interest-bearing bonds, redeemable at par at varying dates of maturity, which took the form of stock in the American government and functioned in the interim as cash. He wanted the debt paid by domestic taxes, mostly on things he called "luxuries." The report listed as many as twenty-five taxable items, ranging from thirty-five cents on the gallon of London Madeira to twenty-five cents on the pound of Bohea tea. He wanted the proceeds of the Post Office plowed into a sinking fund, administered by the Vice-President and members of the Cabinet and Congress, from which the government could invest in its own stock—a forerunner of the intermixture of state and private enterprise that he later sponsored and endorsed. It was very federal, energetic and audacious, and the blend of aggression and ingenuity was his own. As President, Jefferson later complained to Du Pont de Nemours that the startling success of Hamilton's program had derailed at the beginning his own plans for a pastoral republic, entailing upon him the execution of policies that he distrusted, but found himself powerless to interrupt.

Jefferson was suspicious of his plans for industry, counting them a plan to bribe a corps of corrupt followers while perverting the morals of the state. Hamilton was one of the first to link economic self-sufficiency to political independence, and considered self-sufficiency the sine qua non of national integrity, without which independence was a sham. Jefferson thought the country could live as a supplier nation, exchanging raw materials for finished goods. Hamilton saw that as the condition of a helpless debtor, a colony in everything but name. "Not only the wealth, but the independence and security of a Country, appear to be materially connected with the prosperity of manufactures," he insisted, claiming that a free country must contain the means to produce its necessary goods within itself. "The possession of these is necessary to the perfection of the body politic. . . . the want of either is the want of an important organ of political activity."[1] He was vindicated a very few years later, when the wars of Britain and the French republic choked off the flow of European

144

goods. Emotional factors figured too in his position; dependence was not to be borne, open as it was to betrayal and contempt. And haunted by the memory of the Revolution, he feared weakness if another war should happen, and insisted that his country must be strong enough to arm itself.

Jefferson and the Republicans saw taxation as an incursion of the state into the domain of the private citizen, a practice which must be carefully curtailed. Hamilton saw it as essential, the fiscal underpinning of the state. To the kind of government he planned, income was necessary; he saw taxes as the debt of honor which the honest citizen must pay. But here he made distinctions between "good" and "evil" taxes, based on moral judgments of his own. Among the taxes he disapproved of were taxes on essential items (he called them "necessaries"), taxes on scarce items, taxes on industries that were new and struggling or that he deemed valuable, taxes that struck at the ability to invest in industry, or that pinched the pockets of the poor. He especially disliked poll taxes, which either gave too much power to the tax assessors, or if fixed, operated to the disadvantage of the poor. Calling them "despotic," he asked they not be used save in emergencies, when all other sources had been tapped.

The items he chose to tax—and tax heavily—were what he called "pernicious luxuries," such as coffee, tea and alcohol, and here he came close to detailing what sounded like a moral code. This was due perhaps to latent puritanism, or at the very least a revulsion for some forms of excessive consumption that he may have seen among the speculators or the leaders of the "Federalist Court." This response may have related to the simplicity with which he lived in the midst of sometimes flagrant luxury, and in which he seemed to take a form of pride.

Certainly his words have more the tone of the pulpit than of the state paper, suggesting that his urge to make improvements in the human condition could move to intangible matters and embrace the nation's moral health. Calling them "pernicious luxuries . . . a source of national extravagance, and impoverishment," he detailed a mild temperance program.

> The consumption of ardent spirits, particularly no doubt very much on account of their cheapness, is carried to an extreme which is truly to be regretted, in regard to the health and morals, as well as the economy of the community. Should the increase in duties tend to a decrease in con-

145

sumption . . . the effect would be in every way desireable. The saving . . . would leave individuals more at their ease, and promote a more favorable balance of trade.

He stated flatly that he intended to keep taxes on these items as high as they would safely go:

This will lessen the necessity, both of having recourse to a direct taxation, of accumulating duties where they would be more inconvenient . . . and upon objects which are more to be regarded as necessaries of life.[2]

Here he was to run into resistance to his experiment in social engineering. The distillers and drinkers of western Pennsylvania, no doubt deeming moonshine as among life's "necessaries," rebelled against his taxes and his moralizing in 1794.

Hamilton later levied taxes on many other items, including tobacco, which he considered surplus, and carriages, which he did not think essential to the maintenance of life. Complaints from producers and consumers did not move him, and he saw the objections as examples of the selfishness and private interests to which men as individuals were prey. As a taxpayer as well as an imposer of taxes, he made no objections to the inconvenience caused himself. At a hearing later on the carriage tax, he said quite cheerfully that when carriages became too costly, he simply gave his up.

Few at the time understood his major purpose: to knot the states together with ties so powerful that nothing could force them apart. When he told Robert Morris in 1780 that a national debt could be "a powerful Cement to our Union,"[3] he envisioned a train of results flowing from it that would subtly alter the system of government and the way that people conceived it. He wanted the debt combined because it was efficient to do so, but also because it inclined the states and people to think and act as one. He wanted people to pay taxes and collect funds from the central government to solidify the ties between them, to undermine the traditional attachments to the state and local governments, and make them look to the nation as the source of their security and wealth. He wanted the growth of industry to bind the states together in a web of mutual reliance. "Mutual wants," he wrote hopefully, "constitute one of the strongest links of political connection, and the extent of those bears a natural proportion to the diversity in means of mutual supply."[4] Poignantly, inces-

146

santly and sometimes desperately, he implored a hostile South to realize that his aids to northern industry would rebound to its advantage, creating a sustained internal market for the products of the earth. The South did not listen, and when his programs began to divide the country on the lines of class and section, he was hurt, perhaps surprisingly, and his arguments assumed a plaintive tone.

> The idea of an opposition between these two interests is the common error of the early periods of every country, but experience gradually dissipates it. Indeed, they are perceived so often to Succor and befriend each other that they come at length to be considered as one.[5]

Hamilton was slipping here into the sin he scorned in others—that of being idealistic and naive. He was asking a vast section of the country to give its money for a purpose it did not believe in, for a cause it saw as hostile, and whose benefits did not immediately extend to it. His concept of a greater good, sometime in the future, was not concrete enough a prospect to convince the South. For once, his theory of binding men by interest was not applied. He did not offer the South—or the landed interests—enough in the way of tangible assets to overcome their accumulated fears.

Hamilton paid dearly for this lapse of judgment, nearly with his plan itself. The bill for assumption of the state debts was defeated repeatedly in the House and Senate and was not passed until mid summer, when a deal was struck with the connivance of James Madison to trade assumption for a permanent national capital, placed where Virginia wished it, in the South. He did not learn from this experience. Time and time over his policies were to split the nation, in a prelude to the schisms that were to wrack it until the final break in 1861.

Very little furor over the report had faded in December 1790 when Hamilton presented Congress with his plan for a national bank: a semiprivate corporation chartered by the government in which the government would own one fifth of the stock. His aims as before were the linkage of the financial community to the central government, and the augmentation via borrowing of funds. "The money of one individual," he wrote in his defense of his program, "is in a condition to minister to the needs of others, without being put out of his own reach." Here, his language becomes rich and vibrant:

147

> Gold and silver, when they are employed merely as instruments of exchange and alienation, have been not improperly designated as Dead Stock. . . . when deposited in Banks, to become the basis of a paper currency, they then acquire Life.[6]

This time, he had a third and vital reason. The assets of the Bank, "under one direction, and gathered to a point," could be put at the disposal of the central government in the event of any of those sudden and disastrous emergencies he believed constantly at hand.

When the bill passed the Senate by a vote of thirty-nine to twenty (on an ominous division between the northern and the southern states), Jefferson sent Washington an anxious letter, asking him to veto it, and calling the Bank an assault upon the limitations of the Constitution and a wedge through which dictatorship could slip.

> Perhaps indeed bank bills may be a little more *convenient* vehicle than treasury orders, but a little difference in the *degree* of convenience cannot constitute the necessity which the Constitution makes the ground for assuming any non-enumerated power. . . . It would reduce the whole instrument to a single phrase, that of instituting a Congress with power to so whatever would be for the good of the United States. . . . as they would be the sole judges of the good or evil, it would also be a power to do whatever evil they please.[7]

Much else troubled Jefferson about the Bank, which he called an engine of corruption, but his attack touched on questions that even Hamilton knew were troubling, and to which he was obligated to respond. Respond he did, in a remarkable paper written over three days of late night sessions, which changed forever the limits of the Constitution he had faulted and the destiny of the United States.

Jefferson had attacked the Bank on the grounds 1) that chartering a corporation was not a power conferred directly by the Constitution on the government; 2) that as it was not expressly conferred, it was implicitly forbidden; 3) that it was not necessary to the degree that would make an exception defensible; and 4) that an exception here would start a trend to extralegal power, insensible of reason or control. Hamilton chose to

148

defend it, not in itself, but as the means to an end lawfully comprehended in the Constitution, and therefore legal in itself. Declaring that a Bank "has a natural relation to the power of collecting taxes, to that of borrowing money, to that of regulating trade," he claimed that it "affirms a power . . . within the sphere of the enumerated powers,"[8] and did not intrude into frightening new fields. He dismissed Jefferson's theory of necessity as a criterion—few measures could pass so stern a test. And he reemphasized the doctrine he had stated in the *Federalist*: the relation between the measure and the purpose envisioned is the test of constitutional legality. The Bank was a function of allotted power and was therefore legal in itself.

Hamilton did not stop his argument at the defense of the Bank. He went on to evolve a sense of government sweeping in its nature and awesome in its scope. He insisted that government had the right—and one feels he also meant the duty—to intervene in all matters touching the general welfare, to contrive plans to further the national well-being and to spend liberally to bring these plans to life. He also implied a right that would be confirmed by later Presidents: the right to seize extraordinary powers in times of crisis for the purpose of survival and defense. He did not deny the chance of danger, and in two sentences defined the quandary in which his and all other governments were caught:

> The moment the literal meaning is departed from, there is a chance of error and abuse. And yet an adherence to the letter of its power would at once arrest the motions of the government.[9]

While conceding Jefferson's point, he came down squarely on the other side of the argument. If the perils of strength were troubling, demanding thought and judgment, the dangers of weakness, with the certainties of dissolution, were worse.

Washington, whose doubts about the Constitution were almost as great as Hamilton's, agreed with his arguments and on February 25 signed the bill into law. In so doing they added the amendment to the Constitution that they had been unable to obtain at Philadelphia—a gigantic broadening of its writ of power, which generations of succeeding Presidents were to seize and endorse. The Bank itself was to flourish into the first quarter of the following century. So successful in all its enterprises was it that when its charter came up for renewal, Congress was urged to

149

approve it in a message from the President—James Madison—who had fought it in 1791.

Hamilton's third and final report, the Report on the Subject of Manufactures, was presented to Congress on December 5, 1791. It was at once a program for the revision of the political structure of the nation and a plan for the intervention of the government in every aspect of national life. In the late eighteenth century, in a country overwhelmingly agrarian, he urged that the government not only promote the conversion to an industrial economy, but embark on the control and regulation of the nation's economic product, using rewards, taxes and bounties to encourage the growth of some industries, discourage others and monitor the flow of trade and commerce, based on what was judged harmful or beneficial to the nation's political, economic and social health. He urged the adoption of the division of labor (a blow to small farms and household industries) as conducive both to greater efficiency, and to human happiness, as "furnishing greater scope for the diversity of talents and dispositions which discriminate men from each other,"[10] and leaving them free to follow the skills and pursuits for which they were most suited. He asked that the country encourage the growth of industries, those that added to national self-sufficiency or the ability to survive a crisis, by suspending normal taxes on them in their periods of development, and by placing heavy tariffs on competing foreign products until the native industries were totally mature. Such concerns, he said, so vital to the national well-being, were "too important" to be left to the chances of the marketplace alone.

From these tariffs he expected to accrue a financial surplus which could be used to fund a variety of schemes. He wanted a gigantic system of canals and roadways to link the different parts of the country together, diminish the costs of transport (which would reduce the cost of manufactures) and make the back country, once so isolated, accessible to the flow of commerce and of goods. He wanted to encourage the immigration of skilled workers, offering money to artisans in Europe who were too poor to move. He wanted the government to encourage "enterprise"—inventions, discoveries, and indeed, all accomplishments in the arts and sciences—through the regular bestowing of financial honors and rewards. He wanted—in 1791—to establish the first office of consumer protection, in the form of government offices at major port cities, to enforce standards of performance and quality on all American-made goods. The rationale for all of this was the "general welfare" clause of the Constitution, which

Hamilton interpreted as empowering Congress to do anything that was not actually unlawful to improve the well-being of the citizens of the United States. This reading, which was to further terrify the Republicans, seemed to Hamilton the minimum of what a respectable government was expected to perform.

Most of the features of the plan were not passed by Congress, the only one of Hamilton's reports not to be endorsed. A pilot project established to create a model industrial city in Paterson, New Jersey, collapsed in bankruptcy some years later, the victim both of William Duer and of a fatal shortage of capital, experience and skills. Nothing remained but a stand of empty buildings by the river and a statue of Hamilton surveying the wreckage at the summit of the falls. It was the only one of his projects to fail in his lifetime, and it was the victim of his prescience, for his vision had at last outstripped the most extensive resources of his time. He had also run into emotional opposition of a sort particularly tenacious and intense.

In 1782 Thomas Jefferson in his "Notes on the State of Virginia" had written the definitive indictment of commercial society, drawing a firm line of morals between the sinful men of industry and the pious tillers of the earth.

> Those who labor in the earth are the chosen people of God, if ever he had a chosen people, whose breasts he has made his particular deposit for substantial and genuine virtue. It is the focus in which he keeps alive that sacred fire, which otherwise might escape from the face of the earth.[11]

Not only did he link the rural life to private virtue, but also to integrity in government, the disappearance of which meant political decay.

> Corruption of morals in the mass of cultivators is a phenomenon of which no age or nation has furnished an example. . . . The proportion which the aggregate of the other classes . . . bears in any State to that of its husbandmen, is the proportion of its sound to its healthy parts.[12]

Where George Washington proudly wore a suit of American manufacture to his first inaugural and looked forward to the day when industry would make the country self-sufficient, Jefferson deplored the inroads that European wars had allowed commerce to make in American society

151

and longed for a return to the status of supplier nation, exporting food stuffs and raw materials and importing manufactures from abroad.

> For the general operations of manufacture, let our workshops remain in Europe. It is better to carry provisions and material to workmen there, than to bring to them the provisions . . . and with them their manner and principles. The loss by transportation . . . will be made up in the happiness and permanence of government. The mobs of great cities add just so much to the support of pure government, as sores do to the health of the human body.[13]

And he would write to Madison from Paris, "When we get piled upon one another in large cities, as in Europe, we shall become corrupt, as in Europe, and go to eating one another, as they do there."[14]

Jefferson as President maintained a guise of great simplicity, greeting his guests in worn clothes and slippers, denying his complexity and power, masking his political mastery with an appearance of innocence that was not wholly true. In his speeches he evoked a mood of idyllic simplicity, of a government of "plain duties . . . performed by a few servants," in which the guiding hand of man was barely seen. The fantasy was irresistible; the reality of rural life was often brutal, a battle for survival against unfriendly elements in conditions of scarcity and stress. But the image was another matter, whose magic persists into this day. Its appeal predated their era by millennia. In biblical legend Eden was the garden from which man was driven by his thirst for knowledge, equated then with sin. In rejecting rural innocence for the lure of progress, Hamilton cast himself in an unappealing role. Destroying a dream is a crime for which few men have been forgiven. It is certain that Alexander Hamilton was not.

XII

ONE MORNING in the summer of 1791 when Hamilton entered his Treasury offices at Chestnut Street, he found among the usual crowd of clients and petitioners a woman of great beauty and a distracted air. She told him that she was the daughter of a respectable New York family (her sister had married Gilbert Livingston), alone in the city with her daughter; that her husband had left her to live with another woman, and that she was too poor to return to her home. Hamilton said later that he sensed "something odd" about her story, but he was moved by her beauty, her simplicity and her obvious distress. He told her that he would bring her money that evening and arrived at her lodgings with thirty dollars in his purse. He was met there by a landlady and shown to her bedroom, which was at the head of the stairs. There, he said, "further conversation ensued, in which it quickly became apparent that other than pecuniary compensation would be acceptable."[1] Alexander Hamilton went to bed with Maria Reynolds that night and many nights thereafter, sometimes in his own house (Eliza having gone to Albany for the summer) and in the bed that he had shared with his wife.

Maria was beautiful, but she was also in need of comfort, for her life had been a tale of grief and disarray. Married at fifteen into a family that already had a history of debt and of imprisonment—her father-in-law, a commissary in the revolutionary army, was in jail when she married in

1783—she had plunged further into a world of extortion and shabbiness. James Reynolds, a criminal who lived on the monies he could suck from others, was part of the web of intrigue spun by William Duer, and had been one of the number who swarmed through the back country in 1790, buying certificates from veterans on specious stories that bore little resemblance to the truth. The circumstances of their private life were also sordid, for he deserted her often to live with other women and he spent frequent intervals in jail.

James Folwell, a young man at whose mother's house she had sought refuge, testified later that she had arrived in Philadelphia in a state of desolation. "Her mind was at this time far from being tranquil or consistent . . . for at the same time that she would declare her respect for her husband, cry and feel distressed," her mood would change, and she would berate him in harsh and bitter terms. He had, she told Folwell,

> frequently enjoined and insisted she should insinuate herself on certain high and influential characters—endeavour to make assignations with them, and actually prostitute herself to gull money from them.[2]

Soon after, Reynolds appeared, and they moved into a house on North Grant Street, where they "lived, as the family said, but did not sleep together." Whether Reynolds then again left Philadelphia—as he and Maria claimed later—or whether they stayed and planned together to entrap Hamilton is now unknown. All that Alexander Hamilton knew for certain was that sometime that fall Reynolds appeared, was introduced to him by Maria and began to extort favors and then cash from him.

No incident in Hamilton's life is documented more completely than the next phase in the scandal, which was to envelop and absorb his life. It is preserved in the letters of the Reynoldses, ill-spelled and almost incoherent, in the memoranda of the three Congressmen who later entered to investigate, in the depositions collected five years later by a distracted Hamilton and in the extraordinary pamphlet published by Hamilton himself. All are written with great immediacy and a certain raw quality. Hamilton's in particular is composed with the peculiar and self-flagellating candor that marks so much of his speech. As the story now becomes a bizarre tale of secret meetings and letters passed in a false handwriting, of contradictory evidence and midnight rendezvous, it is possible to unravel it only with a careful tracing of sequential evidence, letting each participant speak in his own voice.

Hamilton's version of the start of the intrigue (and here his is the only evidence) is that sometime in early autumn Maria told him that her husband had appeared and asked for a reconciliation, and shortly after, that a reconciliation had been made. After that, she told him that her husband, who had been dealing in securities, knew an "important secret" concerning leaks within the Treasury that he was willing to disclose. The leak turned out to have been William Duer, who had been forced from office eighteen months before. "This discovery, if it had been true, was not very important," Hamilton said later, "yet it was in the interests of my passions to appear to set value on it," and to have Reynolds see him as a friend. Reynolds then asked for a job in the Treasury, which Hamilton refused.

> I parried it by telling him . . . that there was no vacancy
> in my immediate office. . . . But the more I learned of this
> person, the more inadmissable his employment in a public
> office became.[3]

Hamilton was frightened by what he had learned of Reynolds, which may at the same time have increased his attachment to Maria, whom he saw now as a helpless creature caught in a burgeoning spiral of intrigue. That it might in fact be otherwise he learned only on the morning of December 15 when he received two letters, one from Reynolds and one from his wife. Reynolds, who said he had been hitherto ignorant of the adultery, now claimed to have discovered all:

> She fell on her knees, and asked forgiveness, and discovered
> everything to me. . . . She was a woman I should as soon
> have sespected as an angell from heaven. . . . I am robbed
> of all happiness in the world.[4]

There was more talk of heartbreak and dishonor, but Hamilton could not have missed the threat in the sentence: "There is no person that knows any thing as yet." Maria also sent a letter, with the sentence "He ses if you do not come . . . . he will write to Mrs. Hamilton"[5] buried in a stream of lurid prose. Any doubts that might have lingered were dispelled two days later, when Hamilton received another note from Reynolds suggesting a meeting at the George Tavern: "Your house or office is no place to converse about these matters. . . . You may rest assured that the matter is as yet not known."

Hamilton said, "I could no longer be at a loss to understand he wanted money,"[6] and gave him $1,000 in two payments of $600 and $400. He was to write later of the

> amiable concert between the husband and wife to keep alive my connection . . . to spare no pains to levy money on my passions . . . the duress upon me in consequence . . . and the forced loans which were levied on me from time to time.[7]

He did not mention what was perhaps his greatest burden: that he would be forced for twelve months to say nothing and to keep his fear and desperation to himself.

He tried to break his bondage, but with only limited success. Maria's hysterics continued to confound him, along with her intermittent ardor, and he was plunged into a frightening uncertainty of what was real.

> I have kept my bed these two Dayes, and now rise from my pillow, which your neglect has filled with the sharpest thorns [she wrote him]. . . . On my kneese let me intreate you to read my letter. . . . Gracious God had I the world I should lay it at your feet.[8]

She claimed to be dying and begged to see him as her last request.

> Her conduct made it very difficult [Hamilton wrote later]. . . . the appearances of a violent attachment and of a genuine distress . . . were played off with such infinite art . . . that though I was not completely the dupe of the illusion . . . yet I was made to doubt as to the real state of things.[9]

When he did not come, she threatened suicide and said that Reynolds planned to have him killed.

> I could not be absolutely certain whether it was artifice or reality. . . . In the workings of human inconsistency, it was very possible that the same man might be corrupt

156

enough to compound for his wife's chastity, and yet have
sensibility enough . . . to hate the cause.[10]

He was guilty about both of them, which mixed with his resentment to
paralyze him and keep him angry and confused.

Then, on January 17 he received another letter containing "an invitation to me from Reynolds, to *renew my visits to his wife*."[11] ("I find that
whenever you have been with her she is Cheerful and kind," Reynolds
had written, "but when you have not . . . she is to reverse, and wishes
to be alone by herself.")[12] Hamilton did not respond until he had received
more letters from Maria, in which she threatened once again to kill herself. When he returned, Reynolds complained that he did not come suf-
ficiently often and insisted he enter the house through the front door.

Hamilton had believed as long as possible that Maria loved him, but he
was genuinely horrified by her husband's letter, and by the sense that
Reynolds was in the crudest sense selling her, trading her body for his
gain. He did not respond to the next round of letters, and he let his visits
slacken off. Perhaps because he was genuinely out of money, he refused to
give Reynolds $300 to invest in the Lancaster Turnpike in July. But he
did give him $200 in August, as a "loan" toward the purchase of a board-
ing house that the Reynoldses pretended to wish to buy. It was the last
claim they made on him, and he thought for some months he was free.
Then in November 1792 he received two letters from Reynolds, then in
jail for trying to attach the estate of a dead veteran, insisting that Hamilton use his influence to secure his release. Hamilton ignored him and
soon learned from Oliver Wolcott and others that Reynolds and his partner Jacob Clingman had gone to his political enemies with charges of
speculation against him.

Jacob Clingman was Reynolds's partner in this and perhaps in other
schemes. He is a dim figure about whom history tells little, and whom
this episode still leaves in mist. Details about his background and his
relationships with the other principals are shadowy. In view of later
developments, there is the added possibility that Reynolds had for some
time shared his wife, not only with Alexander Hamilton, but with Jacob
Clingman, too.

Clingman said that he had met Reynolds in September 1791 and that
they had been on terms of confidence and intimacy since. This was at the
height of the intrigue with Hamilton. Clingman, by chance or otherwise,
had been at the Reynolds's house frequently when Hamilton was calling,

first to pay his visits to Maria, then to pay her husband his forced "loans." Clingman recalled being there in January when "he saw Colonel Hamilton at the house of Reynolds: immediately on his going into the house, Col. Hamilton left." Days later Clingman was there, this time with Maria, and alone. "Some person knocked at the door; he arose and opened it, and saw that it was Col. Hamilton. . . he delivered a paper to her, and said he was ordered to give Mr. Reynolds that."[13] Clingman asked Maria who could "order" a member of the Cabinet, and she had answered "she supposed he did not want to be known." She told him that Hamilton had given her husband money over a period of months, and Reynolds himself elaborated on the tale.

> A little after Duer's failure [in March, 1792] . . . Reynolds told Clingman in confidence that if Duer had held up three days longer, he should have made fifteen thousand dollars by the assistance of Col. Hamilton . . . that Col. Hamilton had made thirty thousand by speculation: that Col. Hamilton had supplied him with money to speculate . . . that if he wanted money, he was obliged to let him have it; that he [Clingman] had occasionally lent money to Reynolds, who always told him that he could always get it from Col. Hamilton to repay.[14]

He once saw Reynolds go into Hamilton's house and return with one hundred dollars, which he then gave to Clingman as repayment on a loan.

Clingman had once been employed in the office of Republican Congressman Frederick Muhlenberg, and when Hamilton refused to release Reynolds, Clingman began to pressure him.

> Clingman, unasked, frequently dropped hints to me, that Reynolds had it in his power very materially to injure the Secretary of the Treasury [Muhlenberg testified]. I paid little or no attention . . . but when they were frequently repeated, and it was even added that Reynolds said he had it in his power to hang the Secretary . . . that he was deeply involved in speculation, and that he had frequently advanced money to him . . . it created considerable uneasiness in my mind, and I conceived it as my duty to consult with my friends.[15]

Greatly disturbed, and perhaps as greatly excited, he called on two other members of his party, Senator Abraham Venable and Jefferson's friend, James Monroe.

The next day the Congressmen paid two visits: to Reynolds in prison, and to Maria at home. There, Reynolds told them "he had a person in high office in his power, and has had, a long time past: That he had written to him in terms so abusive that no person could have submitted to it, but that he dared not resent it," that he asked Hamilton for help, but that it had been denied him, and that the persecution had been started "to keep him low and oppress him, and ultimately drive him away."[16] Maria told them that she had burned a large number of letters from Hamilton to her husband at Hamilton's request, that Clingman possessed other notes from Hamilton written in a slightly altered hand (which she gave the Congressmen), and that Hamilton had tried to bribe her husband to leave town. She did not mention her own letters or her amorous affair. She did tell them that she had gone for help to Jeremiah Wadsworth, her father-in-law's employer in the Revolution, and quoted some of their conversation. Wadsworth had told her that Hamilton "had enemies, who would try to prove some speculations on him, but when inquired into, he would be found immaculate: to which she replied, she rather doubted it."[17]

On December 15 the Congressmen called on Hamilton, first at his office and later at his home. There, with Oliver Wolcott as his witness, he told them the story in detail. Sparing nothing, he told them of the seduction, the affair and the "discovery"; of the demands on him and of the extortion; of his vanity, his confusion and his fear. Several times Venable and Muhlenberg interrupted him to beg him to stop his recital, but he remorselessly went on. There seemed to be a sense of purging and a need to punish and to cleanse himself. So grueling did Muhlenberg find the experience that he later stopped Wolcott repeatedly on the sidewalk to express his own embarrassment and his wish that he had not been present, and to insist that though he disagreed with Hamilton on politics, he admired and liked him as a man. Muhlenberg, Venable and Wolcott had refused to keep notes of the proceedings, as if the papers themselves might exude the odor of humiliation and disgrace. Hamilton too refused to keep copies, dumping them into the hands of Monroe. He did not at the time realize that copies had passed into the hands of John Beckley, clerk of the House of Representatives, who did not consider himself bound by the oath of silence Wolcott and the Congressmen had taken. He did not know either that Monroe had been unable to resist telling the story to Thomas Jefferson, who made a note of the interview in his journal on December

17. Jefferson later took Monroe's papers with him to Virginia, where he kept them under seal.

Reynolds was released under the terms of a deal made previously with Wolcott to give him his freedom in exchange for the return of the extorted money and the name of the clerk in the Treasury Department through whom the speculations had been made. He then vanished, but Maria and Clingman remained in the city, where they turned on Hamilton and Reynolds both. When Clingman discovered that the Congressmen refused to prosecute, he called on Monroe in a rage. Maria, he said, had been deeply shocked and had wept greatly; she had denied the romance, saying "it had been a fabrication of Colonel Hamilton, and that her husband had joined it." In May 1793 she filed for divorce in New York City, charging her husband with adultery, and was granted a divorce on February 13, 1795. Her attorney in the case was Aaron Burr. On the same day she married Jacob Clingman, who later told Beckley she had divorced her husband "in consequence of his intrigue with Hamilton," and was eager to tell all she knew of both. The pair then vanished, though Clingman surfaced two years later to spill his poison into Callender's and Beckley's ears. Maria herself returned to Philadelphia one year later to ask Folwell to help her clear the "bad character" she had gained in Cecil County, Maryland, where she had been living near his distant kin. When Folwell protested that "as it had been bad before, she had certainly increased it,"[18] she replied that she knew of one fault only—she had married half an hour before she obtained her divorce.

Hamilton was out of government and living in New York in the summer of 1797 when he learned to his horror that a pamphlet, "The History of the United States for the Year 1796," had been published in Philadelphia, containing in it a full account of his traffic with the Reynolds family, including the charge that the adultery—real or fictitious—had been the cover for financial crimes. The pamphlet was the work of James Thomson Callender, one of the most virulent propagandists of his generation, who took a special delight in defamations of a sexual variety, suggesting that his work filled for him not only the necessities of the pocketbook, but of some twisted inner need. Callender was then in the pay of Thomas Jefferson to damage Federalists, and also attacked both Adams and Washington before turning viciously upon his former patron, printing in 1802 the first written charge of a long whispered rumor—that Jefferson had carried on a long affair, and by it had several children, with

Sally Hemings, an exquisite mulatto who was a slave on his plantation and was the half-sister of his long dead wife.

Callender now claimed that the Republican Congressmen had "found various reasons for believing that Mrs. Reynolds was in fact innocent," and called Hamilton's explanation of the reason behind his payments to Reynolds—his fear of exposure—a lie.

> The accusation of an illicit amour, though sounded in notes louder than the last trumpet, could not have defamed the conjugal fidelity of Mr. Hamilton. It would only have been holding a farthing candle to the sun. On that point, the world had already fixed its opinion. In the Secretary's bucket of chastity, a drop more or less was not to be perceived.[19]

He suggested the "adultery" was the cover for a darker sin:

> So much correspondence could not refer exclusively to wenching. No man of common sense will believe that it did. . . . It must have implicated some connection still more dishonorable in Mr. Hamilton's eyes, than that of incontinence.

When Hamilton protested, Callender sent him a savage letter, mocking him as a statesman and lover, calling him incompetent and false as both.

Hamilton would have been best advised to have done nothing, as all his friends had urged. But he was driven by the need to save at least his public reputation, as well as the urge, perhaps deeply buried, to be punished for his sins. He harassed Venable and Muhlenberg with endless letters. He threatened Jefferson with the disclosure of an old scandal— that Jefferson in 1768 had tried repeatedly to seduce Betsey Walker, the wife of his neighbor and close friend. When he was convinced at last of Jefferson's innocence, he turned his furies on James Monroe. To the horror of John Church, he burst into Monroe's lodgings, called him a liar when he protested his innocence and challenged him to a duel, which was averted only by the terrified intervention of his friends. Knowing that his wife was pregnant and fearing the results of his desperate temper, they formed a conspiracy to urge him to withdraw. "Monroe thinks the cor-

161

respondence which has passed between you and him . . . should be withdrawn & destroyed," wrote William Jackson, who was acting as his intermediary. "He never intended to become your accuser, nor is he now so disposed."[20] Monroe himself was stupefied by his behavior and watched him with incredulity. He told Aaron Burr that Hamilton, in making his private gaffe into a public matter, had been extremely indiscreet.

Having averted the disaster of a potential duel, Hamilton's friends now warned him against a measure that they feared could wreck his public reputation and leave his moral character in shreds. They begged him not to answer Callender, and to content himself with a public statement from Monroe, Muhlenberg and Venable that they found Clingman's story incredible and believed Hamilton innocent of public crimes. They knew, as Hamilton did not, that his lurid tale of adultery with Maria Reynolds, blackmail by her cuckolded husband and shakedowns by a pair of swindlers would embarrass his friends, delight his enemies and appall that large segment of the political community who viewed adultery as a mortal sin. "No one . . . can suppose that you are called upon to furnish the Presbyterian pulpits with subject matter of declamation," Jackson warned him. "A detailed publication . . . would only furnish fresh *pabulum* for virulent invective and abuse."[21] They warned him that it was suicidal, but he ignored them and plunged ahead.

Hamilton's rebuttal was published on September 27, 1797. As a psychological document it is one of the most peculiar in American history, and one of the most self-hating. In it he savaged himself with a dedication Callender could have only envied, and a thoroughness he could not have hoped to match. Hamilton told in detail not only of his adultery, but of his vanity, credulity and gullibility; his ineptness, his desperation and his fear. He lingered on them with an exaction that was almost loving as he examined each incident of folly. If he had ever wished to punish himself for his role in this incident, this intention surfaced here.

The story of the damage done to his political reputation belongs to the succeeding chapter and will not be related here. But James Madison, his one-time friend (and a friend perhaps also of Eliza), called it "a masterpiece of folly,"[22] and there was unexpected compassion in a note to Jefferson from one John Barnes:

> Mr. H—has assuredly reduced his Consequence to the most degrading & contemptible point of view . . . such a ridiculous piece of Folly—never was Man guilty of—first

in committing himself via his Dear (dear indeed) Maria; and then to publish it himself . . . how it must on Reflection torture him, on poor Mrs. H. Accot whose feelings on the Occasion must be severely injured, if not expressed.[23]

No one can know how Hamilton broke the news to Eliza, then pregnant with the sixth of her eight children, first of his adultery, and then of his decision to publish it publicly and at length. Her knowledge was the one thing he had genuinely dreaded. Though he admitted that he had given her much reason for suspicion concerning his physical fidelity, he had argued also in his own defense that there was a considerable difference between "vague rumors" and the publication of established fact. The scenes, if any, that passed between them were covered over, as were the first reactions of their Schuyler kin. The extent to which these had been buried was related to Hamilton by John Church with perhaps some incredulity:

I am just this Instant Return'd from your House. Eliza is well, She put into my Hand the newspaper with James Thomson Callender's letter. . . . It makes not the least impression on her, only that she considers the whole Knot of these opposed to you to be Scoundrels.[24]

He might have reflected that the reaction of his fiery Angelica might not have been the same.

Both of them knew that Eliza, in leaving him or condemning him by the slightest word or gesture, could have destroyed him totally and ruined his reputation beyond repair. She did neither, but accompanied him through their social rounds with fierce dignity and a self-possession that did as much as anything could have to restore his public character and make bearable this moment in his life. It may have been an act of love or of charity, but it also was an act of power, for now he was securely in her debt. One sign of this sharp but covert knowledge appeared in a letter he wrote her one year later: "I am much more in debt to you than I can ever repay; but my future life will be more than ever devoted to your happiness."[25]

Their later years appear to have indeed been happy, and their closeness helped sustain them through the tragedies that soon befell their lives. At his death, she buried or otherwise destroyed the papers relating to the scandal that she found among his baggage, as if to bury both her pain and

163

his disgrace. The one clear result of her suppressed anger was its displacement to James Monroe. When the aged ex-President called on her in Washington years later in an effort to make up their ancient quarrel, she had her grandson show him to the door.

The mystery of why Hamilton chose to commit this act of harm against himself, his reputation and the people he most cherished remains a puzzle. He was a child of the eighteenth century, an aristocrat by temperament and a sensual man of great physical magnetism, who could be predatory in his attitude toward women, who accepted pleasure easily and had previously shown no guilt. But in his case there were special complications: he was the bastard child of an irregular connection that had been called lustful, sinful and immoral. His mother before his birth had been imprisoned for "whoring"; his very birth had been a sin. In their warm nature, he had inherited the traits of both his parents, but he had acquired also a desire to refute their failings, to overcome their shortcomings as he saw them replicated in himself. In all instances but one he had been successful: he was serious, dutiful, ordered and diligent; but he was also lustful, and in this one aspect he had failed. In failing he had duplicated their error and brought on himself and on his helpless family the mark of scandal they had brought upon themselves and him. For this, he had sought an extraordinary punishment and brought his vengeance down upon himself.

Hamilton from early adolescence had a premonition of betrayal by the siren and Circe, by the "artful little slut." If Eliza had been the most faithful of women, forgiving him beyond all just expectation, Maria, emerging from the netherworld, had indeed entangled him, soiling him in her corrupt embrace. By a special irony, she had brought him into contact with something he considered far worse than carnal error—the world of dishonor and dishonesty, of trickery and fraudulence and greed. This connection, which he despised above all others, was the final measure of his disgrace. He could forgive himself for sexual excess, but this had been extreme defilement. Long ago in an adolescent poem he had drawn a picture of the intriguing woman as a cat, sleek and beautiful, with the treachery and coldness of her breed. The premonition of his youth had now fulfilled itself. The velvet paws sheathed talons of the most deadly nature. His "jade" had poisoned claws indeed.

XIII

TENSIONS in the government mounted, eroding friendships and straining nerves until they snapped. The friendship of Hamilton and Madison had died completely, without a formal break or declaration, as Hamilton's early reluctance to admit the differences between them gave way to the recognition that he had made an enemy for life. He said little of it, the Carrington letter being the one expression of his unhappiness, but his children bore Madison a special hatred, calling him a traitor and a moral weakling whom Jefferson had cannily seduced. Jefferson himself had broken with John Adams, ending a tie begun years before in Europe that did not mend until both men were aging ex-Presidents. The rift went beyond them to their families, for the Adamses and Jeffersons had become close in Europe, and the quarrel caused them all distress.

Adams was now on only the most formal terms with Washington, for the President, who had disliked him since the Revolution, had coolly cut him off from all access to power, and his name disappeared from policy meetings after 1791. Jefferson's relations with the President, still nominally courteous, were fraying badly. Washington blamed him for Freneau's attacks on the administration and in one Cabinet meeting came close to a direct rebuke. Jefferson rightly took this to imply that he should suspend Freneau's salary from the State Department, thereby cutting off his source of funds. "But I will not do it,"[1] he wrote in his journal, adding

165

that Freneau's paper had saved the country from Washington's and Hamilton's mistakes.

As tensions rose among the Cabinet, Washington had taken to consulting his secretaries in private, keeping them as much as possible apart. But in April 1793, with the outbreak of war between Great Britain and the French republic, the Cabinet was thrown into almost daily sessions and the sniping became open and profuse. Each was reacting to primitive emotions, for Jefferson's hatred of traditional authority matched Hamilton's fear of disorder and anarchy, and their fights assumed an intensity they were frequently unable to control.

Both had lost many friends among the French nobility, but their reactions were dissimilar. Jefferson saw them as soldiers, fallen in a war with tyranny and sacrifices to the greater good.

> I deplore them as I should have done had they fallen in battle [he had written]. Rather than it [the French Revolution] should have failed, I would have seen half the earth desolated: were there but an Adam and an Eve left in every country, and left free, it would be better than it is now.[2]

In other letters, he expressed his hopes that the revolution would ignite a mass uprising, to "kindle the wrath of the people of Europe . . . and bring at length kings, nobles, and priests to the scaffolds which they have been so long deluging with human blood."[3]

Hamilton saw the revolution as the sweeping away of order before a tide of murderous passions and looked at the slide to anarchy with horror. In numerous writings he called France the "GREAT MONSTER," a "prodigy of wretchedness and folly," a "frightful volcano of atheism, depravity and absurdity," a "hateful instrument of cruelty and bloodshed," an "engine of despotism and slavery," a despotism "swelled to a monstrous size, and aping Rome except in her virtues," and a monstrous plague, which had "laid waste provinces, unpeopled regions, and crimsoned her soil with blood."[4] He was appalled by the executions of Louis XVI and Marie Antoinette (which broke a line of legitimate succession and was thereby especially frightening), and he denounced the call of the French Assembly for universal insurrection as "an act of hostility against mankind." He sought out French refugees in New York and Philadelphia, giving them gifts of food and money and telling Angelica, who met many of them as they passed through London, of his sorrow that he could not afford to give them more.

166

Cabinet meetings became increasingly ferocious as they gave vent to their emotions and their fears. There were battles over the wartime treaty made in 1778 between France and the United States, and whether it carried over to the present French government; over the nuances of neutrality in the war between France and Britain, and recriminations with both, as they pulled in American ships and cargoes; over the Democratic Societies, formed on the model of the Jacobin Clubs, which Washington and Hamilton considered most sinister; and over the reception of Edmund Genet, the French ambassador, who traveled through the country urging the people to overthrow Washington, and whom Jefferson in great embarrassment was forced to disavow. Hamilton found the efforts of France and her friends to appeal to Americans as republican brothers infuriating, and France's claims to represent enlightened government absurd. The increasingly truculent tone of Cabinet meetings was recorded in Jefferson's notes in his journal for November 28:

> [Hamilton] denied that France had ever done us favors, that it was mean for a nation to acknowledge favors; that the disposition of the people of this country towards France he considered as a serious calamity; that the Executive ought not, by an echo of his language, to nourish that disposition in the people . . . that he could demonstrate that Great Britain had showed more favors than France.[5]

Jefferson believed that Washington, who was daily becoming more appalled by French atrocities, was being poisoned by Hamilton and by Gouverneur Morris, then American ambassador in Paris, whose dramatic reports of the Terror showed the French government in a lurid light. The sessions became so tense and savage that Jefferson described them later in terms of bloody conflict. In 1810, he would tell a correspondent, "Hamilton and myself were daily pitted in the Cabinet like two cocks."[6] So harrowing were the scenes, that Washington had fits of rage that left the others shaken. All three began to dream fervently of retirement, of exchanging "labor, envy and malice, for ease, domestic occupation, and domestic love."

Hamilton's battle with yellow fever in September 1793 undermined both his waning zest for battle and his already precarious state of health. It came in the middle of an epidemic that had driven the government into nearby Germantown for much of the month of September, and took before the siege abated more than three thousand lives. "Death has plad,

167

such havock that the streets seem desolate," a Philadelphia merchant wrote to Rufus King, as people fled, or barricaded themselves inside their houses. "This ruthless fever spares not even the Bloom of Youth."[7] Doctor Benjamin Rush fought the plague with purges, but Edward Stevens, the friend of Hamilton's boyhood now living in Philadelphia, prescribed icy baths into which he was plunged daily, and the Washingtons sent bottles of Canary wine. So ill was he that he was rumored to be dying, and it was not until three months later that he could tell Angelica that he was truly on the mend.

> My health, which has suffered a severe shock by an attack of the malignant disease lately prevalent . . . is now almost completely restored. The last vestige of it has been a nervous derangement, but this has nearly yielded to Regimen, a certain degree of exercise, and a resolution to overcome it.[8]

There is no clue to the nature of this "derangement," but it may have evidenced itself in an irritability born of weakness and an inability to handle stress. At Albany, where he had gone to recover, he complained at length to Philip Schuyler of his troubles. He no longer had the resources to continue an exhausting struggle that had long since lost its appeal.

The effects of his illness seemed to turn some balance in him, from contentiousness to resignation and fatigue. He had nothing to say when Jefferson retired in December 1793, though the acid Adams was to comment:

> Jefferson thinks by this step to get a reputation as an humble, modest, meek man, wholly without ambition or vanity. . . . But if the prospect opens, the world will see and he will feel that he is as ambitious as Oliver Cromwell.[9]

This very likely was Hamilton's feeling, but he was concentrating on his own retirement, which only Washington's pleadings had managed to postpone. He spoke longingly of a trip to Europe, and of his office in terms of imprisonment. "I am just where I do not wish to be," he told Angelica in April 1794. "I know how I could be much happier, but circumstances still enchain me. It is however determined that I shall break the spell."[10]

One thing alone could rouse him briefly—the chance in autumn to lead a federal army against rioting farmers in western Pennsylvania, who had rebelled against his tax on whiskey (enacted by the Report of 1790), burning the offices of federal tax collectors and putting the officers themselves to flight. He saw this as a test of the ability of the government to keep order, a cause dear to him, but he was lured also by his oldest fantasy—the vision of himself as a hero and conquerer fighting for his country at the head of a vast force of men. He won on the first point, but the second fizzled badly: the farmers fled at the first sight of the army, and he brought back only a small catch of "rebels," some of them feebleminded, who were pardoned with his concurrence by the government.

Personally, the toll was devastating. The one-thousand mile march in damp autumn weather brought on an attack of chest pains, and Eliza, frantic with worry, became ill.

> She has had, or has been, in danger of a miscarriage, which has much alarmed her [Henry Knox wrote from Philadelphia]. As she is extremely desirous of your presence in order to tranquillize her, this note is delivered at the President's request.[11]

He returned, but she miscarried anyhow, and this disaster complicated his distress. On January 30 he sent an apologetic note to Washington, mentioning a "struggle, which would have been far greater, had I supposed that the prospect of future usefulness was proportioned to the sacrifices to be made."[12] In his view he had given too much for too little, to a country that had not been grateful for his work. Hamilton, after four years of great achievements, considered himself a failure as a public man.

Was it the failure to attain the projected ultimate that made his triumphs turn to ashes in his mouth? At bottom he lacked the politician's sense of compromise: he walked a tightrope between surface buoyancy and innate pessimism, and a setback could make him slip into despair. Perhaps it was this that led to his outburst over the failure of Congress to pass a credit bill, three days after he left government for good.

> This unnecessary, capricious, & abominable assassination of the national honor haunts me every step I take [he told Rufus King on February 3]. . . . To see the Character of the Government and the Country so sported with, exposed to such a blot, puts my heart to the torture. Am I then more

169

of an American than those who drew their first breath on American ground? . . . What is it that thus torments me at a circumstance so calmly viewed by almost everybody else? Am I a fool—a romantic Quixot—or is there a constitutional defect in the American mind?[13]

This cry enclosed a note that mirrored his despondency: "There is something in our climate which belittles every Animal, human or brute."

Hamilton's return to New York, law and domesticity did not bring him the tranquillity he sought. He was feted by members of New York's commercial and professional communities at a series of glittering receptions, and he moved at once to the top of his profession, becoming the most prestigious lawyer in the state. But the effects of strain and illness did not leave him. There were spells of fatigue and of intense depression, and the balance of his nerves began to slip. Soon there were two ugly incidents. He picked a quarrel with William Nicholson, father-in-law of Albert Gallatin, the Swiss émigré and financial expert who had bedeviled Hamilton in Congress and would later serve with great distinction as Secretary of the Treasury in the Jefferson regime. Nicholson was an ardent Republican, perhaps because of his family connections, and in the middle of an argument he had flung at Hamilton the old canard from his early years in the Treasury: the charge that he had used his office to embezzle public funds. Hamilton could not ignore this insult and challenged the old man to a duel, which their friends averted after six weeks of mutual threats.

In the same month, he had had another run-in. At a political meeting he exchanged harsh words with the Republicans, and when Brockholst Livingston approached him, he "threw up his arm, & declared that he was ready to fight the whole Detestable faction one by one." when Livingston's cousin Maturin offered to meet him in the field in half an hour, he accepted the challenge, but he soon backed off. He said he could not act while the affair with Nicholson was pending, and the matter was quietly dropped. But it was an ugly incident. "I mention this," Brockholst Livingston had told his mother, "that you may judge how much he must be Mortified . . . before he would descend to language that would have become a Street Bully."[14] But it was not "mortification" but a deeper disturbance, masking doubts as to his future life.

Hamilton had lost office, but he had not yet lost power, for his ties to

Washington and Philadelphia remained intact. They were now stronger than ever, for Washington, lonely and deprived of men he trusted, turned more and more to his old friends for consultation and support. When John Jay brought a treaty back from England that privately appalled both of them, Washington turned to Hamilton for advice on presenting it to Congress, and Hamilton defended what Angelica scathingly called "Mr. Jay's LITTLE Treaty" in New York to violent and angry crowds. They worked together on Washington's Farewell Address, revising drafts and exchanging copies filled with notes and revisions through many months by mail.

By the end of the year Hamilton's power had multiplied through no overt actions of his own. Upheavals and replacements had transformed the Cabinet: Henry Knox had left the War Department soon after Hamilton, and Edmund Randolph, Jefferson's successor, was caught in a secret correspondence with the French ambassador, and after an ugly quarrel forced to resign. Washington was unable to find men of talent to replace them and was forced to settle for third best. At State he placed Timothy Pickering, an intense young man of fanatical politics, and at the Treasury, Oliver Wolcott, who had been Hamilton's assistant and devoted follower since Duer's fall. The Secretary of War was James McHenry, a sweet-natured man of literary leanings, but, as his friends soon discovered, out of his depth in dealing with executive affairs. All three were docile men and somewhat limited. They admired Washington, but they worshipped Hamilton. Not long after his resignation, they deluged him with letters, asking his help in running their departments, referring questions about policy to him for his advice. Within months Hamilton was all but running three departments in the evenings from his drawing room, between his duties at the bar. Washington for his part listened to none of them and continued making policy with Hamilton, whose views he studied and carefully wove in with his own. All five men took this development as perfectly natural, the outgrowth of Hamilton's genius. What did not occur to Hamilton was that this could not go on forever and that the end would surely bring him pain.

Oddly, he had made no effort to establish a political future that did not depend on other men. In fact he now appeared to flee from it, turning down requests to run for office and refusing the offer of a Senate seat, when one fell vacant, from Governor John Jay. It was part of a life-long pattern: for all his wartime talk of self-sufficiency, he had consistently shunned an independent place in public life. Part of this may have been self-knowledge: his genius was creative, not political; he lacked perspec-

171

tive, diplomacy and tact. He was happier with space between himself and the public: he preferred dealing with one man (or with four men) who understood him to facing a large and hostile crowd. In his career he had always been under other men's protection, and he had now come to rely on it.

Hamilton's position in 1796 was most precarious, resting on the favor of four people, three of them appointed, and one of whom would step down the next year. He had his friends, some of them in Congress, but they would be no protection against the powers of a hostile President; and when he made no effort to secure himself a base of power, he had sealed his fate. Hamilton would find it intolerable to live without connections to the American government. What became increasingly apparent was that for a variety of reasons he was finding it equally intolerable to strike out on his own. It is not certain how much of this he admitted to himself. He seemed unwilling to face the fact of Washington's retirement and the limitations it would place on his own life. Part of his troubles stemmed from the refusal to face the reality of this approaching future. The others stemmed from the inner knowledge that it was surely closing in.

Angelica Church and her family returned to America, this time to settle, late in 1796. It is not certain why they left England, though her incessant pleading may have figured in it, along with her husband's failure to shine in politics—for he had not won the power that he sought. Doubtless this made him shine less than ever in the eyes of his wife, who pursued her friendships with artists and statesmen and continued to write letters home. Her correspondence with Hamilton and with Eliza continued its old mixture of teasing, flirtation and genuine longing, for she was wretched away from her country and family and never ceased in her entreaties to return. With great delicacy she had contrived to retain the friendship of Thomas Jefferson, though with diminished intensity. There are tender letters until 1806. There was no more talk, however, of trios together, or of visits to each other's houses. By 1791 the incongruity of Thomas Jefferson as a guest in the home of Philip Schuyler had become evident to all concerned. Though Jefferson wrote to her of his pains in office, he did not mention the leading cause of them. There was a tacit agreement not to mention Hamilton at all.

Church became an outdoor insurer, though his real profession was gambling. He soon was heavily in debt. He lived beyond his means in palatial houses in which he held balls and parties, extravagant beyond measure, at which games went on through the small hours and fortunes vanished overnight.

> Church is working hard at cards [wrote Robert Troup, who watched his career with horror]. How his constitution stands it is a matter of amazement. He has at least four regular card games to attend every week. Sometimes they do not break up until morning. There is as little respectability attached to him as to any man among us. Unfortunately, the whole family is enveloped in such a cloud, that they enjoy little of esteem.[15]

The Hamiltons took no part in the heavy gambling, but their proximity to their glittering in-laws was enough to spread a cloud of worry that they might be drawn to ruin in their wake.

> Church is said to be pushed for money [Troup continued], and family affairs are in a train which will cause an explosion which will spread genuine ruin. . . . I mean the ruin of the whole connection. I consider it unfortunate that he ever removed with his family to this country. . . . I had ventured at every risk to communicate this with a friend of ours upon a certain subject, [but] I feel notwithstanding that things continue in the same course.[16]

The attachment between Hamilton and Angelica became more noticeable than ever, and the connection with Church further tarnished his name. Both added force to the impact of the Reynolds pamphlet, published in September 1797, which did incalculable damage. Declamations against Hamilton as an adulterer were frequent and vehement, and friends who did not chastise him for his moral failings raised questions about his judgment. It was widely taken as the sign of an unstable temperament. Noah Webster, speaking for them, scourged him not for his adultery, but for a disturbing lack of sense.

> What shall we say to the conduct of a man who has borne some of the highest civil and military appointments, who could deliberately write and publish a history of his private intrigues, degrade himself in the estimation of all good men,

173

and scandalize a family . . . to vindicate an integrity which a legislative act had pronounced unimpeachable, and which scarcely a man in America believed?[17]

Thomas Jefferson, himself vulnerable (and himself to become a target of Callender's rages) exonerated Hamilton of both public and private moral failings in a sensitive passage written after Hamilton was dead:

> He was, indeed, a singular character. Of acute understanding, disinterested, honest, and honorable in all private transactions, amiable in society, and duly valuing virtue in private life.[18]

"Duly valuing" is a loaded comment, conceding abundant room for human error, and applying perhaps no more to Hamilton than to himself.

The Adams family was less compassionate. Abigail called him "wicked" and "lascivious." Adams, who would write later of Hamilton's "fornications, his adulteries, his incests"[19] (the last a slighting reference to Angelica), now called him "a proud Spirited, conceited, aspiring Mortal, with as debauched Morals as old Franklin, who is more his Model than anyone I know."[20] Benjamin Franklin had been Adams's rival when both were in Europe in the 1780s, and his popularity, charm and gallant manners had won him an undying hatred from the Adams family that had never been expunged. To have Hamilton thus mentioned as his successor was not an encouraging sign. Adams had become President on March 4, 1797. The enmity of a sitting President was not a thing that Hamilton was used to. It was an unsettling new fact of his life.

XIV

ADAMS AND HAMILTON fought for Washington's power like angry, disputatious heirs. Each in fact had only half his power, for Adams, who took office in March 1797, was not close to Washington, had the allegiance of only half his party and little of his glamour or prestige. Hamilton, who at Adams's accession had not held public office for two years, was adored by the Cabinet and by a large corps in Congress, and was acknowledged as Washington's favorite, gilded by intimacy and regarded by many in the party as his heir.

Adams had been an early, forceful leader of colonial independence, but he had since slipped into the eddies of power and was handicapped by qualities of physique and temperament that did not add to his prestige. Where Washington was tall, possessing even in age the muscular grace of the born athlete, Adams was rotund and portly, giving him a chipmunk-like appearance, and his prowlike nose was oversized. He was touchy, proud and painfully self-conscious. Where Washington was courtly, ever charming diplomats, Adams could be tactless and abrupt. "His vanity is a lineament in his character I had not noticed," Jefferson told Madison in 1782. "His want of taste I had observed."[1] Hamilton's friends regarded him as an interloper, to be embraced with caution; Jefferson, who had returned as Vice-President after his own three-year retirement, had entrenched himself in opposition, quietly preparing for his own campaign.

Hamilton would have been hostile to anyone who had succeeded Washington, but his relations with Adams were particularly tense. The year before he had backed Thomas Pinckney (then Federalist candidate for Vice-President) against Adams in a gesture of resentment and hostility that added new stresses to a simmering distrust.

> There is no cordiality on the part of the President to Hamilton [Robert Troup told Rufus King in 1798]. Hamilton publickly gave out his wishes that Pinckney should be elected President. These were communicated privately and publickly to the President, and occasioned, I suspect, more than a coolness. . . . I blamed Hamilton at the time for making the declarations . . . and foresaw that evil would arise from them.[2]

Adams did see Hamilton as intriguing and hostile. Whether he blamed him also for his exclusion from power in the eight years of the Washington administration is not clear. Washington at the inauguration had acted with great courtesy, insisting that not only Adams but Jefferson precede him from the chamber, but such gestures could not atone for eight years of coldness. Adams wrote later of the "contracted principle of monopoly and exclusion . . . to which I had often been compelled to submit"[3]—a principle that had embraced a man who was a bastard and an alien, while it had left no room for him.

Abigail was still more hostile. "Beware that spare Cassius, has always occured to me when I have seen that cock sparrow,"[4] she told her husband. "I have ever kept my eye on him."[5] Adams, about to take office in January 1797, had replied with like venom, "I shall take no more notice of his puppyhood, but return to him the same conduct that I always did—that is, to keep him at a distance."[6] Hamilton for his part found the idea of this small, blunt, graceless man in Washington's office ludicrous, and perhaps an insult that he was not prepared to take.

Adams also stayed aloof from Washington, either from necessity or choice. Abigail told Benjamin Rush in April 1798 that the two men had had no contact in thirteen months, though whether she spoke with pride or with resentment is unclear. What she did not know was that the Cabinet was in constant contact with Hamilton, asking his advice on a whole range of matters and receiving in return voluminous programs that they passed on to the President as theirs. Unlike Adams, they also wrote to Washington, keeping him informed, confiding in him and asking his advice.

Adams kept them on because he did not dare to do otherwise, fearing their dismissal would seem a slap at Washington and rebound unpleasantly on him. Jefferson wrote to Adams later of the "legacy of Secretaries which Gen. Washington left you, and whom you seemed to consider as under public protection," naming specifically "the Pickerings, the Wolcotts, the Tracys and the Sedgwicks [the last two friends of Hamilton's in the Senate] with whom we supposed you in a state of Duresse."[7] This duress was self-inflicted. If it was hard for most Americans to realize that Washington was no longer at the head of government, it was equally difficult for the President himself.

Perhaps if times were peaceful the tensions might have remained hidden, and the rivalries simmered underground. But the war in Europe, raging on with great ferocity, now involved the United States. Rival warships continued to devastate American commerce. France, outraged by the Jay Treaty, considered it tantamount to a declaration of war. In 1797 Adams (with the secret backing of Hamilton) had sent a mission of Elbridge Gerry, John Marshall and Charles Cotesworth Pinckney to Paris in a last effort to avert hostilities, and for a time peace seemed in sight. But in March 1797, Americans learned to their horror that France had dismissed the embassy on terms verging on insult, demanding a bribe of $250,000 to begin to talk settlements, and had massed a vast force of armed and naval power on its northwestern coast. Alarmed, Congress in April passed a program of war measures, including harsh laws against foreign and domestic dissidents, an enlarged navy, fortifications in the exposed eastern seaports and, fatally for the lives of the three principals, an army of twelve thousand.

The shattering prospect of war with France brought a crisis to the new administration and to the complex truce among the three uneasy men. Adams was afraid of Washington, of his power and of the overpowering nostalgia which the threat of war increased. On June 22 he sent him a letter—the first in the sixteen months since the inauguration—asking for his assistance and the use, as Adams put it, of his "name." But he did not nominate him to lead the army and astounded Timothy Pickering by suggesting as candidates Daniel Morgan, Benjamin Lincoln and Gates—three relics of the Revolution who were old and ailing, and one of whom Washington despised. Pickering was stunned, for none was suitable. He did not yet realize that this was the point. Adams was trying to remove himself from Washington, Washington's friends or anyone who might surface as a rival, fearing they might overshadow him. He did not know that Hamilton had already written twice to Washington, insisting that he must return as commander; or that Washington had answered, naming two conditions that were to prove incendiary: that he would serve only if given absolute power to appoint his own underlings, and that he expected Hamilton to serve with him.

Hamilton did not contact Adams. His lines were to the Cabinet, which was loyal to Washington and to himself. What the three now said to Adams is uncertain, since neither he nor they kept records, but on July 6 McHenry left the capital to travel to Mount Vernon, bearing with him a signed commission naming Washington commander-in-chief. Adams's letter was a remarkable blend of candor and of self-abasement in which he revealed his uncertainties, his lingering fear of Washington and what indeed may have been his wish—that Washington would return to his old office, relegating Adams to the security of the vice-presidential chair. But he did not answer Washington's letter, in which the ex-President carefully detailed the only terms on which he would accept the post. He sent Washington's nomination to the Senate quickly, without informing Washington himself—gestures of anger and of a barely masked hostility which he did not dare to express openly.

Days later, Adams fled to Braintree, where he stayed inured for months together, returning only under pressure when Congress reconvened. His excuse for part of the time away was the health of his wife, which in the fall of 1798 was very serious: she suffered from recurrent fevers and was thought at times to be near death. But it is likely too that it was a flight from a capital that was passing by degrees into enemy country, controlled by forces he resented but did not yet know how to fight. Doubtless he had been told, perhaps repeatedly, that Washington would take the nomination of Gates as a personal insult, and that the nomination of another while Washington was living would create a public outcry that his administration would be unable to withstand. He could not argue without confessions of weakness, which he did not at the time acknowledge and could not bring himself to make.

Washington and Hamilton had no misgivings. They picked up the reins of power as if they had never left their hands. When Adams had not objected to Washington's conditions (indeed, had not even answered them), Washington took this as tacit agreement and proceeded to mold the army to his tastes. On July 26 Robert Troup told King in London what Hamilton, perhaps in great excitement, had told him: that Washington was prepared to promote him over both Henry Knox and Charles Cotesworth Pinckney, the young soldier-diplomat then en route home from the disastrous French mission, to make him second in command. Pickering meanwhile was keeping up a steady drumbeat for Hamilton, though without his knowledge, peppering Washington with pleas. "Knowing Mrs. Adams's *aversion* to Hamilton," he wrote later, "I took the liberty of writing to General Washington. . . . I had no sort of communication with Hamilton on the subject, and it was a spontaneous action on my part."

The two were now in constant communication on every aspect of the army, Washington working directly through Hamilton when he found McHenry slow. The secretaries, shuttling between them, were now ecstatic, writing only sporadically to the President, who daily seemed to fade from view. Their letters are vigorous and show a new delight in power. There is much mention of themselves and their associates; there is very little of the President himself. In Braintree, he seemed a distant and a dreamlike figure, tangential to the work of government and largely out of its concerns. His absences from the capital, often in times of crisis, were to become chronic and lengthy. He was eventually to be out of Washington for nearly one third of his term. The calendar seemed peeled back to the early 1790s with Washington in power, Hamilton beside him and Adams in formal make-work, ornamental office, on the fringes of government, out of sight and largely out of mind.

Adams and Hamilton were now locked in a struggle for precedence in which the true objectives had not yet come to the fore. Neither would admit his ambitions or his fears. They sought refuge in shadowboxing, in night maneuvers that had not reached the stage of open war. It was not a fight for power only, but for something more elusive: a form of legitimacy once held by Washington which each only partially possessed. Hamilton was not after rank, for he had told Washington that he would refer to Knox or Pinckney if either should refuse to serve. But he did care for recognition—for an ongoing place in the American government, which he now demanded as a right. He believed that no President of his own party had the authority to dismiss him from the place that he held under Washington—as advisor, confidant and son. In this he was supported by the Cabinet, and by his friends in Congress, who believed him a genius and thought, with him, that if Washington had sought his counsel, lesser men had no right to refuse. Thus he was also judged innocent in his contact

179

with the Cabinet—he had not seduced another man's advisors, he had simply answered questions from his friends.

By July there was another source of trouble. Hamilton, his dreams inflated by this infusion of power, was drifting perilously close to the schemes of Francisco de Miranda, a Latin American patriot, incendiary and incorrigible dreamer, to join the American army to the British navy, march west across the Alleghenies, and liberate Latin America from Spain. It had been an *idée fixe* of de Miranda's for twenty years, but it had lately taken on new credence in the fact that France and Spain were allies, and that Spain's possessions might become a hostile military base. De Miranda was now in London, trying to sell Pitt and Rufus King on the project, baiting it further with the promise that the masses writhing under Spain's oppression were waiting for the signal to rebel. It was very close to Hamilton's boyhood dreams, and the diverse elements—adventure, hitting France and becoming the savior of an oppressed people—had an irresistible appeal. By late fall he was picturing a role in something other than defensive warfare. He wrote to friends of an aggressive war on his own continent; of tempting prizes in the west.

De Miranda, inflamed with hatred of the Spanish empire, had made this cause the center of his life. Such was his charm that the cool James Madison spoke of his great eloquence, and he was to infect the sober Rufus King to such an extent that his letters became a drumbeat calling for attack. Despite the fears of military danger (or of French possession, which became a fact soon after), there were problems of logistics that could not be overcome. Washington, whose adored half-brother had died at thirty-six from a disease caught in a British war in Venezuela, thought the idea madness, as did Adams, who read King's letters with dismay. "I did not know whether to laugh or weep," he said of these dispatches. "Miranda's project is as visionary, though far less innocent, than . . . an excursion to the moon in cart drawn by geese."[9] King's letters could not sway him on the project, and the prospect of Hamilton as a military hero was enough to demolish its appeal.

De Miranda, who had won Hamilton with his dash and glamour, lost him on another count—the bias built into Hamilton's character to legitimacy and order, and his identification with the government of the United States. He was not Aaron Burr, who urged Hamilton the next year to use the army to overturn the government, saying when Hamilton demurred in horror, "All things are moral to great souls." To Hamilton, nothing was moral that did not bear the imprimatur of the American nation, and when the scheme was dead to the government, it was also dead to him. Though he continued to brood about the French menace, to urge expansion and to dream of military ventures, he did nothing at all to make them happen. His behavior in the years after suggests strongly that his itch for empire was secondary to his need to remain close to the government, the ruling passion of his life.

Though this dream faded, the West remained central to the American imagination, the backdrop against which dramas of character were played. Hamilton, drawn by thoughts of glory, was to dream of conquest, building paper armies, but retreating when national backing was withdrawn. Aaron Burr plotted to sever the country from its western holdings, linking them via Mexico to a vast southern empire, which he planned to rule as emperor with his daughter as queen. He was well on his way to raising an army through a fantastic web of lies and misrepresentations when arrested near the Mississippi in 1807. Thomas Jefferson as President lifted the threat of France entirely by annexing the Louisiana territory, the vast midsection of the continent from the Mississippi to the Rocky Mountains, quietly, peacefully and undramatically, by purchase, with one stroke of his pen.

On September 6 McHenry received Washington's nominations of his under officers and sent them to Adams in their stated order of Hamilton, Pinckney and Knox. When the President returned them, the order had been magically reversed. Adams told McHenry that Hamilton could not rank above Knox or Pinckney, that McHenry must write to Washington to get his agreement and issue the commissions at once. Before the stunned McHenry could contact Washington he received a second letter: he must issue the commissions in the order named by Adams, without consulting Washington at all. When the secretaries protested, Adams answered that Hamilton was not popular in the country or the Federalist party, that he was not a native of the United States, but a foreigner, and that his rank in the revolutionary army was comparatively low. Then they argued that the order was Washington's directive. Adams answered that he would allow no one to usurp his authority and that his orders must be carried out at once. Alone at Braintree with the hostile Abigail, his fears had crystallized into intense suspicion that the alliance of Washington with the bastard foreigner was once more taking root. But he had allowed things to go too far among people who had grown too powerful. When Hamilton threatened to resign rather than to accept this insult, McHenry sent him a letter asking him to do nothing until further notice and threw his whole correspondence with Adams into Washington's lap.

Washington reacted with a volcanic fury that nearly blew the government apart. Not since his days as a young soldier on the frontiers of Virginia had he been superseded by anyone, much less his own Vice-President, and a man he did not like. He had regarded what he saw as Adams's acquiescence in his demands as a sacred promise, the word of a gentleman, which the President was now about to break. His irritation with Adams had grown through the summer, beginning with the failure to inform him of the nomination, proceeding through the flight to Braintree and the resulting neglect of the army. He was beginning to find Adams laggard or inept or both. He now sent Adams an infuriated letter: if Adams did not rescind his orders to the Cabinet, he himself was ready to resign. He said the projected loss of Hamilton to the army would be "irreparable"; he called him a genius, known in Europe and America, and ended with the description that has become famous:

> He is considered an ambitious man, and by some a dangerous one. That he is ambitious I shall readily grant, but it is of that laudable kind, that prompts a man to excel in whatever he takes in hand. He is enterprising, quick in his perceptions, and his judgment intuitively great.[10]

The disdain of this blast is in contrast to the hot fury of his letters to McHenry and Pickering in which he made explicit what he had implied: if Adams did not back down on the matter of the officers, he would take his case to the country and allow the people to decide.

Days later came an absolute capitulation. The President would defer to the wish of the commander, as it had always been agreed that he would do. What would have happened in the case of such a contest Adams did not need to have explained.

John Adams had surrendered as President to the man he had succeeded, and whose coldness had tormented him for eight years in the past. He had also been forced to reinstate his enemy—the "Cassius," the "Bonaparte," the "puppy," the "cock sparrow"—at his tormentor's right hand. Time alone uncovered the extent of his anguish—in retirement he disgorged retrospective vituperation over a twenty-year period in a never ending stream. The immediate reaction was political malaise. "He keenly felt the circumstances of *duresse* under which this result had been brought upon him," wrote his grandson, Charles Francis Adams, "and he foresaw it was only the prelude to worse things."[11] What these were he discovered shortly when in private interviews Washington refused commissions to two men Adams asked for, Peter Muhlenberg, who applied to the President directly, and Aaron Burr. Washington described Burr as gifted, but far too agile at intrigue.

When Theodore Sedgwick told Adams of the Senate's plan to confer new titles upon Washington, he burst out, "What! are you going to appoint him general over the President?"[12] and complained of combinations among sinister forces to undermine his office and prestige. He called Washington, Hamilton and Pinckney the "Triumvirate," spoke disparagingly of "their favorite little army," and talked darkly of plots against the state. The executive and the army had become opposing forces, at war within the government, unable to make peace.

Adams now realized that if he did not take steps quickly to reclaim his government, his power, now eroding, would be altogether lost. He was now searching for a way out of his dilemma. When France, battered by defeats in Europe, sued for terms in a more humble manner, he did not hesitate to take them up. On February 18, 1799, he stunned his government with the announcement of another embassy, and a three-man mission, which was to settle the dispute without bloodshed, sailed for France in November of that year. The immediate effect at home was to destroy the army—as the threat of war receded, so would the edifice of renewed power so precariously erected on its base. Enlistments would cease, funds dwindle, power fade—and private men, called out of retirement into public office, would sink back into retirement again. As maddening to Hamilton's friends, and in the long run, far more sinister, was the secrecy in which the plan was hatched. For the first time they had not been consulted on a matter of high policy. They had been cut off from power and from influence with a single blow. "The measure was secret, & without advice, which has also contrived to make it more disgusting,"[13] Robert Troup told Rufus King in April. No one found it more disgusting than did Hamilton himself.

Hamilton committed nothing rash to paper, so startled was he. But the rage among his friends, who were not silent, unmistakably revealed three things: their distress at what they took to be a grave mistake in policy, their anger at their own exclusion, and their belief that the mission was an act not of policy but of malice aimed at Hamilton.

> The origin [Senator George Cabot told Rufus King, March 10] may be sought in the weakness to which the best of men are liable—Egotism—vanity—wounded pride—distrust of men who lay too much stress on the *public* welfare. . . . I

183

am full of fears, lest it be used with success to divide us anew.[14]

Robert Troup also complained of Adams's behavior, calling him fitful and influenced by jealousy and pique. Suspicions that the motivation had been personal were deepened by rumors that Adams continued privately to rail at France. Cabot told King in April that Adams's hatred of Hamilton had descended to his friends.

> Who are now suspected of having too much influence, and of not knowing how to appreciate his merits. . . . his ears are shut to his best friends, and open to Flatterers, time servers, and even to some Jacobins. These things, not yet extensively or very much known, give infinite pain to me.[15]

Signs of a split within the party began to surface early in the year. Troup had written King as early as April 19 of an incipient rebellion— "There will definitely be serious difficulties in supporting Mr. Adams"[16]—and later of a move to draft Washington. There was an impassioned meeting at Trenton in August, in which Hamilton made a desperate plea to postpone the mission, which Adams stoically ignored. Weeks later Cabot made a trip to Braintree to play peacemaker but was beaten back at every turn. The Adamses read his mind and his intentions and every time that he edged closer to his subject, turned the conversation away. "I was treated with great kindness," he reported, "but every heart was locked." Despairingly, he counted the chance of unity as impossible. "We have hitherto sought in vain for a remedy, & from the nature of the case, I think an effectual remedy is not to be found."[17]

George Washington died suddenly at Mount Vernon on December 14 of a throat infection of astounding virulence that had lasted less than one day. On his desk when he died was a letter from Gouverneur Morris begging him to save the country by running against Adams. In other letters he had declined an open battle, but he had not endorsed Adams either, and strongly suggested he might back someone else. To Hamilton, it was a devastating loss. He was now unprotected, in the year his luck had started to run out.

Adams's feelings were more complex. There are signs that he shared the national emotions of shock and sorrow, but his dominant feeling was the sense that an immense weight had fallen from his back. "I was no more at liberty than a man in prison," he told Benjamin Rush years later, "chained to the floor and bound hand and foot."[18] Years later, he reworked his grievances, saying repeatedly to his friends on paper what he could never say to Washington himself:

> I ought to have said No to the appointment of Washington and Hamilton, and . . . Yes to the appointment of Burr and Muhlenberg. . . . I ought to have appointed Lincoln and Gates and Knox. . . . But if I had said Yes and No in this manner, the Senate would have contradicted me in every instance . . . Washington would have been chosen President at the next election, and Hamilton would have been appointed commander-in-chief.[19]

Often he distorted reality, and his claims became exaggerated and grotesque.

> My popularity was growing too splendid. . . . the great eulogium, "First in war, first in peace, first in the hearts of his countrymen," was believed by him and all his friends to be in some danger. . . . I believe he expected to be called in again.[20]

Hamilton, he believed, had destroyed him out of blind ambition; Washington out of jealousy and spite.

Through the winter and into the spring, Adams continued to revile Hamilton, often in the presence of his friends. His fury spilled over to include Hamilton's associates, in and out of Congress, whom he described as being in a plot to ruin him.

He spoke at times of an "oligarchic faction," at others of a Tory junto, determined to break him and drag the country into war. On May 5 he fired McHenry and Pickering, accusing the former of having been too good a friend to Hamilton and of having praised Washington in a recent speech.

"He became indecorous, and at times outrageous," McHenry reported to Hamilton. "I had done nothing right. . . . Everybody blamed me for my official conduct, and I must resign."[21]

On May 10 Hamilton wrote of Adams to Theodore Sedgwick:

For my part, my mind is made up. I shall never more be responsible for him by my direct support—even though the consequence may be the election of Jefferson. . . . If the cause is to be sacrificed to a weak and perverse man, I withdraw from the party & act upon my own ground—never against my principles, but in pursuance of them in my own way.[22]

On June 7 Hamilton left for Massachusetts, ostensibly on a mission to disband the remnants of his troops. In fact, it was a political mission, and he had gone not to disband troops but to raise them—against the President of the United States. For three weeks he traveled extensively through Massachusetts, Rhode Island and Connecticut, speaking continually to his friends. He spent six days in Boston where he held court like a reigning prince. The height of this wooing came at a banquet there on June 19, where he dined in splendor with a host of Adams's enemies, including the mayor and lieutenant governor, Cabot, Higginson and Ames. His message everywhere was similar. Adams had betrayed the country and the Federalist party. He had no strength where the friends of Hamilton held power. The one course for the party was to ignore Adams in the presidential election and vote instead for the vice-presidential candidate, Charles Cotesworth Pinckney, who happened to be Hamilton's good friend.

This was watched with morbid fascination by the Adams family, which saw its fears of ten years' standing come to life.

Thus has this intriguer been endeavouring to divide the federal party [Abigail wrote to her son Thomas], to create divisions and heart-burnings against the President, simply because he knows he cannot sway him . . . until he can be instrumental in getting a President to his own mind.[23]

Adams in the capital stormed with renewed passion. He had tantrums in the presence of Cabinet members and Congressmen, and the mere mention of Washington could send him into a rage. There were rumors of a coalition between Adams and Jefferson against Hamilton and his friends. His rages were excessive and profane. "His language is bitter even to outrage and swearing," Ames told King on July 15. "He inveighs against the British faction . . . like one possessed."[24]

McHenry described Adams as ridden with distrust of all but flatterers, and said that "at times he would speak in such a manner of certain men and measures as to persuade one he was actually insane."[25] Bayard told Hamilton that Adams was prone to "gusts of passion little short of frenzy, which drive him beyond the control of any rational reflection. I speak of what I have seen."[26] To Goodhue, Adams said the Senate had rejected the application of his son-in-law to join the army purely to injure him—"Saying we had killed his [Adams's] daughter"—and had vetoed the nomination of another man to a small post in the Stamp Office because his daughter married Adams's son. Goodhue said his resentment of the Senate was "implacable . . . in those instances which resulted, he said, with no other view but to hurt his feelings," and called the interview "a perfect rage of passion . . . one continued theme of the most bitter complaint."[27]

His fury focused upon Hamilton in an outpouring of impassioned rage. Goodhue told Pickering of a conversation with Adams, in which he said

> Mr. Jefferson was a very proper person to be president. . . . he would sooner serve as vice-president under him, or even as resident minister at the Hague, than be indebted for his election to *such a being* as Hamilton, whom in the same sentence he called a bastard, and as much an alien as Gallatin. . . . Mr. Goodhue had forgotten some things which he recited to me the next morning, among others the charge against the Senate in this elegant expression, "And you crammed Hamilton down my throat."[28]

Exactly how much of this Hamilton's friends dared to tell him is unknown. But much had doubtless trickled through in gossip and touched him on an unhealed wound.

Hamilton's first response was to write Adams a letter, asking him to account for his remarks. When two months passed without an answer, he wrote another letter, calling the attacks "a base, wicked and cruel calumny, destitute even of a plausible pretext to excuse the folly, or mask the depravity which must have dictated it."[29] The words indicate the depth of his emotions, and he spoke now of attacking the President in print. "I could predicate it on the fact that I am abused by the friends of Mr. Adams," he told Pickering, ". . . and would give it in the form of a *defence*."[30]

Using materials compiled by the ex-secretaries, Hamilton wrote a twenty-thousand-word essay on the shortcomings of the President, which he published on October 21. He had meant it, he said, for the electors of South Carolina, to influence them in their deliberations. But with its discovery and printing by Aaron Burr it became public property, and the world at large could see the storms within the decomposing party, and the hatreds of its leading men. Hamilton spoke of Adams's egotism, jealousy and indiscretion, the "great and intrinsic defects in his character," and his "vanity without bounds." There was some confused reference to public matters, but the core lay in this supporting sentence:

> If Mr. Adams has repeatedly indulged himself in virulent and indecent abuse of me . . . denominated me as a man destitute of every moral principle . . . I have a right to think that I have been most cruelly and wickedly trad-uced.[31]

It was this note that was so frightening: of enmities gone too far and deep for reason, of great hurt on either side.

Hamilton was at court in Albany when news of the publication struck. "At first, he was apparently confused," reported Robert Troup, who was in chambers with him,[32] "but soon afterwards he recollected himself, and I think he appears pleased." As it happened, the only others pleased were the Republicans, who watched happily as their enemies dissolved before their eyes. "We are all thunderstruck here by Hamilton's pamphlet,"[33] wrote Bushrod Washington, the general's nephew, adding that the piece would devastate the party in Virginia, where the electors would hesitate to vote for Pinckney, fearing an intrigue.

> At Albany, they lamented the publication [Troup wrote to Rufus King]. On my return I found a much stronger disap-probation of it expressed everywhere. . . . Not a man in our whole circle of friends but condemns it. . . . In point of imprudence, it is coupled with the pamphlet published by the General concerning himself.[34]

Few cared to defend Adams, but all agreed Hamilton had matched him in malice and intemperance, and it brought back memories of the Reynolds pamphlet, which had also made a wretched situation worse. Noah Webster wrote that Hamilton's pride and ambition had made him the "evil genius" of America. Troup was forced to record the opinion, now all

188

but universal, that "his *character* is *radically deficient in discretion* . . . hence he is considered an unfit head."

George Cabot, after much hesitation, broke the news to Hamilton:

> I am bound to tell you that you are accused by some respectable men of Egotism, & some very worthy & sensible men say you have exhibited the same *vanity* . . . which you charge as a dangerous quality & great weakness in Mr. Adams. . . . I should have left it to your enemies to tell you of the Censures of your Friends, if I was not persuaded that you could not possibly mistake my motives, or doubt of the sincerity of my affection, or the greatness of my Esteem.[35]

Hamilton continued his erratic, self-destructive course. To the horror of his friends, he spoke of new pamphlets in which he would answer his critics in the press.

> The press teems with replies, and I may find it expedient to publish a second time [he wrote to Timothy Pickering]. In this case I shall reinforce my charges by new anecdotes . . . You probably possess some which are unknown to me. Pray let me have them without delay.[36]

He seemed incapable of understanding the damage he had done his party and himself. "I cannot describe to you how broken and shattered our federal friends are," Troup wrote despairingly to Rufus King. "Shadows, clouds and darkness rest on our future prospects. . . . no mortal can divine where or when we shall again collect our strength."[37]

By now Adams and Hamilton were prisoners of their own demons, reason overrun by hate. Four years after he had left the presidency, Washington's party had shattered, torn by a series of explosions from within. In its noisy dissolution, it had created a catastrophe which no one in either party had foreseen. In December, when all the votes were counted, there was a new impasse of frightening dimensions. From some misunderstanding among the Republican electors, seventy-three votes apiece had been cast for each of their candidates—Thomas Jefferson and his vice-presidential running mate, Aaron Burr.

X V

THE SUDDEN EMERGENCE of Aaron Burr as a candidate for President in the election of 1800 came as a shock to the Federalist and the Republican parties, and to no one more than Thomas Jefferson himself. Till then no one had dreamed that a candidate for Vice-President could connive against his running mate with that man's most obstinate enemies, plotting with them not only his destruction but the frustration of the will of the United States. The episode revealed unexpected flaws in an electoral system that many had guilelessly thought perfect, and resulted at last in the Twelfth Amendment, passed with Hamilton's blessing in 1804. It also revealed for the first time Burr's immense capacities for destruction, and the talents for chaos hidden in this small man with the sloed eyes and the rapier slimness, and the ivory pallor that contrasted so strikingly with the midnight darkness of his hair. Burr to this point had been a largely hidden quantity, a political adventurer of charm and guile, a one-time senator and current New York state assemblyman, but one whose opinions and motivations were unknown.

Jefferson had never liked the man he picked to run with him, preferring as confidants and possible successors his friends and neighbors, Madison and James Monroe. When Burr's efforts had secured the vote of New York state in May 1800, he had accepted him with misgivings he did not make public, believing from his own experience that Vice-Presidents once in office were easily controlled. These misgivings had not been one-sided. Burr disliked the group he referred to as the "Virginia junto," and had with difficulty been persuaded to run. William Nicholson told his son-in-law Albert Gallatin that Burr thought Jefferson could not be trusted, and Nicholson's daughter told her husband that "Burr says he has no confidence in the Virginians,"[1] because he believed he had once been deceived. Burr may have hoped that once in office he would succeed Jefferson in power, as had happened to the other two Vice-Presidents, but the tie, so sudden and so unexpected, opened enticing broad new vistas to his eyes. Sometime in December Jefferson realized to his horror that Burr was not willing to take himself out of the election, and that the Federalists in Congress, who would control the House of Representatives until March 1801 and were thus empowered to break the deadlock, in a last effort to keep their enemy from power, were prepared to throw their votes to him.

The intrigue had a special twist of irony. Unlike the sons of farmers or small planters (or, like Hamilton, of the embarrassed lesser gentry), Burr came from a lineage of exceptional distinction—in his father, an honored president of Princeton College, and in his maternal grandfather, Jonathan Edwards, the distinguished preacher of the Awakening, he united two lines of extraordinary accomplishment, if not in power, in morality and thought. But with this brilliance went a troubling legacy: a deep vein of hysteria. Burr's parents and his grandfather had undergone religious conversions in their teens. Edwards wrote of "God's choosing whom he would to universal life, and rejecting whom he pleased, leaving them eternally to perish, and be everlastingly tormented in Hell"[2]—a sentiment that found an eerie echo in the statement of Burr's father, "God saw fit to open my eyes, and show me what a miserable creature I was. . . . I was brought to the footstool of divine sovereign grace, saw myself polluted by nature and practice . . . and was made to despair of help."[3]

Esther Burr had "divine impressions" from the age of seven and made public professions of religion at fifteen. When her husband died after five years of marriage, she fell into a dream of death.

> In the greatest freedom and delight I did give myself to God [she had written]. . . . in talking of the glorious state my dear departed husband must be in, my soul was carried out in such a large desire after that glorious state that I was

191

forced to retire from my family to conceal my joy. When I was alone, I was so transported that I think my nature would not have borne much more. . . . I slept but little, and when I did, my dreams were all of heavenly and divine things. Frequently since I have felt the same in kind.[4]

There was an iron edge to this devotion that stripped it of its gracious quality. Their God was cold, capable of intense and almost careless cruelty, disdaining the value of human effort and unfeeling in the face of pain. Much of this, divorced from its religious context, was to be transmitted to their son.

Burr as a child was described by his mother as "dirty and noisy," "sly and mischievous," "stubborn," and "requiring a good governor to bring him to terms."[5] When she died, he was given to her brother, a harsh, repressive guardian who beat the child "like a sack." Burr, taking refuge in secrecy, began writing to his sister in cipher and running away from home. At fourteen he escaped to Princeton, an intense, precocious child, and began almost at once his break with the piety of his forebears, if not with their hysterical approach.

At first, we are told by Matthew Davis, his protégé and first biographer, he was pathologically afraid of not meeting expectations and drove himself to near exhaustion, fasting to preserve his mental clarity and studying seventeen hours a day. When, inevitably, he outstripped his classmates, his awe turned to derision and contempt. He fell into a life of idleness, pursuing pleasure as he had once sought knowledge and running heavily into debt. He also started what would become a lifetime of seduction, beginning, most likely, with a very young girl. "Miss Moncrieff, before she reached her fourteenth year, was probably a victim of seduction," Davis wrote. "The language of her memoirs . . . leaves little room for doubt."[6] It was to become a constant pursuit, undertaken with his customary intensity, and lasting to his late seventies.

In this particular Burr appears to have been unfeeling and heartless [Davis has written]. With females, he was an unprincipled flatterer, prepared to take advantage of their weakness, their credulity, or their confidence. . . . She that confided in him was lost.[7]

Burr himself had paid tribute to his capacity for ruin, of himself and others, in an essay called "The Passions" written while he was still at school.

> Do we not frequently behold men of the most sprightly genius, lost to society, and reduced to the level of misery and despair? Do we not frequently behold persons of the most penetrating discernment . . . blasted in the bloom of life? . . . The most charming elocution, the finest fancy, the brightest blaze of genius . . . call out for louder vengeance, and doom them to lasting infamy and shame.[8]

Like Hamilton, another small, frail boy with an unhappy childhood, Burr had also sought refuge in dreams of conquest and reveries of military fame. He enlisted early in the Revolution and had gone with Richard Montgomery and Benedict Arnold in 1775 on their doomed assault on Quebec. But he quarreled with Arnold and later with Washington, flying into a tantrum (rumor had it) when Washington found him rifling the papers on his desk. It was the beginning of a lifelong antipathy. "There is no doubt," says Davis, "that the short residence of Major Burr with General Washington laid the foundation for those prejudices which at a future day ripened into hostile feelings on both sides."[9]

Burr later joined the Secret Service, which gave him a new outlet for his passion for mystery, but left the army around 1780, pleading reasons of ill health. Hamilton among others found this questionable, writing later:

> At a critical period, he left and resigned his commission . . . and went to repose at Paramus. . . . If his health was bad, he might without difficulty have obtained a furlough . . . the circumstances excited much jealousy of his motives. . . . He was afterwards seen in his usual health.[10]

The implication was that Burr, who had written before of his "certain love of novelty," had simply gotten bored.

In 1782 Burr, whose reputation as a rake was legendary, astonished everyone by marrying Theodosia Prevost, the widow of a British officer, a bookish woman with a scarred face and little beauty, who had five children by her former marriage and was ten years older than himself.

193

But it was truly a marriage of passion and intellect, and for a time their bonds seemed close. On her part her attachment reached the level of obsession. She wrote him passionate letters when he was gone on a day's errand; she begged him to leave a route of his intended progress so that she could follow him in her imagination and think herself with him. "Love in all its sweet delirium hovers about me," she wrote on one of their short partings. "Like opium, it lulls me to soft repose. . . . surrounding objects check my visionary charms. I fly to my room and give the day to thee."[11] Perhaps this woman might have steadied him, but when she died in 1794 there were already signs of estrangement and restlessness. He turned again to his compulsive wenching, loving only their daughter, also named Theodosia, who became his confidante and one attachment, and to whom he later described the course of his *amours*. Burr had already moved his family into Richmond Hill, a pretentious mansion in New York at Greenwich Village which had been Washington's headquarters in 1776 (and was perhaps the site of their quarrel), and had begun to furnish it in an ostentatious style, going heavily into debt.

Burr had moved to New York at the end of the Revolution, entering the newly opened market for lawyers and becoming one of the profession's stars. But unlike Jay and Hamilton (or Madison and Jefferson), to whom social organization was a compelling passion, he did not go immediately into politics, preferring to hold himself cynically aloof. He took no part whatever in the debate about the Constitution, his only comment being the cryptic remark, as Hamilton recalled later, that the government was at once "too strong and too weak." When he did enter politics four years later, it was as a loner, with a cold delight in technical proficiency, and the technique of the hired gun. In a state dominated by great families, their allies and satellites, he had made himself an independent power, drawing on what his friends referred to as the young and rising, and his enemies as the facile and corrupt.

> Gradually, the young men of the town, who had nothing to hope from the ruling power, were drawn into his circle [Parton wrote]. This party was merely a personal one. Its objects were victory and glory. Consisting at first of half a dozen of Burr's personal friends, it grew in numbers with his advancement. . . . the Burrites formed a fourth party in the state, and were a recognized power in it years after the leader had vanished from the scene.[12]

As disturbing as the rootless nature of this organization was the cool precision with which Burr worked on voters. The calculation others had noted in his courtroom practice was translated here into the manipulation of the vote. In long lists of voters, meticulously detailed and carefully tended, he kept close track of his supporters, noting "not only a man's opinions . . . but his degree of zeal, his temperament, his habits," to wring the maximum amount of use from each. What made him especially dangerous was the mixture of this calculation with the mesmerizing nature of his charm. Neither too familiar nor too patronizing, he treated even the humblest of his followers with an ingratiating courtesy that completely won their hearts. Nor were these charms visible only to the female or the low. Nathaniel Hazard, a friend of Hamilton's, had written him this discerning and somewhat fearful letter in 1791:

> This Person has an Addresse not resistable by common clay; he has Penetration, Fire, Incessant Perseverance; animatedly active Execution, & could, if so unwise as to pursue so wrong a course, mar Councils & Systems, more I suspect, than any Individual I know.[13]

Burr was a challenge to more conventional politicians, who wished to control him while making use of his skills. The thought had occurred to Hamilton and was surely in the mind of Thomas Jefferson when he and Madison journeyed to New York in 1791 to join forces with Burr and Livingston to form the Republican party as a national force. Burr as a tool in the hands of Thomas Jefferson was one thing, but Burr in power, with his "little band," his ambition, his debts, his calculation, and above all his deadly and persuasive charm, was quite another—a knife pointed at the heart of the republic, glittering and deadly sharp. Jefferson, to whom it posed a personal as well as a political crisis, called it "an abysse, at which every patriot must shudder."[14] No one shuddered more than Hamilton himself.

Hamilton had known Burr since the Revolution, as a soldier, a dazzling member of New York society and an ornament of, and sometime rival at, the bar. They struck many as similar in their size, their gallantry, their ambition, and their techniques of courtroom mastery. Burr, Davis said, admired Hamilton for his rich imagination and the "poetic" nature of his mind. But if Burr looked up to Hamilton with admiration, Hamilton did not look up to him. For fifteen years he had traced the career of this small, dapper man with the piercing eyes and courtly manner with a fascination that partook of obsession and of dread. He was secretly repelled by some of Burr's private qualities, for he found his profligacy and his debts distasteful and his avarice unseemly. Burr habitually milked his clients for the highest retainers and charged the most exorbitant of fees. But it was not Burr the private but Burr the public figure that disturbed him. He thought Burr had a taste for despotism. He considered him amoral and corrupt. For years, it seemed, he had been tracking him, collecting evidence for his suspicions. Burr, while denouncing the government as "weak," had assiduously courted the lower classes, the classic move of the aspiring dictator; in 1800, when Hamilton still controlled the army, Burr had urged him to a coup d'état.

> What fixed the General in his opinion of Burr's designs [Troup recalled] was a conversation he had had with him not many months before. Burr had the affrontery to confront him in terms substantially like these: "General, you are now at the head of the Army. . . . Our Constitution is a miserable paper machine. You have it in your power to demolish it, and give us a proper one, and you owe it to your friends."[15]

When Hamilton said that he could not without violating every moral precept, Burr replied [in French] "Poh, poh, General—all things are moral to great souls." So appalled was Hamilton that he repeated this at once not only to Troup, but to Richard Harison and Nathaniel Pendleton, with further warnings to beware of Burr.

Frightened at the thought that this man might reach power, Hamilton sent a flood of letters to his friends. He differentiated here between Burr and other politicians of either creed or party who observed the rules of political morality and could be trusted to abide by them. "He has no principle, public or private," he told Gouverneur Morris, then a senator from New York,

> could be bound by no agreement—will listen to no monitor but his own ambition, and for this purpose, will use the worst part of the community as a ladder to climb to permanent power, and as an instrument to crush the better part.[16]

It was to John Rutledge, Jr., that he sent the most virulent of his assessments of what the country had to fear in Burr:

> Like Cataline, he is indefatigable in courting the young and profligate. He knows well the weak side of human nature, and takes care to play in with the passions of all with whom he has intercourse. By natural disposition the haughtiest of men, he is at the same time the most creeping to his purposes. Cold and collected by nature and habit, he never loses sight of his object, and scruples no means of accomplishing it. He is artful and intriguing to an inconceivable degree.[17]

To James Bayard, the Congressman from Delaware, whose vote in the end was to be decisive, he called Burr "more *cunning* than wise . . . more *dextrous* than *able*," adding:

> He will endeavour to disorganize both parties and to form out of them a third, composed of men fitted by their characters to be conspirators and instruments. . . . Ambition without principle was never long under the guidance of good sense.[18]

He begged Oliver Wolcott to back Jefferson, after having first wrung from him assurances on some vital points: preservation of the navy and the fiscal system, neutrality between France and Britain, and the continuance of Federalists in government offices, "except in the great departments, in which he ought to be left free."[19] He now spoke of Jefferson as a man of ability and "pretensions to character," whose radicalism had been exaggerated, sometimes by himself.

> It is not true [he told Bayard] that he is an enemy to the power of the Executive. . . . While we were in the administration together he was generally for a large construction . . . and not backward in acting upon it in cases which coincided with his views.[20]

Jefferson was, as Hamilton, gifted, moderate and incorruptible, none of which he could say of Burr.

Jefferson was to Hamilton a "trimming" politician. He cared too much for popularity; he would not push his actions beyond what he thought the public mind would bear. To Hamilton, this was a contemptible sign of moral cowardice. In reality, it was the mark of the instinctive politician, skilled at the direction of free men. By nature cautious, he lacked Hamilton's flair for suicide in public, but he too possessed a core of principle, a pattern of conscience from which he could not be swayed. Hamilton knew this, and through his letters ran a vein of grudging admiration for the man who had been his bitter enemy through most of his public life. Temperate, cautious and subtle in his movements, Jefferson stood at a point apart from the two men who were now drawn into hatred and rivalry: Hamilton, the adventurer tamed by his love for his country and order; Burr, the adventurer tamed by nothing at all. Hamilton and Jefferson were drawn together by the tenacious power of their underlying similarities: their concern for the maintenance of order and liberty, their devotion to the balance of society, their care for constitutional procedure and their insistance that the republic must survive. Hamilton's pleas did move some people. He neutralized John Marshall, the Secretary of State in the last days of the Adams administration, who was Jefferson's cousin and embittered enemy. Bayard, who remained his steady correspondent through the crisis, was chastened and disturbed. He was haunted by the fear that his words were futile, that the row with Adams had eroded much of his authority, that Adams's friends hated him and that his judgment was questioned, even by his friends. The specter of a Burr Presidency haunted him, flooding his mind with visions of chaos. He told Bayard that if Burr should be elected by the Federalist party, "I shall be forced to consider myself an *isolated man*."[21]

Meanwhile in the capital Burr's attitude had undergone a change. When the tie had first become apparent, he had written to Samuel Smith, his friend and Jefferson's, saying that he had no interest in the presidency and had come on the ticket only at the urging of Jefferson's friends. This was made public, as was intended. Even then some people were less impressed by what the letter stated than what had been left out. McHenry told a friend that Burr had not "committed himself *not* to court the office,"[22] and Bayard told Hamilton that no one considered it as closing any doors at all.

It is understood here to have proceeded either from a false

198

calculation, of the results . . . or was intended as a cover to blind his own party. By friends of Colonel Burr, it is clearly stated that he is willing to consider the Federalists as his friends, to accept the office of President as their gift. I take it for granted that Mr. B would not only accept the office, but would neglect no means in his power to secure it.[23]

Burr's tone had altered as the intrigue deepened. By the end of December, he was bristling at letters from Republicans begging him to withdraw formally, calling them "unnecessary, unreasonable and impertinent,"[24] and refusing to answer them at all. In January when Jefferson sent Smith and Colonel Matthew Hitchburn to Philadelphia to extract a commitment from him, they found him evasive. He parried their requests with badinage and insults. All they could report in the end was that Burr had told them that the House must be left to make its own decision, and that if it could not agree on Jefferson, it must of course take him. Jefferson recorded in his journal a chilling note from Hitchburn. He said that Burr had told him that the tie would not be broken until the Federalists had come over to his friends. When Hitchburn asked who in that case would be President, Burr suggested Jefferson.

In December, as the crisis started, Gouverneur Morris told Hamilton that he considered the will of the people as binding on him and was committed to accept Jefferson as their choice. This view was not shared by many of their friends. Some of Hamilton's old allies told him that they could not bring themselves to support Jefferson, that they considered as legitimate all means to keep him from power and that the prospect of sowing hatred among the Republicans by pitting their leaders against one another was altogether too delightful to be missed. There was talk that Burr, if bought by them, would reach an "understanding." There was talk of an "interim president" to fill the office until the next election, elected by a Federalist Congress and thus bypassing both Republicans. When John Marshall showed the letter Hamilton had written him to Henry Lee, Hamilton's old friend from the Revolution, Lee was unimpressed.

Accidentally calling on the S of S, he read to me yr letter [Lee wrote Hamilton]. I feel its force, but am not con-

> vinced. . . . Really, my friend, after due delibera-
> tion . . . I am decidedly convinced that our best interests
> will be jeopardized shd Mr. J succeed.

He insisted that Burr, if elected, would be forced to adopt Federalist policies. Gently, he chided Hamilton for a failure of nerve.

> We have lost the battle of Marengo, and like Melas, you are
> all for giving up. I wish to continue the action by a diversion
> in the enemy's country. Be of better chear.[25]

The anger among the Republicans had erupted into open war.

> He hates them for the precedence given his rival [Senator
> Theodore Sedgwick wrote of Burr to Hamilton]. If Burr
> should be elected by the Federalists . . . the wounds
> mutually given and received will be incurable. . . . The
> jealousy, distrust and dislike will every day more and more
> increase and widen. . . . The breach between them will be
> irreparable. Each will have committed the unpardonable
> sin.[26]

Madison referred to the plot as an attempted "usurpation," almost an act of war. In February, the Virginia legislature announced that it would not rise until after the election, presumably to call out the militia if anyone but Jefferson were named. Expresses were set up between Richmond and Washington for the duration of the crisis. When three mails passed without a message, Monroe wrote to George Mason in a frenzy, suspicious of a coup d'état. Gallatin wrote openly of a potential separation, and when rumors spread of a plan to seat a compromise President, Jefferson told Monroe, "We thought it best to declare openly . . . that the day such an act passed, the middle states would arm."[27] The threat of civil war became a prospect, frighteningly real. Bayard told his brother Andrew that if the stalemate persisted the Constitution would be put in danger, and the country might have no President at all.

Balloting began February 11, in the incompleted chamber of the House. Jefferson's friend Joseph Nicholson, ill with fever, was carried through the snow to ballot and lay in the anteroom bundled on a cot. James Bayard, wrapped in his cloak against the chill of the chamber, scribbled notes from the gallery home:

to Allan MacLane, February 12, ½ past 12, night: The House is in session, and engaged in balloting. . . . 19 times the ballots have been given in, and produced the same result—8 votes for Jefferson, 6 for Burr, and two divided. How or when the affair will end, we know not.[28]

to Andrew Bayard, 12 February, 1 o'clock: Nineteen times the votes have been given in, and the result is still the same. . . . There is a resolution of the House not to adjurn until an election. . . . As to what is to happen, we are all ignorant.[29]

to Andrew Bayard, Friday, February 13: . . . in the course of the day and night . . . we balloted 27 times . . . the result has always been the same. . . . The next ballot will be taken tomorrow at 12 . . . I can say nothing as to the event.[30]

In the end it was Bayard himself who broke the deadlock, casting a blank ballot on the sixth day, thus allowing Jefferson to win. As he later told Hamilton, he had been convinced at last that Burr could not be trusted, and that if the impasse continued the Constitution would dissolve. With the agreement of three other friends in Congress, he approached a friend of Jefferson's, who agreed on his behalf not to gut the navy or the financial system, and to leave some minor Federal officials in their place. This in fact was Hamilton's suggestion. How far he had swayed Bayard is unknown.

Your views in relation to the election differed very little from mine [Bayard wrote Hamilton later], but I was obliged to yield to a torrent, which I perceived could be diverted, but could not be opposed. . . . You cannot well imagine the clamour and invective to which I was subjected for some days.[31]

He reported that the mood in Washington, from exhaustion or from anticlimax, was now calm. More ominously, he reported that the New England states remained in bitter opposition, excoriating him violently and swearing that they would never accept the Jefferson regime.

* * *

201

Thomas Jefferson was inaugurated as third president on March 4, 1801. John Adams was not present. He had left Washington at four in the morning, having signed in the night a series of appointments bequeathing to Jefferson a Federalist judiciary, including his cousin, the hated John Marshall, as Chief Justice of the United States. Hamilton's prediction—that Jefferson would indeed prove moderate—was borne out in the first minutes of his speech. Those who could hear him, for the President spoke in his customary mumble and was inaudible beyond the first few rows, knew from his words, "We are all federalists, we are all republicans,"[32] that he was calling a halt to the brutal first decade of American politics and holding his hand out to his rivals for a truce. His feelings as he contemplated the figure of Aaron Burr, standing beside him as Vice-President, were not immediately expressed.

Bayard, who stayed on to see the spectacle, told Hamilton that he found the speech "better than *we* expected, and not answerable to the expectations of the partisans on either side."[33] George Cabot wrote to Rufus King that "hopes are entertained now which could not have been expected if his speech had partaken of the temper of his party. . . . Mr. J's speech is better liked by our party than his own."[34]

Jefferson, who had monitored the intrigue carefully and was aware of the split within the Federalists, was exultant at the results.

> Our information from all quarters is that the whole body of feds concurred with the republicans [he told his son-in-law]. They had been made to interest themselves so warmly for the choice they had opposed, that . . . they find themselves embodied with the republicans, and their quandam leaders separated from them. . . . I verily believe they will remain embodied with us, so that this conduct of the minority has done in one week what could hardly have been effected by years of mild and impartial administration.[35]

And to James Madison he had written:

> We consider this a declaration of war on the part of this band. But their conduct appears to have brought over to us the whole body of the federalists, who . . . alarmed with the danger, . . . had been made most anxiously to wish the very administration they had most opposed, and to view it . . . as a child of their own.[36]

Jefferson's fury marked the extremists as outlaws, but beneath this lay an upheaval in the political scene. Aside from the antagonism smoldering between Jefferson and his new Vice-President, there was the hatred between Burr and Hamilton, the former having heard of Hamilton's campaign against him, and laying much of the blame for his defeat on him. There was also, as Jefferson had noted, the split in the ranks of the Federalist party—with the moderates, King, Kent, Morris, Jay and Hamilton, edging closer to the center, while the radicals, increasingly embittered, became a party of their own. Splintered and quarreling, the Federalists would soon cease to function. And Hamilton, with Washington dead and his own friends drifting into retirement, would find himself increasingly alone.

X V I

HAMILTON'S RETIREMENT was haunted by loss. Between December 1799 and April 1803 he was to lose, to death or illness, the two men who served him as fathers, the two oldest and most gifted of his children and other members of the Schuyler family whom he had come to think of as his kin. At the same time he was forced to face the growing debility of Philip Schuyler, whom he also thought of as a strong, protective father, and the deterioration of his own health. Fragile as a child and as a soldier, he now faced a state of almost constant illness which weakened him still further and drained his resilience and his will. Compounding his declining physical condition was his loss of power, itself a subtle amputation, which cut the last of his remaining ties to government and made him feel rootless and adrift. He knew this time that his career was over. There was no Washington to give him second chances, and Jefferson was far too canny to succumb to the errors by which Adams had destroyed himself. He could not console himself, as he had done four years earlier, with fantasies of resurrected power. His estrangement from government was all but complete.

He mourned this loss as one would mourn a human being, for America had been more than a nation to him, and the thought that he would play no more part in its destiny came as a devastating blow. Some consolation remained in the fact that Jefferson had quietly retained much of his financial system, giving him the hope his work would live. But in Jefferson's rise he saw the country turning to a creed for which he had no instinctive sympathy, and in which he could find no place. He felt himself isolated, estranged not only from his government, but from much of the Federalist party. He called himself "exotic" and an "alien"; he brooded that his life had been a waste.

> Mine is an odd destiny [he told Gouverneur Morris]. Perhaps no man in the United States has sacrificed or done more for the present Constitution than myself. . . . I am still laboring to prop the frail and worthless fabric. Yet I have the murmurs of its friends no less than the curses of its foes for my reward. What can I do better than withdraw from the scene? Every day proves to me more and more that this American world was not meant for me.[1]

The first of his losses was the death of George Washington on December 14, 1799. Washington was sixty-seven, but fit and vigorous, and its suddenness came as a great shock. The illness was devastating, and its course was brief. On Thursday, December 12, he had gone out in a hailstorm and returned drenched and frozen; on Friday his throat had become sore. On Saturday he had wakened before three in the morning, his throat raw and aching and so congested he could hardly breathe. "He spoke but seldom, and with great difficulty," wrote Tobias Lear, his secretary, who was present throughout the illness, "in so low and broken a voice as to be at times barely understood."[2] The disease was a virulent infection of the respiratory system, and the primitive treatment, including repeated bleedings, did nothing to halt the swelling of the membranes or the inexorable closing of his throat.

Through the illness Washington was detached and stoic, serene at the approach of death.

> He was fully impressed at the beginning of his complaint that its conclusion would be mortal [wrote his friend and physician, James Craik]. During the short period of his illness, he economized his time with the utmost serenity, and anticipated his approaching dissolution with every demonstration of that equanimity for which his whole life has been so singularly conspicuous.[3]

He ordered Martha Washington to arrange his papers and watched calmly as she burned an outdated copy of his will. When kindly doctors tried to tell him that he was not dying, he remonstrated with them gently, telling them it was a debt that he was glad to pay. At eleven in the evening the crisis came.

> He lay quietly [wrote Tobias Lear], withdrew his hand
> from mine & felt his own pulse. . . . The General's hand
> fell from his wrist. . . . Dr. Craik put his hand upon his
> eyes, and he expired without a struggle or a sigh.[4]

Hamilton had been in Philadelphia when he heard of Washington's death. Lear's letter to him of December 15 did not reach him until days after he had returned to New York.

> The very painful event which it announces, had, previous to
> the receipt of it, filled my heart with bitterness [he had
> answered]. Perhaps no man in the community has equal
> cause with myself to deplore the loss.[5]

Hamilton's bereavement was uniquely deep, for in "the best of men" (as he would later call him) he had lost not only a father—strong, protective and eternally forgiving—but the man who had stood like a rock between himself and his enemies, and the cord that connected him to American life. It was his adoption by Washington that had legitimized him in the eyes of his countrymen, neutralized much of his "exotic" quality and permitted him access to the patrimony that was the United States. It was not a loss that he could cope with easily in any of its aspects, and his first feeling was of overwhelming sadness.

"She is sensible that your loss, like hers, is irreparable,"[6] Lear had written him on behalf of Martha Washington; and he himself wrote to Charles Cotesworth Pinckney, "No friend of his has more cause to lament; on personal account, than myself. . . . My imagination is gloomy, my heart sad."[7] He sought consolation in thoughts of an afterlife, when the sorrows and inequities of this world were past.

> For great misfortunes, it is the business of reason to seek
> consolation [he told Lear in a letter]. . . . If virtue can
> secure happiness in another world, he is happy. In this the
> seal is put upon *his* glory. It is no longer in danger from the
> fickleness of fortune.[8]

He envied Washington his escape from a world he was finding increasingly hostile, capricious and unjust.

James Hamilton had also died in 1799. Precisely where and when remain unknown. This man, whom Hamilton remembered only for his charm and weakness, had written himself out of his son's life when he was still a child, and in recent years had ceased to contact him at all. Of this death Hamilton had nothing to say. The contrast between the lives of the two men who had stood to him in some degree as fathers could not have been more poignant or have started more troubling reflections in his mind. If the passing of the wastrel James Hamilton awakened feelings of resentment and pity, it was the death of Washington that had brought with it the vulnerability of the child suddenly bereaved. He now thought much of Washington's great kindness to him, telling Lear wistfully, "He was an *Aegis*, very essential to me."[9] Washington had been his bulwark, without whom a future was difficult to visualize. His shield was broken, shattered in the dust around him, and Hamilton, for the first time since he had joined the "family," was unprotected and alone.

Margarita (Peggy) Schuyler was the third of the five Schuyler sisters, a lively woman with a keen wit and acid tongue. She had never won the place in Hamilton's heart that he had given to Angelica, but he was fond of her and of her husband, a political ally for whom he had done considerable work. Their story had begun on a note of high romance and good fortune: Peggy at twenty-six had slipped from a window in the Pastures to elope with Stephen Van Rensselaer, her distant cousin, and the two settled in Albany, living in power and great wealth. But in the late 1790s their tide had begun to ebb. Peggy, who had lost her younger child in 1797, began to suffer from a draining illness, and at the end of 1800 she was close to death.

Eliza did not make the winter trip to Albany, but Hamilton, who was at the capital for the court session, saw her frequently and sent constant letters home. "Your sister Peggy has grown gradually worse, & is now in a situation that her dissolution, in the opinion of the Doctor, is not likely to be long delayed,"[10] he wrote on February 25, adding that her husband had sent messengers to bring their surviving child home. On March 9 he reported that there was but a "glimmering" of hope. Depressed and worn, he longed for home, but the dying Peggy and her distraught parents had begged him to remain.

> Who can resist these motives for continuing longer? [he asked Eliza] . . . There has been little alteration in Peggy's situation for these past four days.[11]

207

Only on March 10 was he freed from his sad vigil, when he wrote a painful letter home:

> On Saturday, my dear Eliza, your sister took leave of her sufferings and friends. . . . Viewing all that she endured for so long a time, I cannot but feel a relief. . . . Your father and mother are now calm. All is as well as it can be, except the dreadful ceremonies, which custom seems to have imposed as indispensable . . . and which at every instance open anew the closing wounds of bleeding hearts.[12]

There were other things beyond the rituals of the Dutch Reformed Church which saddened him. Peggy at forty-three was younger than himself, the mother of a small child, and her long, slow disintegration had been terrible to watch. Her death was the first crack in the fortress of the Schuyler family, that fierce and feudal enclave which had taken him into its embrace even before his marriage and sheltered him as its own. The Schuylers and Washington, linked as they were by their own bonds of affection, had been his supports through his life in America, sponsoring his work in politics, sustaining him with protection and support. One of the two had already vanished, and he was now forced to watch, with increasing horror, the dissolution of the other force begin. One by one his shelters were crumbling. Little in his world was whole.

Philip Schuyler also had been ill through the 1790s. He suffered from gout and kidney stone, which caused him pain and confined him frequently to bed. He may have imagined his own death imminent, but it was his wife, the indomitable Kitty, who died before him, succumbing in April 1803 and leaving the old man shattered and bereft.

> My trial has been severe [he wrote to Hamilton]. The Shock to me was great, and was most sensibly felt, to be thus deprived of a beloved wife, the Mother of my Children, and the soothing companion of my declining days.[13]

This time it was Eliza who went to Albany while Hamilton stayed at home to tend the children. He had tried to be stoic in her presence, but when she left, his spirits and his nerve collapsed.

> Now you are gone, and I have no effort to make to keep up your spirits, my distress on his account, and for the loss we

208

have all sustained, is very poignant. . . . God grant that
no new disaster may befal us; entreat your father to take
care of himself for our sakes, and do you take care of yourself for mine.[14]

He urged her to console her father, perhaps to distract her from her
grief.

I have anticipated with dread your interview with your
father. I hope your prudence and fortitude have been a
match for your sensibility. Remember that the main object
of the visit is to console him; that his burthen is sufficient,
and that it would be too much to have it increased. . . . I
repeat my exhortation that you will bear in mind that it is
your business to comfort, and not to distress.[15]

He tried to be stern, but the formidable Kitty, as fiery and tough as her
husband, had been a pillar of support to the entire family. His own feelings of anguish, bearing the weight of his accumulated sorrows, were now
very great. His counsel to Eliza was fatalistic and depressed.

Arm yourself with resignation. We live in a world full of
evil. In the latter period of life, when misfortunes seem to
thicken around us, . . . our duty and our peace both
require that we should accustom ourselves to meet disaster
with christian fortitude.[16]

If he had once allowed himself to think of life as generous, he did so no
longer. It had become a burden to be endured.

In 1800 Hamilton had begun the construction of a country house on a
ten-acre plot of ground in upper Manhattan, nine miles north of what
was then New York. It was called the Grange, after the ancestral home of
the Scots Hamiltons. By every standard, it was indicative of a desire to
retreat. When completed it was an imposing building, with a pond, an
icehouse and a barn. There was a dock nearby that he could use for
fishing. He would sometimes take his fowling piece and hunt for small
game in the woods. He had first seen the land in the summer of 1797,
when he and the Churches had shared a summer cottage and had fallen
in love with the river, the wooded country and the gently rolling hills. He

had begun to build it for his retirement, but as time darkened his experience it assumed a new character. It became a retreat from the failures and disappointments, with which his life increasingly was filled.

The house itself was a compact two-story mansion with a sunken subfloor for the kitchens and the storage rooms. Piazzas flanked the house on two sides from which one could sit and watch the river. The rooms facing west and east had wide views of each river, reflected in large mirrors on the walls. He took great care with the fireplaces, which he insisted must not smoke. It was at once his escape from his past and his shrine to it, for it was imbued with memory and filled with relics of his life. Visitors saw at once the huge portrait of George Washington given to him by Gilbert Stuart, with Washington's wine cooler underneath. In his garden he carefully planted thirteen gum trees, symbols of the states that had made the union in his youth.

He wrote to friends who were planters, asking their counsel and advice. He told Charles Cotesworth that he was glad to have this new bond between them as he rejoiced in anything that drew them close. He asked Pinckney to send him melon seeds and parakeets for his daughter Angelica. He asked Richard Peters for cuttings of red clover and for his advice on growing hay. He made elaborate plans to beautify his grounds with raspberry plantings in the orchard, dogwood trees in a grove at the periphery, and a flower garden—a nine-foot circle of tulips and hyacinths surrounded by wild roses, with plantings of laurel at the foot. On trips around the circuit, he bombarded Eliza with instructions on their maintenance:

> It has always appeared to me that the gound on which our orchard stands is much too moist [he wrote in October 1802]. A ditch around it would be useful, perhaps with a sunken fence as guard. . . . If you can obtain one or two more labourers, it might be adviseable to cut a ditch around the orchard. . . . you will consider this merely as a suggestion, and do what you shall think best.[17]

On October 14, 1803, there was another letter, concerning "some things necessary" he had neglected to say at home. He wanted two chimneys installed to ventilate the ice house, of which he had made drawings on the reverse side. He wanted a compost bed made for his vineyard, of black mold, three barrels of "the clay which I bought 6 barrels of," two wagon loads of "best clay," and one wagon load of dung. She must remember the piazzas should be caulked. "I hope the apple trees have been planted so as to benefit from this wet and moderate weather," he concluded. "You see that I do not forget the Grange."[18]

Dung and drains now took much of the attention he had once spent on national finance and on the organization of the state. He knew this transformation was regarded by his friends with astonishment and took some amusement in the fact that he and Jefferson—once the ardent proponent of the joys of rural living—appeared to have changed roles. It was with considerable irony that he wrote to Peters of "this new situation, for which I am as little fitted as Jefferson is to guide the helm of the United States."[19]

He was changing the whole temper of his life. He kept the house at Cedar Street, staying there for concerts or dinners, but more and more his life was lived uptown. By 1802 he was commuting almost daily, driving the eighteen-mile round in a two-wheeled carriage with a single horse. In 1803 Rufus King was writing:

> He lives wholly at his house 9 miles from town, so that on an average he must spend three hours a day going and returning . . . which he performs four or five days each week.[20]

Something powerful was pulling him, or conversely, driving him away. It was a swing from the city, with its clamor and ambition, to an interior existence that he had not lived before. He was conscious of its cause. "A disappointed politician," he told Richard Peters, "is very apt to take refuge in a garden."[21] He had used the same words, almost to the letter, in a note to Pinckney the same year. He was now in full retreat into his garden, hoping to bury there his failed ambition and the increasing sorrows of his private life. But solace as it was, it was not safety. That was one thing he could not find.

On November 23, 1801, Philip Hamilton, Hamilton's oldest child and in some ways his most cherished, was shot and killed in a duel with George Eacker, a friend of Aaron Burr. Philip was then nineteen years old. Felled on the first shot with a mortal wound in the abdomen, he was carried to the Churches' house in Greenwich Village, where he lingered into the next morning, surrounded by weeping friends and family with his anguished parents at his side. Hamilton himself was involved as

211

something more than a shadow participant, for it was his code of honor that had been on trial and it was over him that the duel had been fought.

Three days earlier, in adjoining boxes in a theater, the young men had a quarrel about politics, and Hamilton's policies in particular had been discussed. They had heckled each other through the evening and later exchanged insults in the hall. A day later Eacker had dueled with Philip's companion (neither man was injured), and when Eacker refused his second's pleas to end the quarrel, Philip had challenged him. Here his actions seemed almost suicidal: not only had he challenged a man older than himself, a crack shot and an experienced duelist over insults not applied to him directly, but he had decided also to throw away his shot. His cousin Philip Church said he had declined his first shot, as he had been the first to give an insult. Thomas Rathbone, a classmate who was later quoted extensively in the *New York Post*, said that Hamilton himself had given his son instructions "to reserve his fire until after Mr. E. had shot, and then to discharge his pistol in the air."[22]

These instructions appear objectively given: actually, Hamilton was in an agony of fear. With John Church, he had tried desperately to stop the duel. When he discovered his efforts had been futile, he collapsed.

> When he learned that accommodation was at an end, and that his son had actually gone to New Jersey [Dr. Hosack related] he was so much overcome by his anxiety that he fainted, and remained some time in my family until he was able to proceed.[23]

At the bedside he collapsed again. "The scene I was present at, when Mrs. Hamilton came in to see her son on his deathbed, and when she met her husband . . . beggars all description," wrote Robert Troup, adding that Hamilton in particular seemed overwhelmed by pain. At the funeral he nearly fainted again and had to be supported as he saw the coffin lowered into the earth. His anguish for months after continued to concern his friends.

> Young Hamilton was very promising in genius and accomplishments, and Hamilton formed high expectations of his future greatness [Robert Troup wrote to Rufus King in London]. At present Hamilton is more composed, and is

able again to attend to business, but his countenance is strongly marked with grief.[24]

Philip had died on November 24. It was not until the end of March, four months later, that Hamilton could bring himself to answer the letters of condolence that had poured in on his death. "I was waiting for a moment of greater calm, to express my sense of [your] kindness,"[25] he wrote to Benjamin Rush on March 29. On the same day he had written to John Dickinson:

Till very lately, the subject has been so extremely painful to me that I have been under a necessity of flying from it as much as possible. Time, effort, and occupation have at length restored the tranquillity of my mind.[26]

He seemed at length to take some comfort from their words of kindness—from Rush and Dickinson, who had known the Hamilton children in Philadelphia; from George Washington Parke Custis, who had been Philip's friend and schoolmate; from Rufus King and Charles Cotesworth Pinckney; and from James McHenry, who had lost a child of his own:

I lost my eldest child, a daughter, after she discovered whatever can promise to flatter parental expectations. Is there aught in the world can console for such losses? . . . I can well conceive of the distress this event has occasioned, and of the tender recollections that his memory must long continue to excite.[27]

If Hamilton felt added pain at the thought of his peripheral role in the catastrophe, he did not express it in print. What he did express was a sense of hopelessness. If he had once found solace in the thought that the dead Washington was beyond the reach of life's caprices, he found it now in the stronger thought that the dead Philip was beyond the reach of life itself. His view of life was comfortless and bleak. To John Dickinson he spoke of a world "which holds out to virtue many snares, few supports or recompenses,"[28] and in other letters his despair was more pronounced.

Why should I repine? [he asked Benjamin Rush] It was the

213

will of heaven, and he is now out of the reach of a world full of folly, full of vice, full of danger—of least value as it is most known.[29]

Grief, he said, was the diet of the living in a universe controlled by pain.

Hamilton had another reason for his desolation of which he could not bring himself to speak. His daughter Angelica, next in age to Philip and delicate in mind and body, had been shattered by the sudden, violent death of her brother and had gone hopelessly insane. Little was known outside the family of this new disaster. We know now only that this fragile, gentle and now infinitely pitiable young woman was spared the horrors of the prisonlike hospitals established then for the mentally deranged. She was kept at home through much of her young adulthood and placed later in an invalid home run by a doctor in Flushing. There she was to live to the age of seventy-three, her sweet face set in an amiable expression as she chatted happily to her dead brother or played over and over on her small piano the songs her father had taught her in her teens.

The Hamiltons confided in few about this new calamity and did not tell some of their closest friends. When James Kent visited the Grange in April 1804 and found her alone there with her father, he noted only her "uncommon simplicity," her modest deportment, her shyness and her gentle grace. He did not seem to be informed of her illness. Hamilton, who was prolix in airing his public grievances, was tongue-tied in the face of personal disaster. If Philip's death could draw forth only restrained utterance, his sister's tragedy, a living death that never healed or ended, may have been too terrible for words at all.

Hamilton in his lifetime had reconciled himself with difficulty to the idea of death in wartime, as in the case of John Laurens; or, as in the case of Washington, to the death of the aging hero, gone with years and honor to his grave. These found resonances in the classic values of his early manhood, stressing as they did the qualities of heroism, willing sacrifice and the high ideals of service to the state. But to the death of Philip and the still more senseless crippling of his sister, this creed could bring out little solace, and he began to look for comfort in another source. Into the classic values of duty, honor and heroism began to creep the Christian attributes of compassion, mercy and submission to the will of God. Having himself suffered, he sought a creed that could place his pain within a moral context and make his endurance of it a conscious act of grace. If he

214

was afflicted also with corrosive guilt—with the sense that he had been in some way responsible for his son's death and his daughter's madness—he may have also had a special need for mercy, for the forgiveness of a loving deity of his knowing and of his unwitting sins.

This second plunge into religion was altogether different from the first. The intensity, the noisy fervor, all were gone. If his religion was now more internalized, it had also changed its tone. The God of thunder of the hurricane letter had given way to a compassionate deity. Hamilton did not go to church—perhaps the Sundays in the country had some part in this—but he studied the Bible and read services aloud to his children Sunday mornings in the gardens at the Grange. He pictured Philip—and his other dead—in a "haven of repose and felicity," where their spirits were happily at rest. For himself he took refuge in the contemplation of a realm of changeless values, against which the careless fortunes of the earth were naught. "God does not judge, nor condemn like man," Benjamin Rush had written him at the time of his greatest sorrow. "There are no limits to his mercy."[30] It was the God of mercy that Hamilton now turned to and that sustained him for the remainder of his life.

This change, pervading everything, altered his entire character. He became more gentle. The nurturing, almost feminine side of his nature, so often remarked upon, came more and more to the fore. Obsessed by life's harshness, his acts of kindliness increased. James Kent noted his new demeanor in an April visit to the Grange. "He never appeared before so friendly and amiable," Kent told his wife. "I was alone, and he treated me with a minute affection that I did not suppose he knew how to bestow."[31]

His very appearance seemed to change. The double aspect of his face, in which the fierce and sensitive appeared to alternate, showed a shift in balance, with the latter gaining in ascendancy and the former losing ground. He was less interested in dominating others, and the flashing eyes gave way to a more tender expression. A pencil drawing by James Sharples about this period shows the face in profile, looking mild and gentle with signs of pain about the eyes. The stubborn jaw, the fiery pose are missing. The mouth is vulnerable, showing signs of doubt and struggle. The expression is subdued.

In the years 1800 to 1804 the entire character of Alexander Hamilton had changed. The tantrums of 1799 and 1800, when he clawed frantically at his fraying scraps of power, were unthinkable in the man, matured and chastened, who had emerged by 1803. Early in 1800, with Washington dead and his own power melting, he had written cynically to an

215

acquaintance of the troubles of existence in "*This best of all possible worlds.*"[32] But in April 1804 a very different man had written this letter to a deeply troubled correspondent whose identity is unknown:

> Arraign not the dispensations of Providence: they must be founded in wisdom and goodness; and when they do not suit us, it must be because there is a fault in ourselves that deserves chastizement; or because there is a kind intent, to correct in us some vice or failing, or because the general good requires that we should suffer partial ill. . . . It is our duty to cultivate resignation, and even humility, bearing in mind the language of the poet, "That it was pride which lost the blest abodes."[33]

It took a journey of some distance for Alexander Hamilton to write of the virtues of humility and the blessings of diminished pride. The man who had once thought that life was something to be tamed and mastered, because he had once nearly done so, now believed, when it had nearly shattered him, in the idea of the mastery of fate. He, who once saw himself as the star of his own private drama, now saw himself as a figure in a transcendent pattern whose outlines were beyond the range of his own comprehension. He saw himself as an instrument of greater forces, serving purposes beyond his own ambitions of which he was imperfectly and intermittently aware. Ironically, it was in this submission, more than in any other factor, that he prepared himself for his dramatic ending and for the final shattering close of his career.

XVII

JEFFERSON'S CLEMENCY to moderate Federalists did not extend to Aaron Burr. "We are told, and we believe, that he and Jefferson hate each other," Robert Troup told Rufus King barely one month after Jefferson's accession. "Hamilton thinks that J is too cunning to be outwitted by him."[1] Saying nothing, and writing nothing that could be called conclusive, the President began to plot first the exclusion and then the political destruction of Aaron Burr.

Patronage for New York was channeled through George Clinton, one of Burr's enemies, upon whom Jefferson showered favors and flattery. Burr's pleas for a federal job for young Matthew Davis were discounted, and the post was given to an enemy of Burr. Burr protested to Jefferson in November. After four of his letters had gone unanswered, he was referred to Jefferson's "habit" of never answering letters on policy. "You will readily conceive what scrapes one could get into by saying no, either with or without reasons, or by using a softer language, which might excite false hopes,"[2] Jefferson had told him, saying he used this "silent answer" even with his bosom friends.

In the beginning of 1802 Burr told his daughter, "My life has no variety, and of course no incident,"[3] and to his son-in-law he revealed his bitterness at his exclusion by Jefferson and his friends. "They are all very busy, quite men of business. . . . I dine with the President about once a

217

fortnight, and now and then meet the ministers in the street."[4] At the close of the first session of Congress Burr was reported to have told a member that Jefferson had not consulted him on either appointments or policy, and that "he wished that he would not." Indeed, he had no other choice.

James Cheetham was a New York printer, a friend of Jefferson, and allied to the Clinton family, De Witt and George. In April 1801, one month after the inaugural, a flood of pamphlets appeared in New York City, calling Burr a creature of intrigue and secrecy, a serpent moving through the bypaths of politics, treacherous, insidious and sly. For the first time Cheetham charged to Republicans what Jefferson believed but had never said in public: Burr's involvement in the intrigue of 1800–01 had been direct and purposeful, extending back into the campaign itself. Burr, he said,

> seems to have carried on a secret conversation with the federalists from the period of the nomination. . . . [he] entertained the hope that by able management, he might fill that office before Mr. J.[5]

In "Nine Letters: A View of the Political Conduct of Colonel Burr," he drew a picture of Burr's career that became a damning personal indictment, charging that Burr had used the party only to advance himself. "Your activity was uniformly apportioned to your selfishness," Cheetham told him. "You were never active but when you had personal favors to expect." The next year brought another onslaught, as virulent as was the first. By May 1802, Troup was telling King in London that Clinton and Jefferson "hate Burr as much as the Jacobins in France hate Bonaparte. . . . In this city, the Js and Bs are at daggers points. . . . their feuds in our late election . . . blackguarded B without reserve."[6]

In June Hamilton told King that the hatred between the President and the Vice-President exceeded that between the Federalists and the Republicans at their most intense. Troup told King that "the rancor between these parties is indescribable. . . . Burr is a gone man, and all his cunning will not save him."[7] In December he told King that Burr's power was completely broken. "He is expelled from the J party, and I believe he will never possess any material weight."[8]

Burr himself had begun to stir against his enemies. In the Senate he had opposed the Administration on a judiciary bill in which it had been

218

interested. He was heard in private to complain of the "Virginia faction," which he said mistreated him through jealousy and irritation at the independence of his mind. Restless and angry, he began to search for new allies. At a Washington's Birthday dinner in 1802 (long since known as a meeting for Federalists) he walked in unannounced among the company, asked for permission to give a toast and gave one, to their astonishment, to "the union of all honest men." The toast was taken, Robert Troup said later, "as an offer on his part to coalesce."[9]

The offer in some parts was taken up.

> Burr is trying to place himself well with us and his measures are not without some success [Gouverneur Morris wrote one month later]. His friends the Demos hate and fear him, and he knows it. He intends on making a visit to South Carolina. This will excuse him from any special steps in his own state, and leave him free to take a position according to circumstance.[10]

It was indicative of Burr's reputation that this journey, ostensibly a trip to see his daughter, was widely taken as a mission of intrigue.

"Burr is now in Savannah, doing what he can to *render Jefferson* more popular," Troup had written on June 6. "The real object of the visit is well understood."[11] Burr's debts had mounted beyond all hope of payment, his followers were restive and his future with the Republicans was gone. His only hope now lay in disruption, in forays on the fringes of the law. Such designs were not foreign to his nature, and events were soon to play into his hands.

Hamilton's accommodation to his limited universe was now all but complete. He lived in the country, he built walls and planned gardens, he walked in his orchard and took rambles with his shotgun in the woods. His closest friends also had retired—John Gay was a recluse at his house at Katonah and Rufus King would return soon from London. Gouverneur Morris was still in the Senate, but he spent much time at Morrisania, his ancestral manor in the Bronx which he had made into an elaborate estate. When they met at each other's country houses they could do little but reminisce about their days in power, or comment disapprovingly about a government which they were powerless to influence and from which they were increasingly remote.

Hamilton had long since dropped his apprehensions that Jefferson would run a radical regime. But he did agree with Robert Troup that the administration was a "little contemptible thing" of small steps and sly measures, which he considered minuscule and cramped. He called Jefferson's messages "lullabies"; he said he was not harsh enough with France. When Jefferson scotched plans for a national highway system and began to dismantle his program of internal taxes, he saw an end to his system of innovation and the beginning of a lowered threshold of national activity. He mourned the end of his idea of glory, for his country as well as for himself. But he could still respond with humor. In 1802 he told Rufus King that

> Mr. Jefferson is distressed at the codfish having latterly emigrated to the southern coast, lest the people there be tempted to catch them, and commerce, of which we have already too much, receive an accession.[12]

He assured his friend that this was not a joke.

More and more, he was withdrawing into private life. His public activities were confined to writing: he published articles (under pseudonyms), he invested in the *New York Post*, which he used sometimes as a forum for his views. Often he focused on past matters. He was concerned for his reputation in the cold eyes of history and anxious that his arguments be heard. When he did address the present, it was with moderation and a new emphasis on public trust. He supported passage of the Twelfth Amendment, which moved the election of the President to the people from the states. Apparently without result, he urged his party to cultivate popular good will. His concern for order, always prevalent, became obssessive, and he brooded on his party's tendency to seek remedies for the evils of democracy in measures more disruptive than democracy itself. "Nothing will be done," he told Bayard and Morris, "until the structure of our national edifice shall be such as naturally to control eccentric passions, and to keep in check demagogues and knaves."[13] Neither needed much instruction as to whom the prince of knaves and demagogues might be.

He plunged into his legal practice with a concentration that had been missing in his public years. Despite ill health he pushed himself to the limits of his powers, and his capacities reached astounding heights. "The man's mind . . . seems to be progressing to a greater and greater maturity," Robert Troup wrote in 1802. "His powers are now enormous. . . . The only chance we have of success is now and then when he is on the weaker side."

His approach to his cases had new depth and subtlety; he probed them for nuances he had not seen before. This was especially apparent in the last of his great cases, *Croswell* vs. *the United States*. He had been hired to defend editor Harry Croswell against charges of libeling Thomas Jefferson, but he changed his defense into an examination of the relationship between truth and morals, and an inquiry into the nature of truth itself. Law, he said, must distinguish not only between truth and falsehood, but between degrees of truth. If the truth were used to defame men for malicious purposes, it was indeed culpable; but if it were used to bring public men to account for civic actions, it was legitimate, though the degree of injury remained the same.

> I contend [he said in his summation] for the liberty of publishing the truth, from *good motives* and for *justifiable ends,* even though it reflect on government, magistrates, or private persons. . . . If it have a good intent, it ought not to be a libel, for then it is an innocent transaction. . . . It is impossible to separate a crime from the intent.[14]

Motives, not results, had become dominant in his scale of values. He had moved into a realm of shades and nuance which he would inhabit for the remainder of his life.

His mind was changing from its hard, incisive focus to one more mellow and diffuse. He thought less of power than of happiness, less of the present than of the longer range of time. James Kent recalled a visit to the Grange one stormy night in April, when the two men had been alone. Against a background of howling winds which rocked the house remorselessly, Hamilton, his mood detached and thoughtful, told Kent of a scheme he had in mind—a lengthy study of the institutions of law, religion, science and government, their nature and history, and their influence upon the freedom and the happiness of men. He planned an exhaustive study of their history and power; he wanted to know what could be done in the future to improve their effect on human life. He wanted to assign volumes to King, Kent, Jay and Morris among others. The conclusions would be written by himself.

His mood as he spoke was somber and melancholy. Kent saw him undergoing a profound change of character, the fire, audacity and contentiousness of his youth giving way to a nature more balanced and temperate, more gentle and humane. Hamilton's powers, refined by maturity, were at their height. He was then just forty-nine years old.

He remained fascinated and repelled by Burr. His perspective and maturity increased his contempt for the man whom he believed had neither, and his fears for the nation's future grew. He spoke of his friends as "polluting themselves" with Burr's company, and watched their growing dalliance with apprehension and dismay. "We think there can be no coalition with him without a desecration of all that is honorable in character," Troup told Rufus King in 1802. "If B. should be taken up by the feds and brought forward for any conspicuous office, Hamilton and many of us will secede."[15]

In August 1803 Thomas Jefferson announced the acquisition from France of the Louisiana Territory, at a price of $15 million, or four cents per acre. The United States was now a continental power, from the Atlantic Ocean to the Rocky Mountains, with the Mississippi and its ports secure. Hamilton and Morris approved it as increasing the nation's security and power, but to the ultra-Federalists, who now saw themselves isolated on the rim of what was increasingly a foreign country, it came as a devastating blow.

In the early fall, John Quincy Adams, then a senator from Massachusetts, reported that Timothy Pickering had told him that the United States was now too large and too diverse for the union to continue and that the eastern states—New England, New York and Pennsylvania—should secede from the union and form a country of their own. At the same time a chief justice of Massachusetts was rumored to have said that the Federalists in New England intended to "separate from the Union, and *shake off* the Negro states."[16] William Plumer, Pickering's friend and a senator from New Hampshire, entered in his journal:

> I hope the time is not too far distant when the people east of the North River will manage their own affairs in their own way, without being embarrassed by regulations from Virginia, and that the sound part will separate from the corrupt.[17]

Pickering himself had written King a long and vicious letter, calling Jefferson "a coward wretch" and a "Parisian revolutionary monster," and ending:

> Without a separation, can these states ever rid themselves of negro presidents and negro congresses, and regain their just

222

weight in the political balance? . . . I do not know one reflecting Nova Anglican who is not anxious for the GREAT EVENT.[18]

In discussion the confederacy had managed to extend its boundaries. Plumer told Adams they hoped to include Maryland as well. "This was the maximum. . . . New England with part of New York was the minimum. The Susquehanna, or Pennsylvania, was the middle term."[19] It had also managed to include the threat of violence. Plumer told Adams that while the east was inclined to exit peacefully, it was alert to the fact that it might face problems and was prepared to go to war. It was against this background of intrigue and menace that Pickering had written to a hostile George Cabot:

> The proposition would be welcomed in Connecticut, and can we doubt of NH? But New York must be associated, and how is her concurrence to be obtained? She must be made the center of the confederacy. . . . Who can be consulted, and who would take the lead?[20]

The Congressmen had begun to conspire in late autumn. When it was that they first consulted Aaron Burr remains unclear. He had been their guest at their soirees and dinners, where he had joined them in denouncing Jefferson. He had been increasingly splenetic in his tone. "He speaks in the most bitter terms of the Virginia faction, and of the necessity to resist it," wrote Roger Griswold, a Connecticut Congressman, "but what the ultimate objects are which he would propose I do not know."[21] What Griswold did not mention were the other meetings, at which the outlines of a deal were drawn. The Federalists and their friends were to back Burr as a candidate for governor of New York in the elections in early 1804. Burr, when elected, was to aid them in their plans.

Though this was Burr's last chance at power, he did not commit himself at once. Instead he led them on with tantalizing words. Plumer recorded the conversation at a dinner, at which plans for separation were discussed.

> The opinion was universally declared, that the US would soon form two separate and distinct governments. . . . Burr conversed very freely, and . . . the impression was . . . that he not only thought that such an event

223

would take place, but that it was necessary that it should. . . . Yet after critically analyzing his words, there was nothing in them that necessarily implied his approbation. Perhaps no man's language was so apparently explicit, and at the same time, so covert.[22]

As in 1801, he was throwing out mixed signals, encouraging sedition while technically maintaining innocence. Or perhaps, weighing his own mixed emotions, he had not made up his mind.

On January 26, Burr asked for and received an interview with Thomas Jefferson, whom he had not seen in private for some time. His behavior there was so peculiar that Jefferson recorded the entire meeting in his journal in a lengthy note. Burr, he said, had begun by saying that he had come to New York a "stranger," and that he had found the state controlled by several great families who had conspired at the start to shut him out. Since then the families had become more hostile, and Hamilton had joined them in an alliance to break the little power he had won.

He then amazed Jefferson by declaring his attachment to the President. He said he had taken the vice-presidency, which he had not wanted, from loyalty to Jefferson and a wish to further his career. "He had acceded to it with a view to promote my fame and advancement," Jefferson recorded, "and from a desire to be with me, whose company and conversation had always been fascinating to him."

Burr said next that his own feelings had been constant but that Jefferson's had not. The President's friends were using Jefferson's name to destroy him, and Burr needed a "mark of favor" from him that would let him leave in peace. Quietly, he let it be known that if Jefferson would buy him off with another office, he would leave the ticket without fuss. He wanted only, Jefferson recorded, "to declare to the world that he retired with my confidence. . . . He left the matter with me."[23]

Burr's emotions during this interview are impossible to analyze. He may have been testing Jefferson, or baiting him, or trying one desperate last effort at accord. He may also have believed in the story he told Jefferson: that he was indeed a hounded creature; that the Clintons, Schuylers and Livingstons had conspired for unknown reasons to destroy him; and that Hamilton and Jefferson, who agreed on so very little, had joined forces for malicious reasons to further his disgrace. Jefferson for his part listened with contempt and amusement, noting only that Burr had credited him with little sense and much vanity when he asked him to believe that he acted in concern for Jefferson's well-being and his pleasure in the fascination of his speech.

224

Whatever his feelings on entering the White House, Burr left it committed to the plot. It was only three days after this final rejection that Pickering told Cabot that the conspiracy now could count upon New York. Less than three weeks later, on February 18, Burr's friends in Albany, with the help of the disgruntled Federalists, nominated Burr—still the Republican Vice-President—as the Federalist candidate for governor of New York. Burr's hatred of Jefferson had matured and hardened. He was now saying openly that the North must rule Virginia or be ruled by her, and that her power must be broken at all costs.

In early March when Congress adjourned, Burr met Griswold in New York by prearrangement and the new alliance was discussed. Griswold this time was unsettled by Burr's ambition.

> His prospects must depend upon the union of the Federalists with his friends [Griswold wrote], and it is certain that his views must extend beyond the office of Governor. . . . He has the spirit of ambition and revenge to gratify, and can do but little with his "little band" alone.[24]

Precisely when Hamilton learned of the extent and nature of the conspiracy is unknown. He himself left few records, and no letter of his dealing with secession or related matters exists prior to February 12. It is largely in the records left by others, particularly the correspondence between Plumer and John Quincy Adams, that one finds with certainty that he had learned it early, and that someone, most likely the adoring Pickering, had come to him in the beginning with the proposition later made to Burr—civil and military leadership of the confederation, contingent on the securing of New York.

Adams learned in April 1804, presumably from Rufus King, of the "proposal made to Hamilton for the eventual employment of his military talents" in a projected war against the Jefferson regime. Adams was also told that the conspirators originally had "looked to him as the military leader, in the event that forcible measures should become necessary," and he was told in 1828 by William Plumer that "the plan was so far matured that proposals had been made to an individual [Hamilton] to permit himself, at the proper time, to be placed at the head of the military movements"[25] that the conspirators expected to take place. It was Major James Fairlie who much later told John Church Hamilton that before February 1804 Hamilton himself had been approached. "He said that he had been applied to in relation to that project by some persons in the

225

Eastern States," Fairlie related. To this, he said, Hamilton had responded, "I view the suggestions of such a project with horror. . . . Against such a project we old soldiers must all unite."[26]

His revulsion had been instinctive and acute. To the argument that secession alone could save the Federalists, he burst out to Robert Goodloe Harper, "I would rather see Lansing [John Lansing, his old foe of the Convention] governor, and the party broken to pieces."[27] To another friend he said later, "If this Union were to be broken, it would break my heart."[28] When he learned that Burr had been picked as his replacement, his fear and horror increased.

At Albany at the time of the nomination (preparing his defense in the Croswell trial), he broke off his work to appear one evening at a Federalist meeting for an impassioned harangue against Burr. He told all who would listen that Burr was dangerous, that his ambitions were insatiable, and that his election would lead to the dismemberment of the United States. Dining at Albany on the night of February 16 at the home of Judge John Tayler, he expressed himself in terms that were later quoted by Tayler's son-in-law, Charles Cooper, to his friend, a Mr. Brown.

> General Hamilton and Judge Kent have declared in substance that they looked upon Mr. Burr as a dangerous man, and one who ought not to be trusted with the reins of government. I could detail to you a still more despicable opinion, which General Hamilton has expressed of Mr. Burr.[29]

Desperately he flung himself into the effort to defeat the conspiracy and Burr. He resumed the flood of letters to his friends. He begged Rufus King to become a candidate. When King refused, he embraced the cause of men he had been fighting all his life. He was heartsick when George Clinton (who replaced Burr as Jefferson's Vice-President) declined renomination, for the absence of this war horse, a fixture in state politics, would make it easier for Burr to win. He embraced John Lansing, his *bête noire* of the Convention, and when Lansing withdrew to be replaced by Morgan Lewis, a protégé of the Livingstons, he worked for him instead.

When a Major Hoops, who had heard talk of secession in Philadelphia, called on Hamilton in March in New York City, he found him harried and depressed. "The idea of disunion he would not hear without impatience," Hoops reported, "and expressed his disapprobation . . . in very strong terms." As Hoops listened, he outlined his vision of a dreadful future. The union would split into two rival factions. There would be civil war. The North would win, but the results would matter little. The Constitution, and the experiment in controlled freedom, would have been destroyed. The new governments would form on "principles hostile in their nature to civil liberties," parochial, intolerant and harsh. Hoops described him as obsessed and tormented by this vision.

> The conversation lasted more than an hour, with two short interruptions. The subject had taken such fast hold of him that he could not detach himself . . . until a professional engagement called him into court.[30]

Hamilton's friends among the radicals, focusing on his ambition and his thwarted love of military glory, had miscalculated on his deeper motives and on his most compelling drives. They had not seen, or had not noticed, his dominating passion for order and his fear of disruption, breakage, separation—of divorce. They had miscalculated also on the nature of his fears. Hamilton disliked democracy because of its potential for chaos, for the threat of "passions" ungoverned and undisciplined, raging beyond control. But the hysteria of his friends was what he had feared most in the unlettered multitude; and in Burr's followers, avaricious and predatory, moved by nothing but their own ambitions, he saw selfish and designing "interest" at its worst. In their union under Aaron Burr, the prince of all disorder, he saw the realization of his deepest fears. Thomas Jefferson was his rival, against whom he held grudges, and a politician with whose ideas he disagreed. But Jefferson was neither corrupt nor radical, and he was the duly elected—and legitimate—President of the United States.

> Think not, nor let any of our friends, think of a Separation, [Gouverneur Morris had written, gently mocking his compatriots]. How I admire those wondrous Statesmen, who cry out, perish a World, to save a Principle! When the principle is, as usual, false, the maxim is perfectly sublime.[31]

To Hamilton, the union *was* the principle, beside which all other interests paled. For its sake he was willing to accept Jefferson's republic as the lesser of two evils, or even, by contrast, as a good. For the second time in three years he was prepared to stand beside his enemy, for the sake of law and order, against the desperate incursions of his friends. Gradually, under the pressure of events, he was being pushed into an acceptance of the things he had once feared in and for his country, and he was becoming in the process less foreign, less "exotic," less "alien," less strange.

> The argument showed [wrote Henry Adams] that had Hamilton survived, he would probably have separated from his New England allies, and at last, like his friends, Rufus King and Oliver Wolcott, have accepted the American world as it was.[32]

New York voted on April 25. Burr was defeated by a statewide margin of 8,690 votes. In his stronghold of New York City he clung to a plurality of 100, where four years earlier he had swept the city and the state. The immediate threat of a northern confederacy had vanished, as had Burr's political career. There remained to the plotters only the prospect of an autumn meeting in Boston. Hamilton planned to attend it, to give the plot its coup de grace. Whether the conspiracy would have had the strength to survive this debacle is unknown. Less than two months later, on June 18, Hamilton received a note from Aaron Burr calling his attention to his remarks at the Albany dinner of February 16 (printed in the *Albany Register* of April 24), and demanding satisfaction in the field.

XVIII

FROM THE BEGINNING the terms of Burr's challenge were eccentric and bizarre. By tradition a challenge involved an insult that was specific and personal, but the charge that he was "dangerous" applied to his public character, while the allegation that Hamilton had uttered comments "still more despicable" concerned insults that were unenumerated and unknown. Nothing could have been simpler than to dismiss the matter, but Hamilton, while seemingly aware of the inconsistencies, slipped almost by volition into the trap that Burr had laid.

Instead of disposing of the affair in a few terse sentences, he sent two days later a long and prolix letter that went into extraneous detail. He said he could recall the terms of his conversation at Judge Tayler's: as far as he remembered they were unexceptional, but he could not answer for the impressions they made on other people's minds. There was a long discussion of the words "still more despicable"—the variety of meanings that could be read into them; their nuances, ranging, as he said, from very light to very dark. His tone throughout was rambling and defensive. His precision and attack were gone. He closed with a phrase that seemed to put him in Burr's power. If Burr remained unsatisfied with this explanation, he would "abide the consequences" (the common euphemism for a duel) and follow the course that Burr chose to take.

Burr in his answer showed no disposition to compromise. Instead he seemed to close in for the kill. He dismissed Hamilton's protests as caviling.

> The Common Sense of Mankind affixes to the epithet adopted by Dr. Cooper the *idea* of dishonor [he insisted]. The question is not whether he has understood the meaning of the word, or used it according to syntax, or with grammatical accuracy, but whether you have authorized their application either directly, or by uttering expressions or opinions derogatory to my honor. The time "when" is within your knowledge, but in no way material to me.[1]

Hamilton could not fail to notice that Burr in passing had managed to extend the demands of his first letter. He now held Hamilton responsible not only for what Cooper might have heard from him directly, but for what Cooper might have inferred from comments made by others over a period of years. If Hamilton sensed this, it did not rouse him. He continued on his self-destructive course.

Much of what Hamilton did in the weeks following would later puzzle and confuse his friends. He was not aggressive, nor was he angry, and he showed no signs of concern for his life. William Van Ness, who acted as Burr's emissary, and Nathaniel Pendleton, who acted as Hamilton's, were struck by his passive and fatalistic manner. He told them both repeatedly that he considered himself bound by Burr's decisions, and he drifted almost dreamlike to his fate. When Van Ness brought him Burr's second letter, he read it quietly, said that he found it offensive, and that Burr, instead of clarifying matters, had made it impossible for him to respond. He said that if Burr had asked for details of the Tayler dinner, he would have given them, that he believed they would not have been found exceptionable or to have exceeded the limits of civility deemed acceptable by public men. If Burr would recast his letter, he would try to answer him. If not, there was nothing to be done.

Pendleton also noted his passivity. When Hamilton came to him on June 22 with the first news of the challenge, he had said merely that "Mr. Burr must take such steps as he might think proper,"[2] which he seemed to feel himself unable to evade. He gave Pendleton a letter to be given to Van Ness when called for and went off to spend the weekend at the Grange.

The next round of letters raised tensions to a higher pitch. The two men exchanged insults verging on the personal. Hamilton was irritated by the temper of Burr's letters, which had a tone of cold and brutal arrogance that seemed calculated to anger and provoke. The difference in their feeling was due perhaps to a difference in circumstance: Burr to Hamilton was far less menacing than he had been before April 25, and hence less interesting; and the boil of his venom had been lanced. But Burr's hatred of Hamilton, feeding on failure, had since then grown fourfold.

In the course of a conversation with Van Ness on June 22, Burr gave vent to a burden of festering resentment that his defeat in April had brought to a head. Hamilton, he claimed, had for years allowed his name to be given to the use of slanders, which he never had the grace to disavow. Burr had at the expense of his pride exercised almost supernatural forbearance, but to no avail. Hamilton had increased the volume of his attacks upon him (culminating, one imagines, in the barrage of the gubernatorial campaign). Under the weight of these assaults for which he could find no reason, Burr had been forced to conclude that Hamilton bore him a settled and implacable malevolence," that he would never cease in his campaign of slander and that Burr had no choice but to bring his grievance to the attention of the world. "He [Burr] is incapable of revenge," Van Ness quoted Burr as saying, "still less is he capable of imitating the conduct of Mr. Hamilton . . . but these things must have an end."[3]

It is quite likely that Burr did indeed believe himself a gravely injured party, that he saw nothing odd in his political activities, and thus thought Hamilton was motivated not by fear and passion, but by purposeless and malign spite. Earlier Burr told Van Ness that he had been brooding for some time upon Hamilton's insults and looked for a chance to confront him with them, but that until the discovery of the Cooper letter he had found nothing concrete enough. If Burr had made his challenge at his most aggressive, it had caught Hamilton at his most vulnerable.

Hamilton's early hot-headed aggression, which had led him in the past into challenges so easily, had been dampened down by loss and tragedy, by his newly gentle and reflective nature and by his sense of the value and fragility of life. He no longer found it easy to contemplate the thought of shedding blood. His Christianity had made further inroads into the mystique of violence. He knew the Church regarded dueling as murder, and the death of his son three years earlier had done nothing to increase his affection for a practice that many of his friends, themselves soldiers, had come to see as barbarous and cruel. He was enmeshed further in the intricacies of his emotions about Burr. He knew his remarks had been rash and violent, that Burr had just cause to feel resentment, a feeling that

231

undercut his efforts to protest his innocence, and thus to extricate himself.

Hamilton had all his life been a combination of opposites. He was rash and sensitive, excessive and rational, emotional and just. Now the two sides of his nature had caught him in a trap of his own making from which he was unable to escape. Four years earlier he might have jumped wholeheartedly into Burr's challenge; four years later he might have had the strength to call him on the inconsistencies his challenge was shot with and simply walk away. As it was, he was trapped midpoint, caught by inner conflicts that rendered him passionless and bereft of direction or will. It was into this hiatus of will that Burr had flung his challenge, and which he did not scruple to exploit.

Van Ness and Pendleton, aghast at the acceleration of the quarrel, made desperate efforts to arrest it. They composed papers they hoped would lead to a compromise solution. They tried to soften the messages they were forced to carry. On June 25 Pendleton succeeded in extracting a statement from Hamilton that was his most explicit to date: He could not imagine where Cooper could have obtained his impressions except at the Tayler dinner. While he could not recall the precise terms of his statements, he was prepared to say they were political in nature, touching neither on Burr's character nor on events occurring in the past. On the basis of this Pendleton drew up a paper that was submitted to Burr that day. Burr was to draft a letter asking Hamilton if he had *ever* impugned his honor, at Tayler's dinner or elsewhere, at any "particular instance, to be specified," that might have come to Cooper's attention. This position was delicately calibrated to fall halfway between the demands of both combatants: the charges were to remain specific, but they were now to cover a far wider range—of comments made in Albany or elsewhere, and reaching back indefinitely into the past. To such a letter, "properly adapted," Hamilton was committed to reply.

This measure, which might have proved a graceful compromise, was blown apart by Burr. On June 26 he sent Van Ness a scorching letter in which he called the proposal an insult, an evasion and a further libel on himself. He said that he alone would define the limits of the challenge and resisted all efforts to narrow or define its scope. He objected to the term "properly adapted." He would judge himself of the suitability of any measure and considered his two prior letters perfectly adapted to the purposes he had in mind. He rejected the idea of particular instances: if he named and Hamilton denied ten or twenty conversations, it would still leave room for countless other slanders that he believed Hamilton had

232

made. As Van Ness told Pendleton, the conditions had been changed. Burr was now demanding an accounting, not only for anything Cooper might have heard at Albany or elsewhere, but for *all* comments made of Burr by Hamilton, in the course of fifteen years.

> The denial of a specific conversation only would leave strong implications that on other occasions improper language had been used [Van Ness related]. No denial or declaration will be satisfactory unless it be general, so as wholly to exclude the idea that rumors derogatory to Col. Burr's honor have originated with Genl. Hamilton, or have been *fairly* inferred from anything he has said.[4]

Underlying this response was the whole train of Burr's frustrations: the failure of the scheme of 1801, the ostracism from the Republican party and the cut-off of his future there, his new alliance with the ultra-Federalists and the ruin of this latest dream. It was not the demand itself but the escalation that cast the longest shadow on Burr's motives. When it appeared that Hamilton at last was ready to answer the demand made in the initial letter, it was suddenly declared not good enough. Burr himself acknowledged this in a letter to Van Ness. "If it should be asked whether there is no alternative, most certainly there is, but more will now be expected than would have been asked at first."[5]

The jaws of the trap prepared for Hamilton had now snapped shut. He was cornered, both by Burr's orchestrations and by his own ambivalence. The outlines of the snare he had been caught in were described with great perception by John Quincy Adams after the correspondence between Burr and Hamilton was made public on July 22:

> Mr. Burr began by making a demand of Genl. Hamilton which he must have known that Hamilton could not, and ought not to answer. To make the matter more sure, he couched the demand in terms which a much colder man than Hamilton must have spurned. The substance was so vague and so indefinite as to render impossible the very avowal or disavowal it affected to require. The form was studied to provoke and insult, by an assumption of superiority which a man of spirit could not submit to. Hamilton saw through this artifice, but had not a sufficient elevation over the prejudices of the world to parry it. Had he omitted

233

half a line in his first answer, which must be considered as inviting a challenge, I can see nothing in his part of the correspondence against which any reasonable objection can be raised.[6]

Hamilton was trapped completely. Having seen the snare from the beginning but choosing to play with it, he could not now extricate himself. He could do no more than protest, albeit bitterly. Through Pendleton he told Van Ness that the "expectations now disclosed . . . appear to him to have greatly changed and extended the original ground of the inquiry," making it a "general and abstract inquiry, embracing a period too long for any accurate recollection," and concerning rumors, many of which he had not originated, and some of which he had not even heard. "Frequent allusions have been made to slanders said to be in circulation," he told Pendleton bitterly. "Whether openly or in whispers, they have a form and shape, and might be specified." He was still prepared to answer queries as to specific conversations, but not to rumors, which remained of necessity shadowy, elusive and unknown. He was sorry, he said, to find "nothing short of predetermined hostility"[7] on the part of Colonel Burr.

He ordered Pendleton to meet Van Ness to make arrangements, with the reservation that the welfare of his clients be considered first.

> I should not think it right in the midst of a circuit Court to withdraw my services from those who might have confided important interests to me and expose them to the embarrassment of seeking other counsel who may not have time to be sufficiently instructed. . . . I shall also want a little time to make some arrangements concerning my own affairs.[8]

Depressed at their mission, Van Ness and Pendleton held gloomy meetings through the ensuing week. On Friday, July 6, the circuit ended, and Pendleton informed Van Ness that Hamilton would be ready at any time after Sunday, July 8. The meeting was set for Weehawken, New Jersey—the spot where Philip Hamilton had fallen—on the morning of Wednesday, July 11. On July 10 they drew up their final list.

> 1. The parties shall leave town tomorrow morning about five o'clock, and meet at the place agreed on. The party arriving first shall wait for the other.

2. The weapons shall be pistols not exceeding Eleven inches in the barrel. The distance ten paces.
3. The Choice of positions to be determined by lot.
4. The parties having taken their positions one of the seconds to be determined by lot . . . shall loudly and distinctly give the word "present"—if one of the parties fires and the other hath not fired, the opposite second shall say "one, two, three, fire," and he shall then fire or lose his shot. A snap or flash is a fire.[9]

The psychological dimension of Hamilton's decision has been regarded as extraordinary by men of his own and of a later day. Henry Adams, writing almost a century later, called it a form of suicide. Oliver Wolcott, writing the day after the duel, called it the "derangement of a great mind," referring also to "particular reasons, which rendered it proper for *him* to expose himself to Col. Burr."[10]

Hamilton's decision had been doubly appalling. Not only had he been drawn into a duel he had every reason for refusing, but he had decided not to shoot at Burr.

I have resolved [he wrote the week following the decision] to reserve and throw away my first fire, and I have thoughts even of reserving my second fire—and thus giving a double opportunity to Col. Burr to pause and to reflect.[11]

When he told this to Rufus King, the one man besides Pendleton in whom he had confided, King was horrified. He begged him to drop the challenge, and if he would not, to fire, as he owed it to his family and to himself. Profoundly anguished, King approached their mutual friend Matthew Clarkson to see if intervention would be possible; sadly he was told that it would not. Clarkson too was appalled at Hamilton's decision, as was Pendleton himself. "I very well remember," King recalled, "that he entirely agreed with me of the General's decision to receive the fire of his enemy, and throw away his own." King told Hamilton loudly of his own convictions: that dueling was a poor proof of courage and a sin against Man's duty to his country and to God. Hamilton had not changed his mind.

With a mind the most capacious and discriminating that ever I knew [King wrote later] he had laid down for the govt, of himself certain rules on the subject of duelling, the

235

fallacy of which could not fail to be seen by any man of ordinary understanding. With these guides it is my deliberate opinion that he could not have avoided a meeting with Col. Burr.[12]

Some of the motives pushing him to Weehawken were detailed in a paper written by Hamilton himself. In it he said that he was conscious that he had injured Burr over many years in ways that he could not remember; that he could not deny these words because they had indeed been given; that neither could he retract them, because he believed them to be true.

> It was, as I conceive, impossible for me to avoid it [he wrote of the duel]. There were *intrinsick* difficulties and *artificial* embarrassments from the manner of proceeding. . . . Intrinsick—because it is not to be denied that my animadversions on the political principles, character, and views of Col. Burr have been extremely severe. . . . In proportion as these impressions were entertained with sincerity, and for purposes which might appear to me commendable . . . would be the difficulty of explanation or apology. . . . The disavowal . . . was out of my power, if it had really been proper for me to submit to be questioned; but I was sincerely of opinion that this could not be.

Dispassionately, he tried to put himself in Burr's position:

> He doubtless had heard animadversions of mine which bore very hard upon him, and it is possible that as usual they were accompanied by falsehoods. He may have supposed himself under a necessity of acting as he has done.

There was an admission of potential culpability: "It is possible that I may have injured Col. Burr." There was an apology that was at once an explanation of his motives and an expression of his guilt:

> I trust . . . I have not answered him on light grounds, or from unworthy inducements. I certainly have had strong reasons for what I may have said, though it is possible that in some particulars I may have been influenced by miscon-

struction. . . . It is also my ardent wish that I have been more mistaken than I think I have been, and that he by his future conduct may shew himself worthy of all confidence and esteem, and prove an ornament and blessing to his country.[13]

Hamilton had been immobilized from the beginning by his ambivalence. In his heart he had judged himself guilty as charged of attacks upon his rival, a fit object for his jealousy and rage. As his son had withheld his first fire because he had first injured Eacker, Hamilton would withhold his, because he had first insulted Burr.

There were other things that acted in concert to abort all efforts to escape. He was afraid that he would be thought a coward if it were known he had refused a challenge. It would have reflected badly on his private honor and his chance, if he still had one, to regain a place in public life. He did not think other men would follow one who had refused to face another's fire, and his claim to be a leader would be gone. He did not mention a reason that was still more potent: the damage it would do his inner vision of himself. He could not live without the image of himself as a hero, which a refusal would irrevocably destroy. If he had begun to believe with Pinckney, King and others that dueling was a barbaric relic of a more vicious era, he did not yet have, as Adams said, the courage to parry the convictions of his time. "If we were truly brave, we would not accept a Challenge,"[14] Clarkson told Gouverneur Morris at Hamilton's deathbed, with tears rolling down his cheeks. Ironically, the charge of cowardice was the one thing Hamilton was not brave enough to face.

There was a final reason for Hamilton's decision, which overshadowed all the rest. He had begun to realize that if he were killed or wounded by Burr's bullet, it would end, forever and decisively, the alliance of Burr with the ultra-Federalists that had twice since 1800 brought the country to the edge of ruin. He knew that if he could not sway men like Pickering by reason, he could move them in another way. Whatever the state of their own desperation, men who had called him friend could not clasp hands with his assailant over his wounded body or his corpse. The political blow dealt Burr would then be mortal. Exiled from Jefferson's party since the intrigue of 1801, estranged from all potential allies, he would be stranded with his "little band" alone. That this did not also occur to Burr is a measure of his opacity, that peculiar lack of some varieties of comprehension that was to compromise all his other talents and doom him to an outlaw role.

With this realization Hamilton's decision, born at first of his guilt and of his fear for his reputation, assumes a profoundly moral cast. By the duel and his death in it, he would strike a mortal blow against his enemy, and at the specter of secession that threatened the United States. He could fulfill at the same time the fantasy he had always treasured: of himself as a hero, giving his life for a cause of transcendent value, that he loved better than himself. Since Washington's death he had lived in a wilderness, exiled from his government and mourning a lost influence he could not recapture. By his death, begun by Burr's malice, but now controlled and orchestrated by his own direction, he could regain the power he could never claim while living, crush his enemy, save his country and make his death, as he had always wished it, a historic and a truly moral act.

With the duel and his course determined, Hamilton's mood appeared to change. The indecision and the drift were gone. He was no longer the tool of Burr's contriving, but the architect of his own fate. By the decision to appear but not to fire, he had taken his destiny back into his hands. He was composed and even tranquil and went about his business with a serene composure that would later be the wonder of his friends. The burden of the past seemed to slip from him; friends thought him happier than he had been for years. They did not know that it was the detached serenity of a man who had put his life behind him. After years of frustration he had seized his fate and constructed his own pattern, by which he would consciously arrive at his own ends.

While Hamilton was composed and almost happy, Burr seemed somber and subdued. John Trumbull saw them both at a Fourth of July dinner, Burr sitting by himself, dour and silent, while Hamilton chattered with an almost manic gaiety and sang old military songs. Three days before on July 1 Burr had written to his daughter that he had shivered with the cold all day. "I have just now, at sunset, had a fire in my library. Let us . . . drop the subject, lest it lead to another, on which I have imposed silence on myself."[15]

The last days passed calmly. Hamilton's mood was tranquil, almost conspicuously benign. Saturday he entertained Trumbull and William Smith (John Adams's son-in-law) and their families at the Grange. They wandered in the garden with their children, lost in the beauty of the summer day. Only briefly did the conversation turn on politics. He begged his guests, who were going to Massachusetts, to kill the ghost of the secession scheme. "Tell them . . . for God's sake, to cease these threatenings about the dissolution of the Union. It must be made to hang together as long as it can."[16] Early on Sunday he walked with Eliza in the garden and returned to read the morning service to his children, gathered about him in the grass. It was a day of quiet and domestic pleasures. In the evening the family walked out again in the lawn and garden, lying on the grass together as the summer stars appeared.

On Monday morning he returned to New York. In his office he made up his will. He compiled a list of debts owing to him, which amounted to $2,150. He named John Church, Nicholas Fish and Pendleton as his executors, empowered to sell his properties with the consent of his heirs to apply to the discharge of his debts. These debts he urged his children when they reached maturity to pay.

> I pray God that something may remain for the maintenance and education of my children. . . . But should the contrary happen . . . I entreat my Dear Children, if they or any of them shall ever be able to make up the deficiency, I without hesitation commit to their delicacy a wish that is dedicated by my own.[17]

That done, he went to visit Oliver Wolcott. "He spent the afternoon and evening of Monday with our friends at my house," Wolcott wrote later. "He was uncommonly cheerful and gay. The duel had been determined on for ten days."[18]

Tuesday morning he appeared at his office and finished a complex piece of legal work.

> The last thing he did in his office he did at my desk and by my side [his clerk Judah Hammond recorded]. He came to my desk in the tranquil manner usual with him, and gave me a business paper with his instructions. I saw no change in his appearance.[19]

In the afternoon he called on Robert Troup, who had been confined to his quarters by illness. He stayed some time and was relaxed and cheerful, concentrating on the condition of his friend. Solicitously, he inquired after the details of the illness, and prescribed a course of treatment. Troup noticed nothing but his composure and cheerfulness. There was no shadow of the calamity ahead.

He returned to his house at Cedar Street about six o'clock. The older children, who had come to the city with him, noticed no symptoms of distress. They did not consider it unusual that he spent much of the evening in his study, writing by himself. He wrote another statement of his debts and assets, including a guilt-filled explanation of his reasons for having built the Grange, an enterprise, he now realized, that would leave his family in debt. In a gesture of regret and of gratitude, he asked his wife to look after a cousin, Ann Mitchell, now living in New Jersey, who had done him kindnesses when young. In what was his last public action he wrote to Theodore Sedgwick, echoing his pleas to Smith and Trumbull, begging that the secession move be stopped. Sometime in the night he came into bed with one of the older children and had a few hours of a restless sleep. Before this there had been a final declaration, dated "Tuesday Evening, 10 O Clock," directed to his wife.

> The Scruples of a Christian have determined me to expose my life to any extent rather than subject myself to the guilt of taking the life of another. This must increase my hazards, and redoubles my pangs for you. But you had rather I should die innocent than live guilty. Heaven can preserve me, and I humbly hope will, but in the contrary event I charge you to remember that you are a Christian. God's will be done! The will of a merciful God must be good.[20]

It was seven in the morning when Hamilton's boat, bearing Pendleton and David Hosack, docked below the heights of Weehawken across the Hudson River from New York. There was a short walk through the woods of about twenty feet to where a ledge formed a shelf above the river, like a small stage on a theatre, looking south and east to the river and the sea. Van Ness and Burr were there before them. They had shed their coats in the warm morning sunshine and had begun to clear away small trees and brush. Minutes later Hamilton and Burr were placed facing each other at a distance of ten paces, Hamilton by choice (for he had won the lottery) facing southeast, an unfavorable position, for it looked into the morning sun. Hamilton raised his pistol once, then lowered it. He reached into his pocket and put his reading glasses on. He said he did not wish to have the hair trigger on his pistol set. Pendleton gave the word "present," and they seemed to their seconds to have fired instantaneously. Burr's bullet struck Hamilton in the right side of the abdomen. He spun a little, rose on his toes and fell. His own bullet was later found to have passed through the limb of a cedar tree, four feet to the right of where Burr was standing, and about twelve feet from the ground.

Hosack, running to him, found him on the ground, half-sitting in Pendleton's arms. He looked at Hosack, said, "This is a mortal wound, doctor," and fell into a faint. His pulse was still and his breathing inaudible; the doctor at that moment thought him dead. "We lifted him up and carried him out of the wood to the margin of the bank," Hosack wrote later. "During this time I could not discover the least symptom of returning life." Fifty yards from shore, as Hosack applied stimulants, he began to breathe feebly. He sighed, opened his eyes, which wandered unfocused, and said, "My vision is indistinct." His pulse then became stronger, his breathing more regular; his eyes focused and his sight returned. Hosack, in an effort to search for bleeding, pressed lightly on his abdomen, but stopped when he moaned in pain. Seeing his pistol lying at the bottom of the boat, he said, "Take care of that pistol. It is undischarged and still cocked; it may go off and do harm."[21] He asked Hosack about his pulse rate and said he had no feeling in his legs. Hosack moved them and found them flaccid. In fact the bullet had lodged against his second lumbar vertebra and he was paralyzed below the hips. Near the shore he asked that Eliza be sent for, but that the news be broken slowly, to spare her sudden shock. Otherwise he said very little. His eyes had closed and he lay as if sleeping, lulled by the gentle motion of the boat.

William Bayard had been waiting on the opposite shore of the Hudson. When he saw the boat approach with only two men visible, he began to wring his hands. When he saw Hamilton lying almost lifeless, he burst into a flood of tears. Gently the three men carried him into Bayard's house, but the slightest movement caused him agonies, and he fainted once again from pain. He was fed a mixture of wine and water. When he revived, he complained of pain in his lower back.

> We undressed him, laid him in bed, and darkened the room [Hosack recorded later]. I gave him a large anodyne, which I frequently repeated. During the first day he took upwards of an ounce of laudenum; and tepid fomentations were also applied to these parts nearest the seat of the pain. Yet were his sufferings, during the whole of the day, almost intolerable. I had not the shadow of a hope.

Hosack sent at once for Wright Post, a physician attached to Columbia, who confirmed his melancholy forecast. They applied also to Antoine-Venance Gabriel Rey, the French consul, to consult surgeons from French ships in the harbor, whose experience of bullet wounds was great. Fearing to disturb his patient, Hosack described the wound and symptoms to the surgeons in an outer room.

> One of the gentlemen then accompanied me to the bedside.
> The result was a confirmation of the opinion that had
> already been expressed by Dr. Post and myself.[22]

Bayard's house had filled with people. Some had been called for, others had come of their own volition, having heard the news gasped out in the street. Eliza arrived around noon. She was told at first that he was suffering from "spasms" for fear her nerves would utterly give way. Among the crowd, shock, grief and horror were mingled now with fury, much of it at Hamilton himself.

There is no mistaking the rage in this letter of Oliver Wolcott, who had hurried to Bayard's from his office at his bank:

> He has left his family in perfect health, as if proceeding on
> ordinary business, and with the same deliberation, has
> received a mortal wound.

The defence of all this," he told his wife angrily, "is that there was a chance for an escape, and that it would be wrong to torture his family"[23] with fears of an encounter that might not take place. He described the family as "agonized beyond description," and the company as utterly distraught. Hamilton himself remained controlled and lucid, trying to comfort his distracted wife. At one point he asked for and received—with some difficulty, for the Church condemned dueling—the last rites of the Episcopal Church. The thought of his children alone retained the power to shatter him. At the sight of seven of them gathered at his bedside, his voice forsook him. He opened his eyes, gave them one look, and closed them until the children were taken away. As night fell the mourners continued in their vigil, some napping upon chairs or sofas, others drifting outside to lie down on the lawn.

In the night he had slept fitfully. He awakened weaker, though in less pain. His debility now was mercifully numbing. His nerves were losing sensibility as his body had begun to die. When Gouverneur Morris arrived in the late morning, Hamilton was already beyond speech. Morris found the sight unbearable and was forced to go outside. "The Scene is too powerful for me, so that I am obliged to walk in the Garden to take a

242

Breath," he wrote in his diary. "His wife almost frantic . . . every person present deeply afflicted . . . their children in tears."[24] Composed, he returned to sit by the bedside. Hamilton lived a few more hours, slipping in and out of consciousness. At two o'clock he died.

The autopsy, performed almost immediately, showed the extent and nature of his wounds. The bullet had fractured the first and second false ribs, passed through the diaphragm and liver and lodged in the first or second lumbar vertebrae in the lower quarter of the spine. The vertebrae were splintered so badly that the surgeons could feel the slivers with their hands. The blood vessels in the lower portion of the liver had been torn open. The abdominal cavity was filled with about a pint of clotted blood.

Hamilton's body was taken to the Churches' house that night. Immediately on his death, church bells began to ring throughout the city. Stricken people met to whisper in the streets. Morris, leaving Bayard's house that evening, found the city in a state of shock and agitation; every face he passed was grim. Indeed "agitation" was a mild word for the temper of the city: Hamilton's friends were now gravely worried by the threat of mob violence against Burr. Morris, who had been asked that night to give the funeral oration, made a conscious decision to temper the emotion in his speech. "This indignation amounts almost to a Frenzy already," he wrote in his diary. "How easy it would have been to make them for a moment absolutely mad!"[25]

Arrangements for the funeral were taken out of the hands of the family by officials of the city, who had held anguished meetings as Hamilton lay dying Wednesday night. Citizens were asked to suspend business on Saturday, July 14, the day set for the funeral, and asked to wear black bands of mourning for the succeeding thirty days. Church bells were to be rung, muffled; ships in the harbor were to lower their colors and fire minute guns. Salutes were to be fired by companies of artillery parading in Battery Park. There was to be a vast funeral procession suitable for a great state personage, embracing all the professions and men from every form of public life—the governor and mayor, Congressmen and civil officers, foreign consuls and ambassadors, military and naval officers, bankers and clerics, doctors and lawyers, merchants and students of the bar. Hamilton's coffin was to bear his sword and his general's hat. His gray horse, dressed in mourning, with his boots reversed in the stirrups, was to follow

243

close behind. Of necessity, the arrangements had to be made quickly. It was high summer, and the corpse was beginning to decay.

Tributes from around the world began to arrive immediately, as they would flow in through the succeeding year. "We wept as the Romans did over the ashes of Germanicus," wrote Fisher Ames from Boston, "a thoughtful, brooding sorrow, that takes possession of the heart."[26] Lafayette wrote to Angelica of his sorrow in

> the loss of my beloved friend, in whose brotherly affection I felt equally proud and happy, and whose lamentable fate has rent my heart as his own noble soul would have mourned for me.[27]

But beneath these tributes ran a strain of shock and horror: the feeling that Hamilton had connived and conspired in his death. The sense of mystery remains. Alexander Hamilton, whose birth had been a source of lifelong whispers, had arrived at no ordinary death.

The funeral was held on Saturday, July 14. The procession, which was to leave the Churches' house at ten in the morning, was delayed two hours and did not depart till noon. Then it took two more hours for the train to move through the winding streets of lower Manhattan to the interment at Trinity Church. The streets were packed with people, many of them weeping. Spectators were crowded on the roofs of buildings. Some were seen clinging to the tops of trees. Gouverneur Morris delivered the eulogy, speaking from a specially constructed platform with Hamilton's sons (except for the baby, Philip), sitting at his feet. He was nervous and unsettled, and his voice did not reach beyond the first few rows. The coffin was then moved several yards to a plot at the southern border of the graveyard and lowered into the ground. Alexander Hamilton, the bastard and alien, was home in American earth.

X I X

THROUGH THE REST of 1804 and into the year after, Hamilton's friends raised money to settle what remained of his estate. Since 1800 the Grange had absorbed much of his income, and his western lands, bought largely in the 1780s, had not increased in value and would bring in little cash when sold.

> It appears that his property consists altogether of new lands situate in the western part of New York, and of a house nine miles from the city [King told George Cabot in October]. The General's debts amount to fifty-five thousand, and as the estate is unproductive, and the debts bear interest, it is the opinion of judicious persons that with the most prudent management, the estate will be barely sufficient to pay the debts.[1]

The legendary wealth of Philip Schuyler had proved to be exaggerated, for his estate was tied up in property and he had little cash on hand. But friends in Boston conveyed a gift of lands in Pennsylvania, and King, with John Church and Oliver Wolcott, raised a subscription among friends in New York City which had amassed $80,000 by 1805. These funds were used to buy the Grange at auction and present it to Hamilton's widow, who lived there with her younger children through 1813.

Eliza later received some income from lands deeded to her by her father, and in 1837, through a special act of Congress she received over $30,000 in back pay due her as the widow of an army officer, which Hamilton had waived. This would help to make her old age comfortable, but in the grim years following the duel the family was sustained almost entirely on the monies given by their friends. These people were alive to the irony that the man who had saved the finances of the nation had left his family in a state of financial shipwreck from which it required rescue by his friends.

> To the sorrow that every virtuous man has felt for this distinguished patriot [King wrote] it is painful to add the reflection that this young and helpless family must depend for their support, not on the earnings of their father . . . but upon the contributions of a few individuals, who admired his unequalled worth.[2]

Robert Troup's ironic comment, that Hamilton's friends would have to pay to bury him, at last came sadly true.

For a time there were plans to send Alexander to Boston for an apprenticeship in a prospective mercantile career. Hamilton's friends in Boston had made plans for his welfare, but at the last moment Eliza changed her mind. "Do I not owe it to the memory of my beloved husband to keep his children together?" she wrote Nathaniel Pendleton from Albany on September 29, 1804. "It was a plan he made in the last arrangement of the family that they should not be without a parent's care at all times."[3] She kept them together, and they remained, like the Schuylers, a close-knit and loyal unit up to and beyond her death. Alexander did not become a merchant, but a lawyer, as did three of his brothers including the second Philip, who inherited his father's streak of charity and was known as "the lawyer of the poor." The boys also shared their father's martial temperament. All served in the War of 1812. James Alexander offered to lead a Negro regiment and volunteered for the Union Army in 1861. John Church, who wrote his father's first biography, appears to have been the most docile of the children. Veins of irony surfaced in the lives of the other sons. James Alexander became a Democrat, a friend and follower of Martin Van Buren and Andrew Jackson, and served briefly in Jackson's administration as acting Secretary of

State. Alexander represented Eliza Jumel in her suit for divorce against her second husband, Aaron Burr. William Stephen inherited the fatal weakness of his father's family: as weak, as charming and as undisciplined as Hamilton's father and his older brother, he drifted west into the frontier country of Ohio and Wisconsin, found his way to Sacramento by the time of the gold rush, and died there in 1850. The tainted blood Hamilton had spent a lifetime denying surfaced in this son. Of them all, none matched their father's brilliance, or the vitality and color of their mother's Schuyler kin. It is true that death and madness may have taken off the two most promising, but there was a noticeable diminution of talent. One wonders if the repeated shocks of their childhood had some part in this process of decline.

Eliza's sorrows were not ended with her husband's death. By October Philip Schuyler too was dead, removing in four months and almost in one stroke of fortune the two men to whom she was the closest, and on whom she had consistently relied.

> Hers was a stern ordeal [wrote James McHenry]. Within a few years, she experienced the shock of two violent deaths by duels—those of her eldest son and husband, the death of her sister, mother, and father, and her eldest daughter's insanity, and with this little or no means with which to support and educate her family. . . . No wonder the light of youth had vanished from her face when the widow's cap replaced the Marie Antoinette coiffeur.[4]

But if Eliza went through her own dark crisis, it did not break her. The intense vitality that had first drawn Hamilton to her pulled her through the first days of her terrible bereavement and sustained her into vigorous old age.

The trauma of the years 1801–1804 continued to dominate her life. She could not recover from the loss of her husband and the two oldest of her children, and their absence dictated the direction of her days. She became the relentless patron of the orphaned and the weak. She founded orphans' homes in New York and Washington and gave them money she could ill afford to part with. She dunned her friends relentlessly for funds. "Her engagements as a principal of the Widows' Society and the Orphan Asylum were incessant," wrote James Alexander. "In support of these institutions she was constantly employed."[5] It was not unknown for her to take children off the streets who had been orphaned by fire or accident, send them with her card to the asylum and supervise their education and careers. "Her grief over the two children she had lost took the form of protection over those who were poor and unfriended, as well as orphaned,"[6] wrote James McHenry, tracing her quality of extreme solicitude to the tragedies that she had suffered with her oldest daughter and her first-born son. But it may also have involved the memory of her husband, of the stories he had told her of his desperate childhood, of her sense that without the care of others he never might have come to her at all.

Alexander Hamilton remained her passion, in death as in his life. She could not, or she would not, let him go. She wanted no one to forget that she had been married to a hero, a man who had helped to found, and then secure, a nation, and who had left his giant imprint upon every aspect of its life. In his life she had been his protector; in his death she did not cease.

> She was devoted [wrote her grandson] not only to her numerous charities, but to her ceaseless and vigilant efforts that her husband should receive full justice, that his memory should be vindicated, that his manuscripts should be published. . . . From the moment of his death almost to her own, Mrs. Hamilton was constantly engaged in writing to leading Federalists all over the country, and making inquiries. . . . Besides corresponding, she made long journeys to carry out her quest, with more or less success.[7]

Two of her candidates for the role of first biographer were disappointments. Judge Kent declined the project, and Timothy Pickering, who accepted in 1828, died in the next year. As the nineteenth century wore on, she began to worry as death claimed increasing numbers of Hamilton's associates and their score of memories were lost.

"I have my fears I shall not obtain my object," she wrote her daughter Eliza in 1832, when she was seventy-five. "Most of the contemporaries of your father have also passed away."[8] But she attained triumph in the decade after, when she bullied her son John Church into beginning the first of the eight massive volumes he would write about his father, and Congress purchased the collection of Hamilton's papers in 1846. She was then eighty-nine years old.

In her later years, she was perhaps as happy as she had been since she became his bride. She lived in Washington with her daughter Eliza and her family; she interested herself in politics and in her incessant social work. She became friends with Dolley Madison, the widow of her husband's friend-turned-enemy, and the one-time romance of Aaron Burr. The two old women, frail and lucid, became doyennes of social life. In extreme old age she acquired fragile dignity, time refining the almost Indian cast of her high cheekbones and accenting the beauty of her large dark eyes. Her vitality remained astonishing. At ninety-five she would walk three miles from her daughter's house on H Street to visit her friend Judge Cranch on Capitol Hill, stopping en route to visit schools and orphans' homes.

In 1837 at the age of eighty she went to Wisconsin to visit her son William, undeterred by crude roads and rough river voyages, sending letters home of the strange new western cities, of the Ohio River with its clay-filled waters, and Pittsburgh, a grim industrial city, "gloomy from the use of coal." Everywhere she was received with ceremony and reverence; it would have pleased her to know that her visit was referred to in Wisconsin histories as the state's "first great social event." There she played backgammon with her hostess, and troubled her with her habit of extended strolls. "Every morning before breakfast she would take, unattended, a long walk in search of wild flowers," her hostess recalled. When she objected, "the amiable old lady would shake her head, and say 'I must take my morning walk.' "[9]

Home in Washington, she continued her routine. She was dined at the White House as the guest of seven Presidents. "At a State dinner, we met Mrs. Alexander Hamilton, whom President Fillmore escorted to the table," wrote another visitor, "a plain little old lady, plainly dressed."[10] She was pleased to realize that she was now the sole survivor of the revolutionary generation, a resource to a new generation of historians to whom she could tell her version of the truth. She would entertain them in her daughter's parlor, serve them drinks from George Washington's punch bowl and tell them of the Constitution and *The Federalist*, and that her husband was the greatest man that ever lived. When Julia Miller, a social historian, called on her in 1850, she sat beside her on the sofa, held her hand tightly, "telling me how she knew Washington, 'with whom I was a great favorite,' and Lafayette, 'a most interesting young man.' "[11] Jesse Benton Fremont, wife of a politician of the Civil War generation, saw her in 1854 at the Church of the Epiphany at a ceremony marking the fiftieth anniversary of the Orphans' Home:

> She entered, a small, upright little figure, in deep black . . . As she moved slowly forward, supported by her daughter . . . one common feeling made the congregation

rise and remain standing, until she was seated in her pew at the front.[12]

She died that same year in November, at the age of ninety-seven, lucid and alert until the last. Her body was taken to New York, where she lies buried next to her husband in the graveyard of Trinity Church.

The later years of Aaron Burr were nowhere near as tranquil or benign. He returned to Richmond Hill after the shooting, but he had not anticipated the wave of shock and hatred or the horrified reaction to his deed. He was stunned to find himself not only ostracized socially, but wanted for murder in New Jersey and New York. He saw himself the victim of unwarranted cruelty.

> The event . . . has driven me into a sort of exile, which may terminate in an actual and permanent ostracism [he told his son-in-law on July 18]. Every sort of persecution is to be exercised against me. A coroner's jury will sit this evening, being the *fourth* time.[13]

When the New York indictment was handed down on August 2, he fled to Philadelphia, going from there to St. Simon's island off the coast of Georgia before returning to Washington—he was still Vice-President—on November 5. His exit from Philadelphia had been dictated by necessity. Governor Morgan Lewis of New York had been asked to require extradition from the governor of Pennsylvania, with which he would have been obligated to comply.

From Georgia Burr told his daughter that death threats had been made against him, and he told his son-in-law that Richmond Hill had been sold at auction, leaving him still $8,000 in debt. In Washington he was further affronted to learn that a grand jury in New Jersey had indicted him for murder, making him now wanted in two states.

"The subject in dispute is which shall have the honor of hanging the vice president," he told his daughter with suspect bravado. "Wherever it may be, you may rely on a great concourse of company, much gaiety, and many rare sights."[14] He added in much the same manner, "If any male friend of yours should be dying of ennui, recommend to him to engage in a duel and a courtship at the same time."[15]

On March 5, 1805, his term as Vice-President ended, ridding Thomas Jefferson of a considerable embarrassment, and himself of his last tie to public life.

250

In New York, I am to be disenfranchised, and in New Jersey, hanged [he told his son-in-law]. Having substantial objections to both, I shall not, for the present, hazard either, but shall seek another country. You will not, from this conclude that I have become passive. . . . Or if you should, you would greatly err.[16]

Passive indeed he had not been. In August 1804, one month after the duel, and while he was still Vice-President, he sent an intermediary to the British embassy to discuss with them his newest plan: to detach the Louisiana Territory from the American government and form an empire in the West. He asked for a British squadron to be placed at the mouth of the Mississippi, and a loan of half a million dollars for himself. When he was released from office he approached Ambassador Merry in person with a new series of proposals, relayed by Merry to his government in dispatches labeled "most secret" and somewhat harrowing in tone:

Mr. Burr . . . has mentioned to me that the inhabitants of Louisiana seem determined to render themselves independent of the United States, and that the execution of their design is delayed only by the difficulty of attaining previously an assurance of protection and assistance from some foreign power . . . and of concerting and connecting their independence with that of the inhabitants of the western parts. . . . It is clear to me that Mr. Burr . . . means to endeavour to be the instrument of effecting such a connection.

Merry added that:

I have only to add that if a strict confidence could be placed in him, he certainly possesses, perhaps in greater degree than any other individual in this country, all the talents, energy, intrepidity, and firmness that are required for such an enterprise.[17]

At the same time the French government received this message from its own ambassador in Washington, Turreau:

Mr. Burr's career is generally looked upon as finished, but

he is far from sharing that opinion, and I believe he would rather sacrifice the interests of his country than renounce celebrity and fortune. Although Louisiana is only a territory, it has obtained the right of sending a delegate to Congress. Louisiana is therefore to become the theatre of Mr. Burr's new intrigues.[18]

Burr did not get his loan or his squadron, but he did continue with his schemes. Apparently he believed, as his coconspirator James Wilkinson testified later at his trial, that his plan was not only plausible but just:

Mr. Burr, speaking of the imbecility of the government, said it would molder to pieces, die a natural death—or words to that effect, adding that the people of the western country were ready to revolt.

He went to the western country, where he apparently told people like Andrew Jackson that he was raising a force under the auspices of the American government to fight the Spanish, but he also had fantasies of leading an army in a march on Washington and capturing Jefferson himself. He had raised the beginnings of a sizable army when he was arrested on the Mississippi in January 1807, word of his actions having finally filtered to Jefferson in the east. His trial for treason in March and April, the exhibition of a former Vice-President's plan to dismember his country, was a spectacle almost as dramatic as the duel with Hamilton. He was freed on lack of evidence, protesting to the last his innocence, which he perhaps by then believed.

Burr's last years—he lived to 1836—seem almost morbidly farcical. In June 1808 he sailed for England, where he continued to try to sell his schemes. He had now added the conquest of Mexico to his plans for the emancipation of the West. But his journals were seized on the orders of the ministry, and upon protests of the Spanish ambassador he was ordered by the government to leave. Burr fought the order, first denying that he was engaged in plots against the Spanish government; next claiming that he was a British subject, and not an American; and last, that he was "too poor to remove." Nonetheless he was deported, going to Sweden and then Denmark, embarking thence for Paris, which he reached at the end of 1809.

There he approached the foreign office with a memorandum claiming to prove that with the aid of ten thousand troops in a combined attack from Canada and Louisiana he could guarantee the destruction of the United States. The response of the French government was to revoke his visa and place him under police surveillance. He lived there for more than two years in a state of squalor and semi-imprisonment. Matthew Davis wrote later of the cruelty of the government and the coldness of the French people, of the insults and injuries of the American representatives, and of the "all-pervading vigilance and power" of the French police. Burr's captivity was ended only through the intervention of the Duke of Bassano at the beginning of 1812.

> The conduct of the Duke was most generous [Davis wrote], not limited to what alone Colonel Burr had for more than a year in vain requested, the relaxation of the tyrannical refusal of his passports, but accompanied by a loan of money, which enabled him to leave Paris free from debt.[19]

In August 1812 Burr returned to America and appeared at Albany in his capacity as a lawyer when the fall session of the circuit court began. The indictments against him had expired, and he had ceased to be a figure of notoriety and fear. If he was noticed at all, it was as a curiosity, a figure from a distant and dramatic past. The years of exile had added a layer of self-consciousness to his demeanor. He seemed perennially aware of being watched. He had retained his elegance and his magnetism and maintained a dignified composure among his somewhat raffish associates, whom he sometimes seemed to be trying to ignore. "He always had queer people around him, whose free manners were a strange contrast to his measured correctness," one acquaintance said.

A young lawyer, whom Burr once interviewed for a place in his law office, left this picture of Burr in his old age:

> I was struck with his serpent-like fascination. His head, eyes, mouth were so very snake-like. His habit in talking to you . . . was to have one of his long fingers extended, with which he really seemed to be feeling you all over, while his remarkably piercing small dark eye seemed to have a nail in it that fastened you.[20]

He took only a slight interest in politics, continuing however to rail at the "Virginia faction" and to follow the career of Martin Van Buren, rumored to be his illegitimate son. In 1832 at the age of seventy-six he married Eliza Jumel, a rich widow reputed to have been a successful madam and to have conspired in her late husband's death. She divorced him later on the grounds of adultery, and he was served at the same time with a paternity suit, filed by a young woman who had been working as a servant in his house. While both were pending, he died in 1836. His body was taken to Princeton, where he was buried near his parents' graves.

The secession plan, as Hamilton anticipated, died forever, crushed by the bullet that had lodged against his spine. He had been right in what appeared to be his expectation. His friends, Pickering among them, could not clasp hands with his murderer. The men who had not heeded him when he was alive were forced to acknowledge the shattering drama of his death.

Exactly what he saved the country from remains conjectural, distorted by the manner of his death. Jefferson, who knew of the plot by April, dismissed it later as not serious. He could find, he said, no basis for prolonged agreement between Pickering's group of pious fanatics and the people of Burr's "little band." But this assessment is vulnerable upon two points: first, it was made after the threat was over; and second, the lack of a capacity for constructive action does not negate the potential for destruction, as a maniac can demolish in minutes an edifice it has taken artisans years of careful work to build. One must recall that nullification was advanced as a valid doctrine in 1828, and the idea that there was a legal basis to the "right" of secession was disposed of later only after four years of brutal war. In 1804 the country had existed under its new government for less than fifteen years. Its loyalties were not cemented, its powers not conceded universally, its forms, so fragile, had not jelled. Its ability to survive sustained attack was still uncertain. Thomas Jefferson, whose tranquil presidency had begun in the high drama of potential insurrection, was spared the further high drama of a civil war.

Three times in the history of the secession plot Hamilton had intervened to deflect and severely weaken its trajectory. He had refused at first to lead it, intervened again to deprive it of its second choice of leader and intervened a third time to die and to render the coup de grace. At each point his intervention had been critical, at no point more than at the first. Alexander Hamilton at the head of a northern rebellion, with his prestige and all his friends around him, would have cast the confederacy in a far more impressive light. By a stroke of irony that is almost too perfect, Hamilton, who had helped Jefferson to the presidency in 1801, made certain three years later that he had a country to keep. Jefferson, in a tacit gesture of acknowledgment, installed a copy of the Gerraci bust of Hamilton at Monticello, where it occupies a place of honor in the mansion's entrance hall, across the room from the Houson bust of Jefferson himself.

What had also died with Hamilton on July 12, 1804, was the political viability of Aaron Burr. This curious man, with his infinite powers of seduction and mischief, was exiled forever from the company of serious men. His range of action was dramatically curtailed. It was possible for him in 1806 to beguile westerners, who did not consider dueling murder, with stories about the conquest of the Spanish empire, but it was no longer possible for him to gain a hearing in the drawing rooms of eastern politicians, in whose hands true power lay. The moment his bullet entered Hamilton's body, Burr's career was over. His long slide downhill to treason, exile, squalor and ultimate inconsequence—a fate perhaps more dreadful to him than dramatic infamy—was preordained.

The prospect of Aaron Burr in power, as president in 1801 or dictator-general in 1804 and after, belongs to the realm of the imagination and can be inferred only from his aggregate of acts. The picture is not a soothing one. It is a rare public servant who will twice connive at the dismemberment of his own country, once while sitting in its second-highest seat. If this portrait of Burr shows more a series of sporadic grabs than a cold and concentrated drive at power, it is nonetheless the picture of an unstable personality, unrestrained by conscience and loyal only to itself. Hamilton senses this flaw in Burr quickly, perhaps through Burr's superficial resemblance to himself. If it was Hamilton's acquaintance with the lure of power that made him realize the strength of its seductive qualities, it was his feeling for the things that acted as restraints upon him—his love of order and community, his attachment to the American republic—that made him dread the influence of ambition on men who did not have them, and added to his fear of Burr. It was Hamilton's passion for legitimacy and order that made him dread Burr to the marrow, gave their confrontation a predestined and an almost mythic quality, and made him believe that a life given to keep this man from power was indeed a life well spent.

Finally, Hamilton's motives were internal, stemming from a private lapse of will. He died because he did not wish to live. In the end, nothing—not his friends, his legal career or the adoration of his family—could recompense him for a life from which power, glory and the hope of an heroic destiny had gone. An abundance of the things that constitute the whole of life for other people was not enough to sustain him. In his later years, he had made a valiant effort to construct alternative resources—

religion, domesticity, his country mansion. In the end, they were not good enough.

At least one of his fortresses had helped to undermine him. In his last years he had become deeply Christian, and its gentle doctrines had done much to reconcile him to loss. But the center of Christianity is sacrifice, and this had merged with the classic values of his adulthood to reinforce the glamour of a sacrificial death. If he suffered also from guilt at the thought that he was responsible in part for Philip's death and Angelica's madness, it may have been a form of expiation, a payment of his life for theirs.

It is more likely that the prevailing impulse sprang from another pattern, established early, whose demands he was unable to evade. As a young boy, lacking human comforts and attachments, he had sought refuge in his imagination, in the concept of "honor," in the idea of himself as an heroic figure willing to die in a cause of overriding value, whose worth would dignify his sacrifice. There is some reason to believe that this fixation was never routed from the center of his life. In the war, together with his friends, he had been relentless in his quest for an heroic ending, a quest which fate denied. Then in peace and when he least expected it, at a time when his reserves were weakest, fate had given him a second chance—to die for his country, to make himself a legend and to finish at the same time the career of a man whom he saw as a menacing figure, an enemy of the republic, of his ideals of order and of everything he loved. He took that chance, and died.

Appendix: The Hair Trigger Clue

Several years ago it was discovered by a panel of ballistic experts that the pistol used by Alexander Hamilton in his duel with Aaron Burr on July 11, 1804, was fitted with a hair trigger, permitting the pistol to discharge upon very slight pressure from the hand. On this evidence three things were postulated: 1) that Hamilton entered the duel determined to shoot at Burr; 2) that he chose the pistols to give him an extra and unfair advantage; and 3) that in aiming the pistol under extreme tension, stress caused him to press the trigger prematurely, thus causing the wild shot. This explanation has already entered several publications, as the revised version of the truth.

This postulation strikes me as questionable, both upon consideration of the factual evidence concerning the duel, and upon knowledge of the emotional pattern of Hamilton's life. In the first place, Hamilton did not buy the pistols, but borrowed them from his brother-in-law, John Barker Church. He borrowed them because they had been used by his son, Philip Hamilton, in the duel with George Eacker, in which Philip lost his life. No one has suggested that Philip, who had also stated his intention not to fire at his rival, had secretly intended to shoot at Eacker. And, if as Hamilton's classmate testified, Hamilton had told Philip to withhold his fire, it is unthinkable that he would give his child advice of a most dangerous nature that he would not follow for himself.

No conclusive evidence can be gathered from reports of the duel as to which of the two men fired first. Understandably, Van Ness and Pendleton both asserted that their principal's opponent fired the first shot. The statement that they both signed together states only that the pistols were discharged "within seconds" of each other, and it is likely that they sounded almost as one shot. What was known at the time, however, was the existence of the hair trigger. Pendleton stated as much in a letter to the *New York Evening Post* of July 19, 1804, and said also that it was not in use. "When he received his pistol, after having taken his position, he was asked if he would have the hair spring set?—His answer was, '*Not this time.*'"

Pendleton related further evidence, based on Hamilton's actions in the boat heading back to New York City, which was confirmed by David Hosack in a letter to William Coleman on August 17. "Soon after recovering his sight, he happened to cast his eye upon the case of pistols, and observing the one he had had in his hand lying on the outside, he said, 'Take care of that pistol; it is undischarged, and still cocked; it may go off and do harm—Pendleton knows (attempting to turn his head towards him) that I did not attempt to fire at him.'"

Pendleton stated, "If he had fired *previous* to having received the wound, he would have remembered it, and therefore would have known that the pistol, could not go off . . . *afterwards,* it must have been the effect of an unvoluntary exertion of the muscles, produced by a mortal wound."

I find it incredible that Hamilton, in great pain and barely conscious, could have maintained a falsehood, or that Hosack and Pendleton, friends as they were of Hamilton, would have collaborated on a fabrication.

The overriding disclaimer stems from Hamilton's character. There is ample evidence that a sacrificial death, a death by fire, a death in the service of his country, a dramatic death, which would enshrine him as a hero-martyr, had a great appeal for Hamilton from early childhood, and had intensified and deepened with the years. It was ingrained in his ambitious, honor-loving, deeply romantic character, and the two moral traditions from which he drew sustenance—the classicism of his youth and the Christianity of his maturity—stressed the moral glamour of a sacrificial death. There is evidence also that much had happened to him in his later years to dishearten him and make him doubt life's value: the loss of power and influence, the loss of his heroic self-image, the loss of his connection to his country and government, the death of his son and the madness of his daughter, which must have caused him devastating guilt.

Much in his correspondence from 1801 on suggests that his mainspring had indeed been broken, that he thought of death as not at all unwelcome, and that a death of honor, that would both break an enemy and reinstate his old heroic luster, would seem a most appealing thing.

There is the evidence also of his "honor," which had exaggerated import in his mind. If he had told few of his intimates about the duel, he had by the morning of July 11 told enough people—Pendleton, and Rufus King, who had also told Matthew Clarkson and John Jay—of his decision *not* to fire to commit himself to it publicly and irrevocably. He had also committed this intention to writing in several papers written in the days before the duel, and in the final letter to his wife. To a man of his temperament, such commitment was final. To renege at the last moment, to shoot at Burr, and in a way that implied the taking of an unfair and cowardly advantage, would have branded him forever as a fool and coward—something he would literally have died to prevent.

There is a last piece of practical evidence that works against the charge. Hamilton's bullet was found the day after the duel to have passed through the branches of a cedar tree, twelve and a half feet above the ground, and four feet to Burr's right. No shot so wild could have been fired by a man simply aiming a gun. The common action in aiming a pistol is to raise the arm and slowly lower it. The angle of shot—sharply upwards—indicates the gun was fired as the arm was sharply raised. Nothing accords with these facts so much as Pendleton's assertion that Hamilton fired in "an unvoluntary exertion of the muscles," on impact from Burr's bullet, and that he did not mean to shoot at Burr.

Selected Bibliography

ADAMS, Charles Francis. *Works of John Adams with a Life of the Author*, 10 vols. Boston: Little, Brown, 1850–56.

ADAMS, Henry. *History of the United States of America During the First Administration of Thomas Jefferson*, 9 vols., New York: Scribner's, 1889.

_____. *Life of Albert Gallatin*. New York: Peter Smith, 1947.

ADAMS, John. *Adams Family Correspondence*. Edited by Lyman H. Butterfield. 2 vols. Cambridge: Harvard University Press, 1971.

_____. *The Adams-Jefferson Letters*. Edited by Lester Cappon. New York: Clarion Books, 1971.

_____. *Letters of John Adams*, addressed to his wife. Edited by Charles Francis Adams, 2 vols. Boston: Little, Brown, 1841.

_____. *The Political Writings of John Adams*. Edited by George L. Peek, Jr. New York: Bobbs-Merrill, 1954.

_____. *The Works of John Adams*. Edited by Charles Francis Adams. 10 vols. Boston: Little, Brown, 1851.

_____. *The Spur of Fame*, Dialogues of John Adams and Benjamin Rush. Edited by John A. Schutz and Douglass Adair. Kingsport: Kingsport Press, 1966.

_____. *Diary of John Quincy Adams*. Edited by Allan Nevins. New York: Scribner's, 1951.

_____. *Memoirs*. Edited by Charles Francis Adams. 12 vols. Philadelphia: 1874–7.

BAYARD, James A., *Papers of James A. Bayard*. Edited by Elizabeth Donnan. New York: Da Capo Press, 1971.

BOWEN, Catherine Drinker. *Miracle at Philadelphia*. Boston: Little, Brown, 1966.

BRANDT, Irving. *James Madison*, 5 vols. New York: Bobbs-Merrill, 1944–61.

BRODIE, Fawn M., *Thomas Jefferson. An Intimate Biography*. New York: Norton, 1974.

CALLENDER, James Thomson. *Historical Memories of the United States, for the Year 1796*. New York, 1797.

COLEMAN, William, ed. *A Collection of the Facts and Documents Relative to the Death of Major General Alexander Hamilton*. By the Editor of the *Evening Post*. Freeport: Books for Libraries Series, 1969.

CHASTELLUX, Marquis de. *Travels in North America*. Edited by Howard C. Rice Jr., Chapel Hill, 1963.

DAVIS, Matthew, ed. *Memoirs of Aaron Burr, with Miscellaneous Selections from his Correspondence*. 2 vols. New York: Harper & Bros., 1836–7.

DEMONDS, Alice Curtis. *Alexander Hamilton's Wife*. New York: Dodd, Mead, 1952.

FLEXNER, James Thomas. *George Washington*, 4 vols. Boston: Little, Brown, 1965–72.

_____. *The Young Hamilton*. Boston: Little, Brown, 1979.

GRAYDON, Alexander. *Memories of his own Time*. New York: New York Times & Arno Press, 1969.

HALL, Margaret Esther, ed. *The Hamilton Reader*. New York: Oceana Productions, 1957.

HAMILTON, Alexander. *The Papers of Alexander Hamilton*. Edited by Harold Syrett and others. 24 vols. New York: Columbia University Press, 1961–80.

HAMILTON, Allen McLane. *The Intimate Life of Alexander Hamilton*. New York:, Scribner's, 1910.

HAMILTON, James Alexander. *Reminiscenses*. New York: Scribner's, 1869.

HAMILTON, John Church. *Life of Alexander Hamilton*. 2 vols. New York: Halstead & Voorhees, 1834–40.

_____. *History of the Republic of the United States, as traced in the*

Writings of Alexander Hamilton and his Contemporaries. 7 vols. New York: Appleton & Co., 1852–60.

HENDRICKSON, Robert. *Hamilton,* 2 vols. New York: Mason/Charter, 1976.

HUNTE, George. *The West Indian Islands.* New York: Viking, 1972.

JAY, John. *The Correspondence and Public Papers of John Jay.* Edited by Henry F. Livingston. 4 vols. New York: Putnam, 1891.

_____. *Unpublished Papers, 1745–80.* Edited by Richard B. Morris. New York: Harper & Row, 1975.

JEFFERSON, Thomas. *The Complete Jefferson.* Edited by Saul K. Padover. New York: Duell, Sloan & Pearce, 1943.

_____. *Memoirs, Correspondence and Private Papers of Thomas Jefferson.* Edited by Thomas Jefferson Randolph. 4 vols. London: Coburn & Bentley, 1829.

_____. *Notes on the State of Virginia.* New York: Harper Torchbooks, 1964.

_____. *Papers of Thomas Jefferson.* Edited by Julian P. Boyd. 18 vols. Princeton: Princeton University Press, 1950–72.

_____. *Writings of Thomas Jefferson.* Edited by Paul L. Ford. 10 vols. New York: Putnam, 1895.

KING, Rufus. *Life and Correspondence of Rufus King.* Edited by Charles R. King. 6 vols. New York: Putnam, 1895.

LAFAYETTE, Marquis de. *Lafayette in the Age of the American Revolution.* Edited by Stanley J. Iderdza. 3 vols. Ithaca: Cornell University Press, 1977.

_____. *Memoirs, Correspondence and Manuscripts of General Lafayette,* 3 vols. London: Saunders & Otley, 1839.

LAURENS, John. *The Army Correspondence of Colonel John Laurens.* New York: New York Times & Arno Press, 1965.

LEE, Charles. *The Lee Papers,* 3 vols. Collections of the New-York Historical Society. New York, 1872–5.

LOMASK, Milton. *Aaron Burr, 1756–1802.* New York: Farrar, Straus & Giroux, 1974.

MADISON, James. *Notes on the Debates in the Federal Convention of 1787, as Reported by James Madison.* New York: Norton, 1969.

_____. *The Writings of James Madison.* Edited by Henry Gaillard. 3 vols. New York: Putnam, 1906.

MASON, George. *The Papers of George Mason.* Edited by Robert A. Rutland. 3 vols. Chapel Hill: University of North Carolina Press, 1970.

MILLER, John C. *Alexander Hamilton and the Growth of the New Nation*. New York: Harper Torchbooks, 1964.

_____. *The Federalist Era*. New York: Harper Torchbooks, 1963.

MITCHELL, Broadus. *Alexander Hamilton*, 2 vols. New York: Macmillan, 1962.

MONROE, James. *The Writings of James Monroe*. Edited by Stanislaus M. Hamilton. 4 vols. New York: Putnam, 1898.

MORÉ. Charles Albert. *Chevalier de Pontgibaud, A French Volunteer of the War of Independence*. Edited by Robert B. Douglas. New York: New York Times & Arno Press, 1969.

MORISON, Samuel Eliot. *The Oxford History of the American People*. Oxford: Oxford University Press, 1965.

MORRIS, Gouverneur. *Correspondence and Diary*. Microfilm collection, New York Public Library.

_____. *The Life of Gouverneur Morris, with Selections from his Correspondence*. Edited by Jared Sparks. 3 vols. Boston: Grey & Bowen, 1832.

MORRIS, Richard B. *Seven Who Shaped Our Destiny*. New York: Harper Colophon Books, 1976.

PAREMT, Herbert S., and HECHT, Marie B. *Aaron Burr: Portrait of an Ambitious Man*. New York: Macmillan, 1967.

PARTON, James. *Life and Times of Aaron Burr*, 2 vols. Cambridge: Houghton Mifflin, 1881.

ROSSITER, Clinton. *Alexander Hamilton and the Constitution*. New York: Harcourt, Brace, & World, 1964.

_____. *1787: The Grand Convention*. New York: Macmillan, 1966.

SHAW, Peter. *The Character of John Adams*. Chapel Hill: University of North Carolina Press, 1976.

SMITH, Page. *John Adams*, 2 vols. New York: Doubleday, 1966.

SYRETT, Harold C., and Cooke, Jean G., eds. *Interview at Weehawken, The Burr-Hamilton duel, as told in the Original Documents*. Middletown: Wesleyan University Press, 1960.

WASHINGTON, George. *The Writings of George Washington*. Edited by John C. Fitzpatrick. 39 vols. Washington, D.C.: Government Printing Office, 1933.

_____. *The Writings of George Washington*. Edited by Worthington C. Ford. 14 vols. New York: Putnam, 1889.

WOOD, John. *Suppressed History of the Administration of John Adams*. New York: Burt Franklin Research Source Work Series, 1968.

Notes

Chapter I

1. Hunte, p. 121.
2. John Church Hamilton, *Life,* v. 1, p. 2.
3. John Church Hamilton, *Life,* v. 1, pp. 2–3.
4. John Church Hamilton, *History,* v. 1, pp. 41–42.
5. Mitchell, v. 1, p. 7.
6. Hamilton to Elizabeth Schuyler, August, 1780.
7. Hamilton to Margarita Schuyler, January 21, 1780.
8. Hamilton to Alexander Hamilton, May 2, 1797.
9. Hamilton to James Hamilton, Jr., June 22, 1785.
10. Hamilton to James Hamilton, Jr., June 22, 1785.
11. Hamilton to Elizabeth Schuyler, October 13, 1780.
12. Hamilton to Elizabeth Schuyler, September 25, 1780.
13. Hamilton to John Laurens, May 22, 1779.
14. Probate Court Transaction, no. xxix (in Syrett, v. 1, pp. 2–3).
15. Hamilton to Elizabeth Hamilton, October, 1782.
16. Hamilton to Tileman Cruger, November 16, 1771.
17. John Church Hamilton, *Life,* v. 1, p. 4.
18. Hamilton to Edward Stevens, November 11, 1769.
19. Hendrickson, v. 1, p. 30.
20. Hamilton, *Royal Danish American Gazette,* September 6, 1772.

21. Hamilton to Elizabeth Schuyler, October 27, 1780.
22. Hamilton to Elizabeth Schuyler, September 3, 1780.
23. Hamilton to John Laurens, April, 1779.

Chapter II

1. Graydon, pp. 376–7.
2. Chastellux, v. 1, p. 373.
3. Jay to Robert Morris, September 16, 1780.
4. Hamilton, *Farmer Refuted*, February 23, 1775.
5. Ibid.
6. Hamilton, *Full Vindication*, December 14, 1774.
7. Hamilton, *Farmer Refuted*, February 23, 1775.
8. Hamilton to Jay, November 26, 1775.
9. Hamilton, *Americanus*, February 8, 1794.
10. Moré, p. 147.
11. Hendrickson, v. 1, p. 108.
12. John Church Hamilton, *Life*, v. 1, p. 57.
13. Stevens to Hamilton, November 16, 1777.
14. McHenry to Hamilton, September 21, 1778.
15. Plutarch, p. 864.
16. Ibid., p. 887.

Chapter III

1. Hamilton to Tobias Lear, January 2, 1800.
2. Washington to Adams, September 25, 1798.
3. Plutarch, p. 898.
4. Lafayette, *Memoirs*, 1779.
5. Ibid.
6. Ibid.
7. Ibid.
8. John Church Hamilton, *Life*, v. 1, pp. 391–2.
9. Schuyler to Hamilton, September 10, 1780.
10. Hamilton to Boudinot, July 5, 1778.
11. Troup to Jay, January 21, 1779.
12. Hamilton to James Duane, September 6, 1780.
13. Lee to Benjamin Rush, September 19, 1775.

14. Boudinot, *Diary,* 1778.
15. Hamilton to Laurens, September 12, 1780.
16. Hamilton to Washington, November 22, 1780.
17. Ibid.
18. Laurens to Hamilton, December 18, 1779.
19. Hamilton to Laurens, January 8, 1780.
20. Hamilton to Laurens, June 8, 1780.

Chapter IV

1. Allen McLane Hamilton, p. 95.
2. Ibid., p. 97.
3. Tilghman, Diary, August, 1775.
4. Hamilton, *Royal Danish American Gazette,* April 6, 1771.
5. *Rivington's Gazette,* May, 1778.
6. Hamilton to John Laurens, April, 1789.
7. Hamilton to Margarita Schuyler, February, 1780.
8. Hamilton to Laurens, June 30, 1780.
9. Hamilton to Angelica Church, June 20, 1796.
10. Hamilton to Elizabeth Schuyler, July 2, 1780.
11. Hamilton to Elizabeth Schuyler, August, 1780.
12. Hamilton to Elizabeth Schuyler, October 5, 1780.
13. Hamilton to Elizabeth Schuyler, September 6, 1780.
14. Hamilton to Elizabeth Schuyler, July 20, 1780.
15. Hamilton to Elizabeth Schuyler, Ibid.
16. Hamilton to Elizabeth Schuyler, August, 1780.
17. Ibid.
18. Hamilton to Elizabeth Schuyler, September 3, 1780.
19. Ibid.
20. Hamilton to Elizabeth Schuyler, October 13, 1780.
21. Hamilton to Elizabeth Schuyler, October 27, 1780.
22. Ibid.

Chapter V

1. Hamilton to Elizabeth Schuyler, September 25, 1780.
2. Hamilton to Laurens, October 11, 1780.
3. Ibid.

4. Hamilton to Elizabeth Schuyler, October 2, 1780.
5. Hamilton to Washington, November 22, 1780.
6. Ibid.
7. Ibid.
8. Lafayette to Hamilton, November 28, 1780.
9. Lafayette to Hamilton, December 9, 1780.
10. Hamilton to Schuyler, February 18, 1781.
11. Hamilton to McHenry, February 18, 1781.
12. Mitchell, v. 1, p. 231.
13. Hamilton to Schuyler, February 18, 1781.
14. Ibid.
15. Hamilton to Washington, October, 1787.
16. Hamilton to Elizabeth Hamilton, August, 1781.
17. Hamilton to Lafayette, October 15, 1781.

Chapter VI

1. Hamilton, July 4, 1782.
2. Hamilton, *Vindication of the Funding System,* No. 3, 1792.
3. Hamilton to Washington, February 7, 1783.
4. Washington to Joseph Jones, March 12, 1783.
5. Hamilton to Washington, March 17, 1783.
6. Hamilton to Washington, March 25, 1783.
7. Hamilton to Clinton, May 14, 1783.
8. Hamilton to Clinton, June 1, 1783.
9. Hamilton to Clinton, June 11, 1783.
10. Hamilton to Madison, July 6, 1783.
11. Parton, v. 1, p. 214.
12. Graydon, p. 149.
13. John Church Hamilton, *History,* v. 7, p. 744.
14. Hamilton to Elizabeth Hamilton, November, 1788.
15. James Alexander Hamilton, p. 65.
16. Hosack to John Church Hamilton, January 1, 1833.
17. Allen McLane Hamilton, p. 46.
18. John Church Hamilton, *History,* v. 7, p. 940.
19. William Bradford to Hamilton, July 2, 1795.
20. John Church Hamilton, *History,* v. 7, p. 944.
21. Kent to Elizabeth Hamilton, December 10, 1832.
22. Coleman, pp. 242-3.

23. Morris, July 14, 1804.
24. Kent to Elizabeth Hamilton, December 10, 1832.
25. Parton, v. 1, p. 212.
26. Morison, p. 323.
27. Parton, v. 1, p. 213.
28. John Church Hamilton, *History*, v. 3, p. 161.
29. Hamilton to New York Assembly, January 27, 1787.
30. Ibid., February 6, 1787.
31. Ibid., February 8, 1787.

Chapter VII

1. Hamilton to James Duane, September 3, 1780.
2. John Church Hamilton, *History*, v. 3, p. 275.
3. Hamilton, *Notes*, June 18, 1787.
4. Madison, *Notes*, June 18, 1787.
5. Ibid.
6. Ibid.
7. Ibid.
8. Madison, *Notes*, September 6, 1787.
9. Morris to Robert Walsh, February 5, 1811.
10. Hamilton to Edward Carrington, May 26, 1792.
11. Hamilton, *Notes*, June 18, 1787.
12. Hamilton to Pickering, September 16, 1803.
13. Thomas Y. Howe to John Church Hamilton, March 31, 1840.
14. Hamilton, *New York Post*, February 14, 1802.
15. Hamilton to Pickering, September 16, 1803.
16. Madison to J. K. Paulding, April, 1831.
17. Madison, *Notes*, June 29, 1787.
18. Lansing, *Notes*, June 29, 1787.
19. Hamilton to New York Ratifying Convention, June 23, 1788.
20. Mason to Thomas Jefferson, August, 1787.
21. Hamilton to William Pierce, July 20–26, 1787.
22. Hamilton to Nathanael Mitchell, July 20, 1787.
23. Madison, *Notes*, September 6, 1787.
24. Madison, *Notes*, September 17, 1787.
25. Madison, *Notes*, June 18, 1787.
26. Kent to Daniel Webster, January 21, 1830.

Chapter VIII

1. Hamilton, *Federalist,* no. 15.
2. Ibid., no. 27.
3. Ibid., no. 22.
4. Ibid., no. 15.
5. Ibid., no. 6.
6. Ibid., no. 34.
7. Ibid.
8. Ibid., no. 23.
9. Ibid., no. 31.
10. Ibid., no. 70.
11. Ibid., no. 77.
12. Ibid., no. 78.
13. Ibid.
14. Ibid.
15. Ibid.
16. Ibid., no. 70.
17. Ibid., no. 71.
18. Ibid., no. 6.
19. Ibid., no. 1.
20. Hamilton to Edward Carrington, May 29, 1792.

Chapter IX

1. Hamilton to New York State Ratifying Convention, June 28, 1788.
2. Ibid.
3. Hamilton to Sedgwick, October 9, 1788.
4. Hamilton to Madison, November 23, 1788.
5. Hamilton to James Wilson, January 25, 1789.
6. Jeremiah Wadsworth to Hamilton, February 5–28, 1789.
7. Angelica Church to Hamilton, October 2, 1787.
8. Angelica Church to Elizabeth Hamilton, July 30, 1794.
9. Allen MacLane Hamilton, p. 74.
10. Angelica Church to Elizabeth Hamilton, April 25, 1788.
11. Angelica Church to Elizabeth Hamilton, July 30, 1794.
12. Hamilton to Angelica Church, August 3, 1785.

13. Hamilton to Angelica Church, November 8, 1789.
14. Hamilton to Angelica Church, June 25, 1796.
15. Hamilton to Angelica Church, March 6, 1795.
16. Hamilton to Angelica Church, December 6, 1787.
17. Hamilton to Angelica Church, November 8, 1789.
18. Hamilton to Angelica Church, June 25, 1796.
19. Angelica Church to Hamilton, November 7, 1789.
20. Hamilton to Angelica Church, November 8, 1789.
21. Elizabeth Hamilton to Angelica Church, November 8, 1789.
22. Angelica Church to Hamilton, November 7, 1789.

Chapter X

1. Hamilton to Edward Carrington, May 26, 1792.
2. Henry Adams, *History,* v. 1, p. 186.
3. Jefferson to Washington, May 3, 1788.
4. Jefferson to Madison, December 20, 1787.
5. Jefferson to William S. Smith, November 13, 1787.
6. Jefferson to Washington, September 9, 1792.
7. Jefferson to Lafayette, June 16, 1792.
8. Hamilton to Carrington, May 26, 1792.
9. Jefferson, *Anas,* February 4, 1818, in *The Complete Jefferson.*
10. Hamilton to Jay, December 18, 1792.
11. Jefferson to Washington, September 9, 1792.
12. Hamilton to Carrington, May 26, 1792.
13. Hamilton to Washington, August 18, 1792.
14. Jefferson, *Anas,* February 4, 1818.
15. Hamilton to Philip Livingston, April 2, 1792.
16. Constable to Robert Morris, October 20, 1789.
17. Hamilton to John Holker, January 8, 1790.
18. Hamilton to Duer, August 17, 1791.
19. Duer to Hamilton, August 16, 1791.
20. Duer to Hamilton, March, 1792.
21. Troup to Hamilton, March 19, 1792.
22. Schuyler to Hamilton, March 25, 1792.
23. Hamilton to Duer, March 14, 1792.
24. Duer to Hamilton, January 17, 1799.
25. Duer to Hamilton, February 16, 1792.

Chapter XI

1. Hamilton, *Report on Manufactures*, December 5, 1791.
2. Hamilton, *Report on the Public Credit*, January 9, 1790.
3. Hamilton to Robert Morris, April 30, 1781.
4. Hamilton, *Report on the Public Credit*, January 9, 1790.
5. Hamilton, Ibid.
6. Hamilton, *Report on the National Bank*, December 13, 1790.
7. Jefferson to Washington, February 15, 1791.
8. Hamilton to Washington, February, 1791.
9. Hamilton, Ibid.
10. Hamilton, *Report on Manufactures*, December 5, 1791.
11. Jefferson, *Notes on the State of Virginia*, 1782.
12. Ibid.
13. Ibid.
14. Jefferson to Madison, December 20, 1787.

Chapter XII

1. Hamilton, Reynolds Pamphlet, September 27, 1797.
2. Folwell to Edward Jones, August 12, 1797.
3. Hamilton, Reynolds Pamphlet, September 27, 1797.
4. Reynolds to Hamilton, December 15, 1791.
5. Maria Reynolds to Hamilton, December 15, 1791.
6. Hamilton, Reynolds Pamphlet, September 27, 1797.
7. Ibid.
8. Maria Reynolds to Hamilton, January 23, 1792.
9. Hamilton, Reynolds Pamphlet, September 27, 1797.
10. Ibid.
11. Ibid.
12. Reynolds to Hamilton, ND.
13. Clingman, December 13, 1792.
14. Ibid.
15. Muhlenberg, December 13, 1792.
16. Monroe and Venable, December 13, 1792.
17. Ibid.
18. Folwell to Jones, August 12, 1797.
19. Callender, *History*, pp. 218–20.

20. William Jackson to Hamilton, July 24, 1797.
21. Ibid.
22. Madison to Jefferson, October 20, 1797.
23. John Barnes to Jefferson, October 3, 1797.
24. Church to Hamilton, July 13, 1797.
25. Hamilton to Elizabeth Hamilton, November, 1798.

Chapter XIII

1. Jefferson, *Anas*, May 23, 1793.
2. Jefferson to William Short, January 3, 1793.
3. Jefferson to Tench Coxe, May 1, 1794.
4. Hamilton, the Stand, April, 1798.
5. Jefferson, *Anas*, November 28, 1793.
6. Jefferson to Walter Jones, March 5, 1810.
7. Isaac Wharton to King, September 23, 1793.
8. Hamilton to Angelica Church, December 27, 1793.
9. Brodie, p. 263.
10. Hamilton to Angelica Church, April, 1793.
11. Knox to Hamilton, November 24, 1794.
12. Hamilton to Washington, February 3, 1795.
13. Hamilton to King, February 21, 1795.
14. Hamilton, Syrett, v. XX, p. 42.
15. Hendrickson, v. 2A, pp. 555-6.
16. Ibid.
17. Webster, November, 1797.
18. Jefferson, *Anas*, February 4, 1818.
19. Adams to Rush, September 11, 1807.
20. Adams to Abigail Adams, January 9, 1797.

Chapter XIV

1. Jefferson to Madison, February 14, 1783.
2. Troup to King, November 16, 1798.
3. Adams to James Lloyd, December 11, 1815.
4. Abigail to John Adams, January 28, 1797.
5. Abigail to John Adams, December 31, 1796.
6. Adams to Abigail Adams, January 9, 1797.

7. Jefferson to Adams, June 15, 1815.
8. Wood, pp. 374-5.
9. Adams to James Lloyd, March 16, 1815.
10. Washington to Adams, September 25, 1798.
11. Charles Francis Adams, v. 1, p. 530.
12. Sedgwick to Hamilton, February 7, 1799.
13. Troup to King, April 19, 1799.
14. Cabot to King, March 10, 1799.
15. Cabot to King, April, 1799.
16. Troup to King, April 19, 1799.
17. Cabot to King, September 23, 1800.
18. Adams to Rush, November 11, 1807.
19. Ibid.
20. Adams to Rush, June 12, 1812.
21. McHenry to Hamilton, May 8, 1800.
22. Hamilton to Sedgwick, May 10, 1800.
23. Abigail Adams to Thomas B. Adams, July 14, 1800.
24. Ames to King, July 15, 1800.
25. McHenry to Hamilton, May 8, 1800.
26. Bayard to Hamilton, August 10, 1800.
27. Goodhue to Pickering, June 26, 1800.
28. Pickering to King, June 26, 1800.
29. Hamilton to Adams, October 1, 1800.
30. Hamilton, Letter, October 21, 1800.
31. Troup to King, November 9, 1800.
32. Bushrod Washington to Wolcott, November 1, 1800.
33. Troup to King, November 9, 1800.
34. Cabot to Hamilton, November 29, 1800.
35. Hamilton to Pickering, November 13, 1800.
36. Troup to King, October 1, 1800.

Chapter XV

1. Maria Gallatin to Albert Gallatin, May 7, 1800.
2. Parton, v. 1, p. 28.
3. Parton, v. 1, pp. 31-2.
4. Esther Burr to Jonathan Edwards, 1757.
5. Esther Burr, *Journal*, January 21, 1757.
6. Davis, v. 1, p. 90.

7. Davis, v. 1, pp. 91–2.
8. Parton, v. 1, p. 171.
9. Davis, v. 1, p. 83.
10. Hamilton to John Rutledge, Jr., January 4, 1801.
11. Theodosia to Aaron Burr, March 22, 1784.
12. Parton, v. 1, p. 170.
13. Nathaniel Hazard to Hamilton, November 25, 1791.
14. Jefferson to John Breckinridge, December 19, 1800.
15. John Church Hamilton, *History*, v. 7, p. 489.
16. Hamilton to Morris, December 24, 1800.
17. Hamilton to John Rutledge, January 4, 1801.
18. Hamilton to Bayard, January 16, 1801.
19. Hamilton to Wolcott, December 17, 1800.
20. Hamilton to Bayard, January 16, 1801.
21. Ibid.
22. Lomask, p. 275.
23. Bayard to Hamilton, January 7, 1801.
24. Burr to Samuel Smith, January 7, 1801.
25. Lee to Hamilton, February 6, 1801.
26. Sedgwick to Hamilton, January 10, 1801.
27. Jefferson to Monroe, February 15, 1801.
28. Bayard to Allen McLane, February 12, 1801.
29. Bayard to Andrew Bayard, February 12, 1801.
30. Bayard to Andrew Bayard, February 13, 1801.
31. Bayard to Hamilton, March 8, 1801.
32. Jefferson, March 4, 1801.
33. Bayard to Hamilton, March 8, 1801.
34. Cabot to King, March 20, 1801.
35. Jefferson to Thomas Mann Randolph, February 19, 1801.
36. Jefferson to Madison, February 18, 1801.

Chapter XVI

1. Hamilton to Morris, February 27, 1802.
2. Lear, December 19, 1799.
3. Craik, December 21, 1799.
4. Lear, December 19, 1799.
5. Hamilton to Lear, January 2, 1800.
6. Lear to Hamilton, January 23, 1800.

7. Hamilton to Pinckney, December 22, 1799.
8. Hamilton to Lear, January 2, 1800.
9. Ibid.
10. Hamilton to Elizabeth Hamilton, March 10, 1801.
11. Hamilton to Elizabeth Hamilton, February 25, 1801.
12. Hamilton to Elizabeth Hamilton, March 16, 1801.
13. Schuyler to Hamilton, April 16, 1803.
14. Hamilton to Elizabeth Hamilton, March 13, 1803.
15. Hamilton to Elizabeth Hamilton, March 16, 1803.
16. Ibid.
17. Hamilton to Elizabeth Hamilton, October 16, 1802.
18. Hamilton to Elizabeth Hamilton, October 14, 1803.
19. Hamilton to Richard Peters, December 9, 1802.
20. King to Gore, November 20, 1803.
21. Hamilton to Richard Peters, December 9, 1802.
22. Hamilton, Syrett, v. XXV, p. 436.
23. Hosack to John Church Hamilton, January 1, 1833.
24. Troup to King, December 5, 1801.
25. Hamilton to Rush, March 29, 1802.
26. Hamilton to Dickinson, March 29, 1802.
27. McHenry to Hamilton, December 4, 1801.
28. Hamilton to Dickinson, March 29, 1802.
29. Hamilton to Rush, March 29, 1802.
30. Rush to Hamilton, November 26, 1801.
31. Kent to Elizabeth Kent, April 26, 1804.
32. Hamilton to William L. Smith, March 17, 1800.
33. Hamilton to _____, April 13, 1804.

Chapter XVII

1. Troup to King, May 27, 1801.
2. Jefferson to Burr, November 12, 1801.
3. Burr to Theodosia Alston, February 21, 1802.
4. Burr to Joseph Alston, March 8, 1802.
5. Parton, v. 2, p. 208.
6. Troup to King, May 6, 1802.
7. Troup to King, June 6, 1802.
8. Troup to King, December 10, 1802.
9. Troup to King, June 6, 1802.

10. Morris, 1802.
11. Troup to King, June 6, 1802.
12. Hamilton to King, June 3, 1803.
13. Hamilton to Bayard, April 6, 1802.
14. Hamilton, *People* v. *Croswell,* February, 1804.
15. Troup to King, April 9, 1802.
16. John Quincy Adams to Plumer, December 31, 1828.
17. Plumer, *Journal,* March 14, 1804.
18. Pickering to King, March 4, 1804.
19. Plumer to John Quincy Adams, December 31, 1828.
20. Pickering to Cabot, January 29, 1804.
21. Griswold to Wolcott, March 11, 1804.
22. Plumber, *Journal,* 1803.
23. Jefferson, *Anas,* January 26, 1804.
24. Griswold to King, March 11, 1804.
25. Plumer to John Quincy Adams, December 31, 1828.
26. John Fairlie to John Church Hamilton, March 21, 1827.
27. Hamilton to Harper, February 12, 1804.
28. John Church Hamilton, *History,* v. 7, p. 822.
29. Cooper to Schuyler, April 23, 1804.
30. Hoops to John Church Hamilton, March 30, 1829.
31. Morris, February, 1804.
32. Henry Adams, *History,* v. 1, pp. 188–9.

Chapter XVIII

1. Burr to Hamilton, June 21, 1804.
2. Pendleton, *New York Evening Post,* July 16, 1804.
3. Van Ness, *New York Morning Chronicle,* July 17, 1804.
4. Van Ness to Pendleton, June 26, 1804.
5. Burr to Van Ness, June 25, 1804.
6. John Quincy Adams to Louisa Adams, July 22, 1804.
7. Hamilton to Pendleton, June 26, 1804.
8. Hamilton to Pendleton, June, 1804.
9. Pendleton, June 10, 1804.
10. Wolcott to Mrs. Wolcott, July 12, 1804.
11. Hamilton, June 27–July 4, 1804.
12. King to Charles King, April 21, 1804.
13. Hamilton, June 27–July 4, 1804.

14. Morris, *Diary,* July 12, 1804.
15. Burr to Theodosia Alston, July 1, 1804.
16. John Church Hamilton, v. 7, p. 823.
17. Hamilton, July 9, 1804.
18. Wolcott to Mrs. Wolcott, July 11, 1804.
19. John Church Hamilton, *History,* v. 7, p. 824.
20. Hamilton to Elizabeth Hamilton, July 10, 1804.
21. Hosack to William Coleman, August 17, 1804.
22. Ibid.
23. Wolcott to Mrs. Wolcott, July 13, 1804.
24. Morris, *Diary,* July 12, 1804.
25. Morris, *Diary,* July 14, 1804.
26. Coleman, p. 239.
27. Lafayette to Angelica Church, May 14, 1805.

Chapter XIX

1. King to Cabot, October 10, 1804.
2. Ibid.
3. Elizabeth Hamilton to Pendleton, September 28, 1804.
4. Allen McLane Hamilton, p. 105.
5. James Alexander Hamilton, p. 65.
6. Allen McLane Hamilton, p. 112.
7. Allen McLane Hamilton, p. 109.
8. Allen McLane Hamilton, p. 115.
9. Desmond, p. 257.
10. Ibid.
11. Desmond, p. 262.
12. Desmond, p. 263.
13. Burr to Joseph Alston, July 18, 1804.
14. Burr to Theodosia Alston, December 4, 1804.
15. Burr to Theodosia Alston, August 11, 1804.
16. Burr to Joseph Alston, March 22, 1805.
17. Henry Adams, *History,* v. 1, p. 403.
18. Ibid., p. 407.
19. Davis, *Journal,* p. 25.
20. Parton, v. 2, p. 299.

Index

Burr's political exclusion and, 217, 218
Constitutional Convention and, 93, 94, 101, 102
eastern states secession plan and, 226
ratification of Constitution and, 118
Clinton, Henry, 67, 69, 75
Coleman, William, 258
Constable, William, 86, 137
Constitution (U.S.), 111–13, 131, 143, 194, 249
  Burr's political intrigues seen as threat to, 200, 201, 227
  function of Supreme Court and, 112, 113
  "general welfare" clause of, 150–51
  plans for, 100, 103
  presidential elections under, 121
  ratification of, 118–19
  signing of, 104
  Twelfth Amendment to, 190, 220
  Washington's view of, 149
Constitutional Convention, 27, 89, 92–104, 114, 120, 131, 226
  effects of Shay's Rebellion on, 130
  opponents of centralized power at, 93–94
  signing of Constitution at, 104
  views on government presented at, 95–104
Continental army, 33–35
  fear of mutiny by, 78–80
  members of, besiege Continental Congress, 81–82
  See also Revolutionary War
Continental Congress, 27, 28, 43, 52, 130, 136
  Hamilton at, 71, 72
    government plan presented by, 82
    national financial system presented by, 78–81
    soldiers' back pay and, 78, 80–81
    soldiers besiege, 81–82
    Washington's replacement considered by, 46, 47
Conway, Thomas, 46, 47
Cooper, Charles, 226, 230–33
Cornwallis, Charles (Marquis Cornwallis), 75, 76

Corny, Madame de, 123
Cosway, Maria, 123
Craik, James, 205, 206
Cranch, (judge), 249
Cromwell, Oliver, 168
Croswell, Harry, 221, 226
Cruger, Mrs. Nicholas, 23
Cruger, Nicholas, 20, 23, 72
Custis, George Washington Parke, 213

Davis, Matthew, 192, 195, 217, 253
Declaration of Independence, 130
Dickinson, John, 213
Dipnal, Thomas, 19
Duer, Lady "Kitty" (Lady "Kitty" Stirling; cousin), 136
Duer, William (cousin), 135–41, 151, 154, 155, 158, 171
Du Pont de Nemours, Pierre Samuel, 144

Eacker, George, 211–12, 237, 257
Earle, Ralph, 86
Edwards, Jonathan, 22, 191

Fairlie, James, 225
Faucette, Ann (Ann Lytton; aunt), 14, 18
Faucette, John (grandfather), 14, 15
Faucette, Mary (first wife of John Faucette), 14
Faucette, Mary (Mary Uppington; second wife of John Faucette; grandmother), 14, 15
Faucette, Rachel (Rachel Levein; mother), 14–21, 24, 25, 67, 98
Federalist, The, 105–17
  views expressed in
    on centralized power, 109–12, 116–17
    on finance, 106–11
    on mankind, 109–10
    on presidency, 113–14
    on secrecy, 111–12
    on state power, 106–8
    on Supreme Court, 112–13
Fenno, John, 133
Fillmore, Millard, 249
Fish, Nicholas, 75, 239

281